ANIMAL-ASSISTED THERAPY

ANIMAL-ASSISTED THERAPY

SUPERSTARS CHANGE TEEN LIVES

Gaby Dufresne-Cyr

Dogue Shop Publishing, Montreal

Copyright © 2023 Dogue Shop Publishing

All rights reserved.

No part of this publication may be reproduced, distributed, or transmitted in any form or by any means, including photocopying, recording, or other electronic or mechanical methods, without the prior written permission of the publisher, except in the case of a brief quotation embodied in critical reviews and other noncommercial uses permitted by copyright law. For permission requests, contact Dogue Shop Publishing.

Book Cover by Gaby Dufresne-Cyr
Edited with Grammarly.

Animal-assisted therapy: superstars change teen lives.
First Edition, 2023.

ISBN: 978-1-7752927-4-6

Library and Archives Canada: 29986
Bibliothèque et Archives Nationales du Québec: 769423

Dogue Shop Publishing
5055 Bessborough Avenue
Quebec, Canada, H4V 2S2
www.dogueshop.com/dogue-s-publishing

I'm #MadeByDyslexia – Expect creative thinking and creative spelling.
We support Made by Dyslexia
www.madebydyslexia.org

Printed in Canada.

For Kathlene

"Childhood, as we ideally think of it, cannot exist without a certain measure of hypocrisy."
— Neil Postman

Table of Contents

Acknowledgements	vii
Introduction	xi
Living with a learning disability	xi
My path to animal-assisted therapy	xvi
Chapter 1	1
AAT definitions	1
Animal-assisted therapy and the law	1
Animal-assisted intervention	3
Animal-assisted therapy	6
Animal-assisted activity	11
Zootherapy	12
Emotional support dog	20
Service dogs	21
DAAT – HAAT – RAAT – WAAT	23
The future of AAI	27
Chapter 2	29
Training an AAT animal	29
A working-class animal	29
Selection	30
AAT socialization	33
AAT training	40
Behaviour maintenance and management	54
Chapter 3	63
Adolescent issues in AAT	63

Common conditions	63
Aggressive behaviour	64
Anxiety disorders	66
Attention deficit & hyperactivity disorder	70
Autism spectrum disorder	75
Body dysmorphia and gender dysphoria	80
Depression	84
Learning disabilities	88
Obsessive-compulsive disorders	93
Post-traumatic stress disorder	95
Substance abuse and addiction	97
Chapter 4	103
Changing lives with animals	103
AAT adolescents	103
Alexander	104
Alessandro	116
Jamal	128
Markayla	132
Rayvon	142
Calvin	150
Karlo	163
Seymour	179
Connor	189
Jacob	196
Wolf Animal-Assisted Therapy	202
Michael	203

Jessie	204
Making WAAT History	205
Chapter 5	213
The future of AAI	213
Making changes	216
The art of living	220
Photo Annex	221
Bibliography	233
References	241
Contacts Information	259
Your Notes	261

A person with dyslexia wrote the book you are about to read.
I intentionally avoided sending it to our editor to encourage
other dyslexics to reach for their dreams regardless of labels.
Be patient; writing is a work in progress for us.

Acknowledgements

I want to thank the Animal Behaviour Apprenticeship and Animal-Assisted Therapy students for contributing to the success of AAT. They generously volunteer their time because they firmly believe in the healing powers of animals. The teens and high school personnel appreciate the contributions made by the Dogue Shop and Dogue Academy collaborators.

I would also like to thank the volunteers personally (dog's name in parenthesis). In alphabetical order: Angeliki Koinis (Gene), Annick Levesque, Ann-Marie Bourassa, Audrey Lavertue (Enzo), Faye Siluk (Trillium), Julie Langlois (Chica), Kathlene Dixon-Dow (Jasmin & Maggie), Katye Garon, Kelsey Deer (Rick & Lua), Laura Lasry Gruszczynski (George), Mark Werenchuck (Reggie), Rachel Nam (Mandu), Sabrina Mignacca (Ivy), Shayne Murray, my indispensable assistants Henri Lamarch and Taighe Strang, and my dogs (Albear & Hariette). Finally, I thank Gilbert Ranger for driving us all over the city with our pet partners. Your extended or curtailed passage means that AAT would not be possible.

To the students who have participated in AAT but I have not mentioned you in the case study section, please accept my most overly articulated Canadian *Sorry!* It was impossible to include everyone and keep the book to a reasonable size. Know that you have changed us forever, and I hope our animals conveyed their joy while working with you. We cherished your presence during AAT, and I will happily chat with you should we bump into one another. You know where to find us, and remember, our door is always open for you.

I thank my family and friends for supporting me and my crazy ideas about people and animals. Thank you for your ideas, input, insights, feedback, and patience with my recollection of the successes the teens and animals have accomplished over the years. We are passionate about work, which tends to spill into every aspect of our lives. Finally, thank you to all the dogs in our program. The volunteer dogs come from shelters, SPCA, and other rescue organizations, except for Hariette and Mandu.

Thank you to the many rat partners who have gone through

the program. The AAT journey is not always easy, but it is the most rewarding. Most days, we laugh, but we have shed our fair share of tears over the years. However, I would not change one moment.

Thank you from the bottom of my heart.

George thanks you on behalf of the AAT animal crew.

Introduction

Living with a learning disability

Animal-assisted therapy is not for everyone, yet something changes when a human enters a relationship with an animal. People let down their guards and revert to a simpler time when positive emotions overcame them. Childhood memories and experiences come racing forward, compelling humans to live in the present moment through interactions. The human-animal bond is essential to the development of children. The connection experienced between child and animal has the potential to teach empathy, impulse control, gentleness, compassion, confidence, and joy. Later in life, when people face complex challenges, the human-animal bond can serve as a catalyzing agent between adult interactions. People experience reduced blood pressure, heart rate, stress, and other negative emotions (Friedmann, Katcher, Thomas, Lynch & Messent, 1983).

Many grade schools, colleges, universities, hospitals, and businesses employ animals to reduce stress or strengthen bonds between employees and management. Team building conducted with animals is rising because of its efficiency and efficacy. When we hand an animal to a person and instruct him to train the animal to perform a behaviour, cooperation and communication are the first parameters that team members put in place. How can people achieve their goals when animals do not talk or repeat, for that matter?

Years ago, I met with a group of professionals who now devote their time to developing relationships between people through the construction of animal enrichment. Team Building with Bite is a fantastic group that goes beyond the call of duty to challenge our understanding of human-animal relationships. During a Team Building with Bites event, participants are placed outside their comfort zone and work with power tools. As a result, communication flourishes, and cooperation becomes steadfast. I have participated in two of their events throughout the years; therefore, I know firsthand how animals and our dedication to their well-being influence human collaborations. People will do just about anything to have a close encounter with animals.

The benefits of animal-assisted interventions reconnect us with nature, affection, sensory stimulation, and an overall sense of well-being. But most of all, animal encounters bring us back to the present moment and the rhythm of living we forget. Our day-to-day fast-paced lives disconnect us from ourSelves[1]; in turmoil, animals make us feel relaxed, satisfied, and humane. The longing for affection and touch has never been greater. Cell phones do not offer warmth and soothing embraces when emotions overwhelm us, but animals can.

For 30 years, I have asked people, clients, family, and friends why they have a dog. The facial expression often yields an empty stare and bewilderment. Most likely, they have never asked themselves that very question. Perplexed, the vast majority of people I interrogate answer me with *companionship*. I often reply with another question, *but don't you have family, friends, or a spouse for companionship?* The summary of their answers boils down to deception, disappointment, disbelief or a combination of all three. Some people go as far as treating their dogs like toddlers. They speak to them as humans and can make difficult decisions or comprehend complex emotional states. Anthropomorphism throws oil into the fire. Dogs have rooms, sophisticated beds, wardrobes, boots, slippers, designer leashes, collars, transport bags, and jewellery.

At the pinnacle of the anthropomorphic practice, dogs are pushed in strollers and inherit financial fortunes. The dog has taken over the companion role to become the surrogate child. Meanwhile, adults treat their children like adults. Kid clothing resembles adult fashion; children drive fancy cars and have cell

---

[1] Note to the reader: throughout this book, you will note some unusual spellings of certain words: ourSelf, yourSelf, mySelf, god, re-member, etc. These are quite deliberate and intended as a gentle reminder to reconsider their ethymology and definition.

phones and Facebook profiles.

Parents dialogue with their toddlers and young children as if they understand the subtleties of language. During the medieval era, kids were treated more like dogs. Then, in the seventeenth century, adults started to worship children. So, we have reached the apogee of offspring glorification in the 1600s. As Postman describes in The Disappearance of Childhood (1994), childhood disappears as a societal and developmental concept. In his book Centuries of Childhood: A Social History of Family Life, Ariès (1962) describes how the idea of childhood did not exist for the better part of human development.

> *"In medieval society this awareness was lacking. That is why, as soon as the child could live without the constant solicitude of his mother, his nanny or his cradle-rocker, he belonged to adult society."*
>
> — *Ariès, p.128*

The idea of childhood as a separate developmental phase arose in the sixteenth century with the invention of the printed press. *"The printing press created a new definition of adulthood based on reading competence, and, correspondingly, a new conception of childhood based on reading incompetency."* (Postman, 1994, p.18). Before the mass production of information occurred, medieval populations saw development as a two-phase process. A person was either dependent or independent of adults. Until the second part of the 20th century, parents integrated children into their daily activities as soon as they could walk. These children actively participated in societal requirements when they were approximately seven. In the Victorian era, it was not uncommon to see children earn wages.

However, in the seventeenth century, adults started viewing children as distinct from themselves. The rise of the *little adult* as a separate identity exhibiting different needs and desires is a concept we still accept and protect in the twenty-first century. However, over the last six decades, the idea of childhood has been threatened again.

> *"And then, without anyone's suspecting it, a goldsmith from Mainz, Germany, with the aid of an old winepress, gave birth to childhood."*
> —Postman, p.19

The adolescent phase of development, as we know it today, began in 1902 with the psychologist Stanley Hall. No longer considered a child yet not recognized as an adult, psychology sees adolescent development as a transitional phase during which identity and social roles form. Erik Erikson discusses the teenage stage of development at length in his book Identity and the Life Cycle (1980). If we use the analogy of the sea to represent adulthood, adolescence is its murky waters.

When I studied for my first degree, I specialized in adolescent development because the government and private institutions offer minimal services to this population segment. My professor once told me that people would wait in line to register if I built animal-assisted therapy programs. He was right. I love teens because I recognize myself in their creative process, insightful questions, analytical discussions, and their place within the world. We can all recall events during our adolescence that forged our personalities.

Suppose you think back to a challenging moment, positive or negative; chances are, you felt alone and scared. For teens, the school system adds to the discomfort. Students feel ostracized by their peers, misunderstood by their family, and, worse, their friends. Friends often minimize emotional reactions because they do not know how to manage their emotions, let alone somebody else's. I certainly felt that way when I was in high school. I was the *Anglophone* amongst the French-speaking, the woman from Labrador/Newfoundland, a province unknown and unfamiliar to most. I was considered an outcast with very different skills and beliefs. Growing up in Canada's great north, I am the perfect representation of what we call *an army brat*.

A nomad way of life is typical for an army brat. However, the most dramatic effect of growing up in the army was the cultural shock between civilian and military lifestyles. Military bases in the middle of nowhere, in the second-largest country on earth, provide a bubble-like life. We were isolated from the world with nuclear drills, fighter planes going Mach-2 or Mach-3, and men in immaculate uniforms discussing with other immaculately dressed higher-ranking men.

The fact that army kids can recognize stripes and stars on uniforms and address personnel with *Yes—Sir—No—Sir!* was surreal. So was playing on tanks, part of an army brat's life. You can imagine a little more easily how life's different experiences influence who we are and who we become over time. If you read Dog in the Mirror is God, a scientifically spiritual approach to treating human and animal behaviour problems, you know I have a learning disability. I was diagnosed in my mid-twenties by the Learning Centre at Dawson College.

I am happy to have grown up in remote places within the Air Force. The first reason is that the remoteness of the location meant television was not an option, but animals were. The presence of our domestic and nature's exotic animals made life bearable. The second reason is that I got to experience amazing things most people never will know. I saw icebergs and flocks of geese so impressive that their chatter was deafening. The Aurorae Borealis, a 360° uninterrupted horizon, snow, so much snow, and planes of all shapes and sizes were unconventional realities. It was a fantastic time in my life.

Before I knew I had a learning disability, I felt lost and confused. Teachers told my classmates to search our math memory drawer to retrieve the information we needed to solve the problem. I recall raising my hand to ask where I looked and if I had no memory drawer, just a pile of data on the floor. She never answered me. My response should have raised a red flag. Still, psychologists did not assess students for learning disabilities when I was a child. Army base did not equip their teachers to identify and assist students with neurocognitive disorders. When this situation arises, students fall through the cracks.

The term learning disability was coined in 1963 in the United States by Samuel A. Kirk. Fourteen years later, students were still not recognized or tested for dyslexia or other learning impairments. Learning-disabled students struggled in class;

therefore, school staff placed them in special needs groups. Thank god I never made it into those classes. The one thing I did notice about myself was that life became much more manageable if our dogs were around. I felt more relaxed and allowed myself to be. I would sometimes rest on our Great Dane's torso and sink my breath with theirs; this made me feel more secure, especially if I had some essay or big assignment due.

When we moved to Quebec, there was a period during adolescence when dogs were absent from my environment; those were my most problematic years. Dogs did not help with my education per se; however, they did contribute to my motivation to learn. I was fortunate in my misfortunes to have very open-minded neighbours. They let me play and train their dogs, which was rewarding itself. I loved those canids as if they were my family members.

I am, to this day, forever grateful for their trust and belief in me and their extreme generosity. During a meditation séance in the late 1990s, I had a vision of my life's purpose. It was so vivid that I drew the plan on paper. It was as if every moment of my life had prepared me for this, good or bad. I was to create an animal-assisted therapy program like no other, which I have set out to accomplish. It took longer than expected, but countless things happened between now and then.

Following the vision, my journey began as an animal-assisted practitioner. My learning disabilities, when coupled with my knowledge of dog behaviour, allow me to make sense of a highly confusing world. Dogs are indeed a god sent.

My path to animal-assisted therapy

The project started in 1997. My first step was to discuss animal-assisted with a professional therapist about my goals and objectives. I needed to know where to start, so I searched for the leading animal-assisted therapy specialist near where I lived. That was the easy part; my research yielded two people, and one had moved to France. Raymond Plouffe from the Douglas

Mental Health University Institute in Montreal was the person I contacted. Our meeting was productive and enlightening. M. Plouffe was kind and generous with his time. I told M. Plouffe I was looking forward to working with teens. He invited me to stay for two of his sessions with autistic teenage boys.

One of M. Plouffe's recommendations was to complete a university degree in any human science program and specialize in my target clientele. When I went back home, I did more research. I needed to find which university program would be best. It took a few years to settle on a degree and a university. After this, I decided to wait a few years for my son to mature and become autonomous. In 2009, I returned to school after an absence of fifteen years. That was challenging.

Following the meeting with M. Plouffe, I listed my intended accomplishments. I am happy to report that I am working on the last three elements of that list. I graduated in 2016 and was readmitted the next day into psychology, more specifically in cognitive neuroscience. My son once said I would still be in university in my nineties. He might be right because I love learning.

During my university internship, I was fortunate to put the animal-assisted therapy program to the test. I had called all the establishments that usually accepted students, but everyone I contacted turned me down. Barbara White, from Perspectives I High School, accepted my internship proposal. My internship teacher was friends with Mr. White, and she convinced her that the AAT program was *amazingly successful*. Thus, I had eight weeks allotted for my internship, so I went to work as soon as possible. Chapter four will discuss each school and the students who participated or are still participating in the animal-assisted therapy programs.

Programs are plural because we work with multiple species. Each animal species has specific protocols for socializing, training, and transporting; consequently, success lies in refining that process with each new animal addition. An element not on the previous list but which M. Plouffe had made me think of was my choice of animal partners. Initially, I thought dogs were the obvious answer, but I concluded that was not the only possibility with research. Rats, too, can make magic happen.

In 2003, I started to breed rats and immediately saw their impact on my teenage son. Rats are hyper-social, fast, funny, agile, fusional, and highly relaxing when they walk directly on your skin. It might appear disgusting to some, but those who have experienced rat massages vouch for them. I introduced rats in my animal-assisted therapy program in 2015 at Focus High School in Montreal. The program structure is the same regardless of the animal species. Rats, dogs, and people learn through the same leading learning theories. Differences lie in species-specific animal behaviour. At the bottom of the food chain, rats prefer safety as their primary reinforcement. At the same time, most canids select food or play. When I add a new species to the program, homework is required.

I must first study species-specific taxonomy, vocal and non-vocal behaviours, biology, and physiology. Rats do not move like dogs. When a rat and a canid flatten themselves to the ground, the significance differs from one species to the next. Similarly, there are many differences between program constructs. Animal-assisted interventions and zootherapy might look or sound the same; however, they are different in their creation. Program designers build AAIs with specific intentions.

The first chapter will describe and explain what the

different terms mean and what laws govern the animal-assisted therapy industry, if any. My goal is to shed some light on the confusion. Chapter two introduces a socializing and training sample week in the life of a working pet partner. The third section will explore the common conditions afflicting our participants. The last chapter explores some of our more notable students and some successful and unsuccessful cases. I added a few photographs of the students who worked with us the longest but did not necessarily end as successfully as other teens.

Most animals I work with reside at the Dogue Shop; animal-assisted programs become who we are. We must constantly care for our pet partners and devote time to feeding, cleaning, bathing, training, and upkeeping their socialization needs. The different forms of animal-related work often define the lifestyle we choose for ourselves and our clients. I designed my programs based on what I would have needed as a teenager. Reading to dogs would have improved my skills twice as fast, if not more. Instead, teachers told me to read out loud in front of a mirror. That never happened. AAIs must include transferable skills to impart long-lasting changes within our student body.

I added extra pages for your note-taking needs at the end of the book. Furthermore, I inserted contact information should you wish to read and expand your knowledge of animal-assisted interventions. Weblinks might change over time; therefore, I will only mention names for your Googling needs. If you have an e-book, you can follow the links. For paper book lovers, you can search the titles; it should bring you directly to the website.

> *"The only tyrant I accept in this world is the "still small voice" within me. And even though I have to face the prospect of being a minority of one, I humbly believe I have the courage to be in such a hopeless minority."*
> —Mahatma Gandhi, 1922, p.1023

I did not write this book to glorify AAI. I aim to present an objective view to further our profession. The human-animal bond is a powerful healing connection we need to protect if we are to guarantee our profession's future. Safety is our priority.

As you read along, remember that you are reading the thoughts of a dyslexic mind. I may repeat myself, present strange sentence structures, and the odd typo. Except for repetitions, blame Grammarly for the editing mishaps. The humour is all mine.

Happy reading.

Albear 2010-2022. In memory.

"What we actually need when we come into a new situation is time—all the time that is necessary in any situation to become fully acquainted."

— *Virginia Satir, 1988*

Chapter 1
AAT Definitions

Animal-assisted therapy and the law

An umbrella term in our field refers to many animal-related services, excluding law enforcement or the military. Animal-assisted interventions (AAI) regroup animal-assisted therapy, animal-assisted activity, and animal-assisted psychotherapy. I will also define service animals and emotional support dogs. Some countries, states, and provinces legally protect specific terms; consequently, I can only write from the perspective of the country and province where I live. In the United States, laws protect those with disabilities under the Americans with Disabilities Act (ADA). The ADA is a federal law passed in 1990. Canada does not have a federal law specific to disabilities. The Canadian Charter of Rights (1982) and Freedoms and the Canadian Human Rights Act (1985) protect people with physical or mental disabilities. The Charter states:

> **15.** (1) Every individual is equal before and under the law and has the right to the equal protection and equal benefit of the law without discrimination and, in particular, without discrimination based on race, national or ethnic origin, colour, religion, sex, age or mental or physical disability.

The Human Rights Act is a little more specific yet highly interpretable regarding animals. While Article 3 describes the basis of discrimination, Articles 5 (a, b) and 6 (a, b) relate to the entry and stay of a public or private establishment. Both articles state:

> **3.** (1) For all purposes of this Act, the prohibited grounds of discrimination are race, national or

ethnic origin, colour, religion, age, sex, sexual orientation, gender identity or expression, marital status, family status, genetic characteristics, disability and conviction for an offence for which a pardon has been granted or in respect of which a record suspension has been ordered.

5. It is a discriminatory practice in the provision of goods, services, facilities or accommodations customarily available to the general public.
 (a) to deny, or to deny access to, any such good, service, facility or accommodation to any individual, or **(b)** to differentiate adversely in relation to any individual, on a prohibited ground of discrimination.

6. It is a discriminatory practice in the provision of commercial premises or residential accommodation. **(a)** to deny occupancy of such premises or accommodation to any individual, or **(b)** to differentiate adversely in relation to any individual, on a prohibited ground of discrimination.

Canada does not clearly define what a service animal is. Consequently, provinces are legally responsible for these definitions. In Quebec, animal rights are under revision; thus, what I am about to write might become obsolete when this book is published. Regardless, I must write the law as it is now. Quebec only recognizes two disabilities: visually impaired and autism spectrum disorder (ASD). Disabled people can enter any public or private establishment with their service dog for these two conditions. The trainer's name should appear on the document along with any relevant documentation about the condition—people with other conditions wishing to have a service dog need a document stating the person's situation. A psychiatrist or other government-recognized practitioner will write a letter and sign it. The document should always accompany the person and dog. If the person wants to enter a governmental establishment, the organization is responsible for stating its position. Government building regulations can refuse animals. Suppose a person with disabilities wishes to bring their pet into a private business. In that case, the decision remains the establishment's owner's choice.

A few federal and provincial parks allow dogs on leashes. Most municipal parks also accept dogs on leashes. In contrast, actual service animals are allowed in all levels of parks. Unfortunately, people lie about their animal's true purpose because we do not have a provincial registry for work animals. The lack of clarity leads to intolerance towards genuine service animals wishing to enter establishments. Moreover, there is a pressing need for an easily accessible registry to verify and protect people who are genuinely disabled and require an animal to fulfill their daily activities.

Animal-assisted intervention

No municipal, provincial, or federal laws govern animal activities within the human intervention or prevention disciplines. In other words, practitioners do not need to design animal-assisted intervention (AAI) programs based on regulations or laws. If you drive a car, you need, by law, to buckle your safety belt. Civil and criminal law applies when suspected of negligence, recklessness, or intent to cause harm. Consequently, insurance companies require establishments and professionals to have their clients sign waivers and assumption of risk documents before starting an AAI program. Provincial civil laws also govern breach of contract. In Quebec, professional orders protect practitioners such as psychologists and psychiatrists. Due diligence legally controls AAIs.

The brick-and-mortar establishment's insurance typically covers their company for those without a professional order. However, practitioners should acquire a *follow-me* insurance policy if they travel outside their establishment to conduct AAIs. I strongly recommend that future practitioners research all applicable laws before designing and implementing AAI programs in their area. Municipal laws dictate which animals are allowed or forbidden on their territory. Furthermore, cities might require a business plan, permits, and occupational licenses to conduct business within their boundaries.

In Handbook on Animal-Assisted Therapy: Theoretical Foundations and Guidelines for Practice (AAI Handbook), Dr. Fine regroups animal-assisted therapy, animal-assisted activities, animal-assisted psychotherapy, and other exercises into one umbrella term called animal-assisted interventions. In the AAI Handbook, chapter two, Kruger & Serpell (2006) cite Kathleen Ray Lajoie (2003) with the following terms:

> *"Pet therapy, pet psychotherapy, pet-facilitated therapy, pet-facilitated psychotherapy, four-footed therapy, animal-facilitated counselling, pet-mediated therapy, companion-animal pet-oriented psychotherapy, therapy, and co-therapy with an animal."*
> —*Kathleen Ray Lajoie, p.22*

Some terms might sound unprofessional, but they all strive to define the animal as a pet partner. The human-animal bond (HAB) is the core of animal-assisted interventions, with or without goals specifically designed within their structure. The term Animal-assisted intervention is much easier to remember because it refers to the interceding process between animals and humans. Researchers Kruger and Serpell (2004) define AAIs as *"any intervention that intentionally includes or incorporates animals as part of a therapeutic or ameliorative process or milieu."* Animal-assisted therapy is still predominantly used as a general term to describe any HAB activity that strives to improve the human condition. I am guilty of this terminology offence and switch between AAI and AAT to describe similar programs.

Think of the word doctor. It is a general term for everyone caring for the human body. Healthcare figuratively cuts the body into segments and attributes a particular doctor to them. These specialists are cardiologists, gynecologists, urologists, and other healthcare professionals. When you tell a friend you have a skin rash, you will probably say *I went to the doctor*. People rarely say *I went to the dermatologist*. Yet, both terms are correct and convey the pertinent information you consulted a professional healthcare provider.

Animal-assisted interventions date back many decades. Konrad Lorenz once said, *"The wish to keep an animal usually arises from a general longing for a bond with nature. The bond with a true dog is as lasting as the ties of this earth can ever be."* (Fine, 2010). I agree with this quote one hundred percent. Being disconnected from nature nourishes anxiety and stress. Access to an endless abundance of information at the push of a button is unnatural and can become overwhelming. I see our students struggle with anxiety and panic attacks. Yet, when they are in the presence of our animals, teenagers relax and take the necessary time to be and develop a positive HAB.

There are sayings on the walls at the Dogue Shop, and one states *Thou Enter Animal Time*. This quote reminds our students and clients that in our establishment, we do not produce behaviour; we train behaviour. The animal has one hundred percent control over its learning. The rationale reaffirms our connection to nature because we cannot force an animal to perform a specific behaviour. We must wait for the animal to offer behaviour and work from there. The human-animal bond secret lies in the animal's decision-making process. The animals chose to make contact. Gary Priest once told me, *"When you put people and animals together, you obtain instantaneous success, even if the animal fails."* The reason is simple: the animal chose to interact, which captivates our species; the result is irrelevant.

Choice is the motivation behind the popularity of close encounters. Ambassador programs in zoos, aquariums, and other facilities are rising worldwide. When the encounter is over, the person leaves with an overflowing feeling of acceptance, belonging, joy, and love. Unconditional love is why people place themselves in dangerous selfie situations with wild animals. The rarity of the natural encounter alone defines our humanity. Above all else, people feel unique because the animal chose to connect with them. When I bring teenagers to work with horses, it is their first encounter with an equid for the most part. The group is always captivated by the sheer size of the animals: horses command presence, self-awareness, and impulse control. You cannot text your best friend and try to interact with them simultaneously. You might lose a body part; conversely, when the animal responds to the exercise, the immediate realization is one of inter-species communication and understanding. It is an *"instantaneous success."*

Animal-assisted intervention programs are rising, and my teacher was right; people are knocking at my door. Animal-assisted therapy (AAT) and animal-assisted activity (AAA) are similar but achieve different results. Some programs do not attempt to reach specific goals and objectives. At the Dogue Shop, we are goal-oriented people. I love to see a person change. I admire the teens' resilience and desire to interact and forge partnerships with the animals. Still, most importantly, I marvel at animals' willingness to form relationships with us.

I affectionately refer to my different programs as dog animal-assisted therapy (DAAT), rat animal-assisted therapy (RAAT), wolf animal-assisted therapy (WAAT), and horse animal-assisted therapy (HAAT). You can make a funny sentence to remind people about our program if you have not noticed it. The phrase is *What's that rat hat*. I love humour; it lightens the mood before we get serious.

Animal-assisted therapy

The following definition of animal-assisted therapy includes Animal-Assisted Education (AAE). Both terms are very similar; therefore, I prefer to group them into one functional description. My classification differs from the literature because the bond developed between humans and animals creates a desire to protect that species. An old Mohawk proverb says humans destroy what they do not know, but if we understand a species, we will protect it. AATs not only create and maintain secure attachments, but they also serve to transform people into ambassadors for other animal species. Consequently, the definition of animal-assisted therapy necessitates a revision.

> *"If you do not talk to them [animals], you will not know them, and what you do not know, you will fear. What one fears, one destroys."*
>
> —Chief Dan George

Fine writes in Handbook on Animal-Assisted Therapy: Theoretical Foundations and Guidelines for Practice AAT that *"A form of therapy that involves using an animal as a fundamental part of a person's treatment."* (2010, p.XV). This definition does not stipulate the role of the animal. Furthermore, I can not entirely agree with the term *using* an animal because it implies we are forcing animals into servitude by participating in therapy sessions. In reality, we invite animals to partake in the therapeutic process and allow them to refuse interactions. Conversely, the refusal of an animal to interact should be considered a healthy outcome. If the animal abstains from contact, I will backtrack and reassess the situation. I will reevaluate the animal, the client, and the environment to see if they have changed and hindered progress.

I prefer to describe AAT as a goal-oriented therapeutic process achieved by developing a secure attachment between a specifically trained animal and a person with psychological or physiological needs. The animal immediately becomes a catalyst between the practitioner and the client or patient. This definition characterizes the role of the animal and assesses the interaction by compiling information and data on the exchange. Each client-animal team and individual animal has a file. Tracking progress is essential to human and animal well-being, especially in therapeutic settings. Without specific goals or objectives, animal-assisted therapy emerges as an animal-assisted activity.

Do not get me wrong; I am not proclaiming one as better than the other; it all depends on the nature of the outcome expectancy. We measure an AAI program against its results; that is the only way to track its validity. If I want orange juice and press lemons, I will have juice, but it will not be the desired kind. Occasionally, a program will yield unforeseen positive or negative goals; we hope for the former, but sometimes we achieve the latter. I witnessed participants change their views towards certain animals from utter disdain to total enjoyment. Although rare, I have documented the opposite.

When appropriately designed, AAT programs rarely achieve adverse outcomes because of the nature of the human-animal bond. The need for protection and emotional safety is the essential survival mechanism for a social species (Bowlby, 1969). Insecure attachments lead to anxiety, stress, fear, anger, and a series of other negative emotions; consequently, animals offer a secure attachment by reducing the negative emotions in people (Nagasawa, Mogi, & Kikusui, 2009). In their paper on Attachment Between humans and Dogs, Nagasawa, Mogi, & Kikusui (2009) summarize the process as follows, *"The activities of the system [safety regulation system] tend to reduce the risk of harm to the individual, for example, predation and anxiety, and to increase the sense of security."* (p. 210).

> *"This suggests the possible elements that form the basis of cross-species empathy and that the development of evolutionary cognitive abilities in a species may depend on not only their genetic dendrogram[2], but also interspecies-specific symbiotic relations."*
>
> —*Nagasawa, Mogi, & Kikusui, 2009*

Since people replicate their attachment style throughout their lives (Bowlby, 1969, 1980; Ainsworth, 1979), there seems to be no end to emotional suffering. The ultimate underlying goal of AAT is to create and maintain a secure attachment style throughout the individual's lifespan (Bowlby, 1973; Zilcha-mano, Mikulincer, & Shaver, 2011). When we look at human-animal interconnectedness, we observe the bond positively impacting the human condition. Science has noticed and kept

---

[2] Dendrogram: is a tree diagram, especially one showing taxonomic relationships.

studying the symbiotic relationship we share with animals and pets. From the 1600s to today, philosophers, psychologists, and psychiatrists have discussed animals' role and impact on humans. However, more research on human-animal attachment is necessary to explain why our interspecies connection with dogs generates the four attachment criteria: proximity seeking, safe-haven, secure base, and separation distress (Ainsworth, 1991; Zilcha-mano, Mikulincer, & Shaver, 2011).

Meanwhile, AAT provides insight into the fact that animals are fundamental facilitators in the Umwelt[3] process. In animal-assisted therapy, the therapeutic approach should correspond to a direct link between the species-specific behaviour and the person's response to the trained behaviour. An example of species-specific behaviour is the *up behaviour*. All dogs can place their two front feet up on something and stay. We teach the *hugging* dog behaviour for the AAT program because it serves the human-animal bond. Most dogs despise hugging because it is not part of their ethogram. Conversely, human hugs establish emotional connections and social affiliations (McClelland, 1951).

Eye gazing is another species-specific behaviour that is not interspecific. Dogs naturally avoid prolonged eye contact because it generates conflicts. Dogs prefer to avoid conflict; thus, they frequently break or avoid eye contact. I have trained my dogs to seek eye contact because humans feel acknowledged through visual connection. Albear, my dog, will go so far as to growl (trained behaviour) to solicit eye contact. It works every time. People make eye contact to seek information: *Am I OK or in danger?* Either way, Albear is reinforced by the actual visual acknowledgement from the person. In my programs, I train all the dogs for specific behaviours common to all pet partners.

In contrast, some behaviours are exhibited only by one

---

[3] Umwelt: in ethology the word refers to 'the world as it is experienced by a particular organism'; form the German word 'environment'.

member of the animal team. Mandu, the dachshund, is the only dog in our program; I trained to display the *Pow!* You're dead behaviour. In my experience, an untrained animal should not be considered an animal-assisted partner. The reasons are multiple. First, the therapist must master dog language to identify whether the animal exhibits a species-specific behaviour. Secondly, the practitioner cannot foresee behaviour regression if it does not have a specific behaviour performance baseline. In other words, how can one assess if the animal's behaviour is progressing, stagnating, or regressing? Here is an example. I trained a dog to *place paw-on-arm* but now performs a *place toe-on-arm*; the behaviour has regressed.

In this case, the human professional evaluates why the dog refused to perform the behaviour or why it deteriorated. Was it circumstantial, boredom, negative sensory input from the clients, or poor reinforcement brought on by inadequate training skills during training sessions? The answer harms the client and the dog's physical and psychological well-being. When I train animals to perform specific behaviours, most likely, it is because I have set goals or objectives for clients and patients. Animal-assisted therapy is probably confused with animal-assisted activities or what people in Quebec call zootherapy. I believe both practices should hold their definitions based on two factors. The first factor is the human science profession field. The second is the level of training the animal received and succeeded. Suppose we are to progress as a profession and prevent our clients from accidents. In that case, we must ensure that the animals in our programs are deemed trustworthy and safe.

> "We need animals as allies to reinforce our inner selves. We must revive our intimate associations with nature and its animals if we are to survive as the dominant species on earth. It is, of course, possible that man can survive without animals, but we would surely be a depleted race, shorn of most of our emotional strength."
> —Levinson, 1972, p.29

Animal-assisted activity

Many people confuse animal-assisted activity with animal-assisted therapy since AAT, AAE, and AAA are practices that include animal partners in their programs. The significant difference between therapy, education, and activity lies in the goals and objectives, or lack thereof, designed into the program plan. (Fine, 2010).

I describe AAA curriculums as inclusive or exclusive. We define an inclusive approach as a multidisciplinary team working towards specific goals and objectives. Animal practitioners work within a group of human science professionals such as psychologists, social workers, teachers, therapists, or any combination of these or other professions. Multidisciplinary teams can work with groups or individuals; I tailor program goals and objectives to the person and group. The animal practitioner often works nearby by involving or soliciting a reaction from the pet partner's interactions. The animal can accomplish certain behaviours but requires the professional's guidance to direct the exchange.

An exclusive approach is quite the opposite. Animal practitioners do not design their programs with specific goals or objectives. Exclusive AAAs intend to entertain rather than intervene. If I observe a change in human behaviour, it is often a corollary outcome, not a direct development achievement. When I see physiological changes within AAAs, such as lower heart rate and stress levels (Friedmann et al., 1983), these benefits are an indirect result, not a sought-after goal.

The following is an example of AAT versus an exclusive AAA within the same program. I would structure the AAT exercise to induce communication between peers as follows. When the students enter the room, I ask them, How do you think your animal feels today? I ask follow-up questions: What makes you say that, and why? Can you describe what behaviours you see that would explain the feeling? The next step would be to ask the pair of students to summarize the exercise we did last time and where we should start this week. I would hand the leash to one team member and the tools to the other. The exercise began with communication endeavours elicited through the animal. Students work in teams of two or three and must agree upon the proper strategy to work through the training exercise. If there is a problem, we encourage the participant, with the help of the pet partner, to solve the situation by implementing an effective strategy. We apply the solution and reinforce a positive outcome. I track and document the progress of an intervention exercise and report its progress.

In AAA, I would structure things differently. First, the students would not work in groups; there would be no formal exercise design; teens would interact with the animals only if they wished to. I would bring a toy and encourage participants to play. Still, I would not force interactions between humans and animals. In inclusive AAAs, if there is an issue to work through, the animal practitioner would seek the help of the multidisciplinary team. In an exclusive AAA, the onset of a problem would inevitably end the session. After the session, there would be no tracking or documentation of the participant's progress.

Inclusive or exclusive AAAs and AATs benefit those involved; thus, we cannot state that one is better. In my opinion, both practices are valuable to those participating in them. Conversely, the term zootherapy, in my opinion, should be discouraged to avoid confusion or misunderstandings. The following section discusses why we should avoid the term altogether. Remember that it is mister and misses everybody we must convince, not the government agencies. Free services undermine professionals.

Zootherapy

People confuse AAIs and zootherapy by establishing them as one and the same. Unfortunately, professionals need constant clarification as to why AAIs and zootherapy differ. The term zootherapy is almost exclusive to the French-speaking population. Anglos never use zootherapy to describe AAIs. The term zootherapy refers to the use of animal-based medicine or nutraceuticals. If you take glucosamine made from shark cartilage, you use zootherapy to address a physical ailment. If you are depressed, glucosamine will not aid in treating your psychological problem. In French-speaking communities, people use zootherapy as an umbrella term for all AAIs. The French term regularly refers to an uneducated and untrained human-animal team visiting establishments for the elderly, ill, or dying. Somehow, people believe that animals who do not display reactions in social interactions make them uniquely qualified to practice this type of *therapy*. People who offer zootherapy[4] do so as volunteers. Typically, unpaid workers do not provide intervention or prevention services. We often refer to this as pet-the-puppy sessions.

Furthermore, volunteers do not track clients or see problems develop. Most zootherapy practitioners do not have adequate insurance policies, nor do their clients sign waivers and assumptions of risk documents. The potential for accidents is extremely high, putting the profession under scrutiny. Significant confusion often occurs between AAAs and zootherapy visits. The difference lies in the human's education and the pet partner's training. Another considerable difference between AAIs and zootherapy is cost; AAI practitioners charge for their services. AAI professionals are highly educated and have extensively trained their animals. Practitioners are ensured and track their clients and pet partners; thus, they frequently visit the veterinarian to offer professional services.

I have observed throughout the years that one out of five professionals burns out with their pets within five years of starting AAIs. The Journal of The American Veterinary Medical Association (Larkin, 2021) shows that five out of ten veterinarians burn out. We can extend this statistic to another professional animal group, zoos. My colleagues in zoo settings

---

[4] Zootherapy can best be described as making people feel better by visiting them with their pets in specific establishments.

are also highly susceptible to work-related emotional problems. The American Psychology Association (APA) states in their opening paragraph (2019) that people who work with animals are at high risk of developing mental health issues.

> *"According to data from the 2016, 2017, and 2018 AVMA Census of Veterinarians surveys, 50.2% of respondents were classified as having high burnout scores. Controlling for other variables, high educational debt was associated with high burnout."*
> —*AVMA, 2021*

The APA says many problems plague veterinarians, technologists, and shelter workers face during their careers. The inability to save animals is a significant contributor. I can attest that working against one's values causes frustration and emotional distress among the clinic staff, all positions included. Working with animals is not for the faint of heart. Caring for an organism that cannot express how it feels is, at best, heart-wrenching to watch it suffer and not be able to say *Everything will be okay, trust me!* Animal trainers, groomers, and pet sitters experience these conditions, too. Therefore, it is apparent that AAI practitioners also face high levels of depression, anxiety, burnout, and even suicide.

> *"While it might sound like fun to work around pets every day, veterinarians and people who volunteer at animal shelters face particular stressors that can place them at risk for depression, anxiety and even suicide, according to research presented at the annual convention of the American Psychological Association."*
> —*APA, 2019*

Finally, professional AAI practitioners regularly reevaluate animal wellness levels to ensure their pet partners do not burn out. I have seen too many dogs come to hate people because AAI therapists ignore the animal's request for boundaries and space or misunderstand the behaviour. I had to pull one of my client's dogs from another company's program because it demonstrated aggressive behaviour toward unfamiliar people. Dogs should not develop behavioural problems from AAI; we owe our animals that much. It is best to stop a session, pull the animal out, and explain to clients why we opted for that strategy.

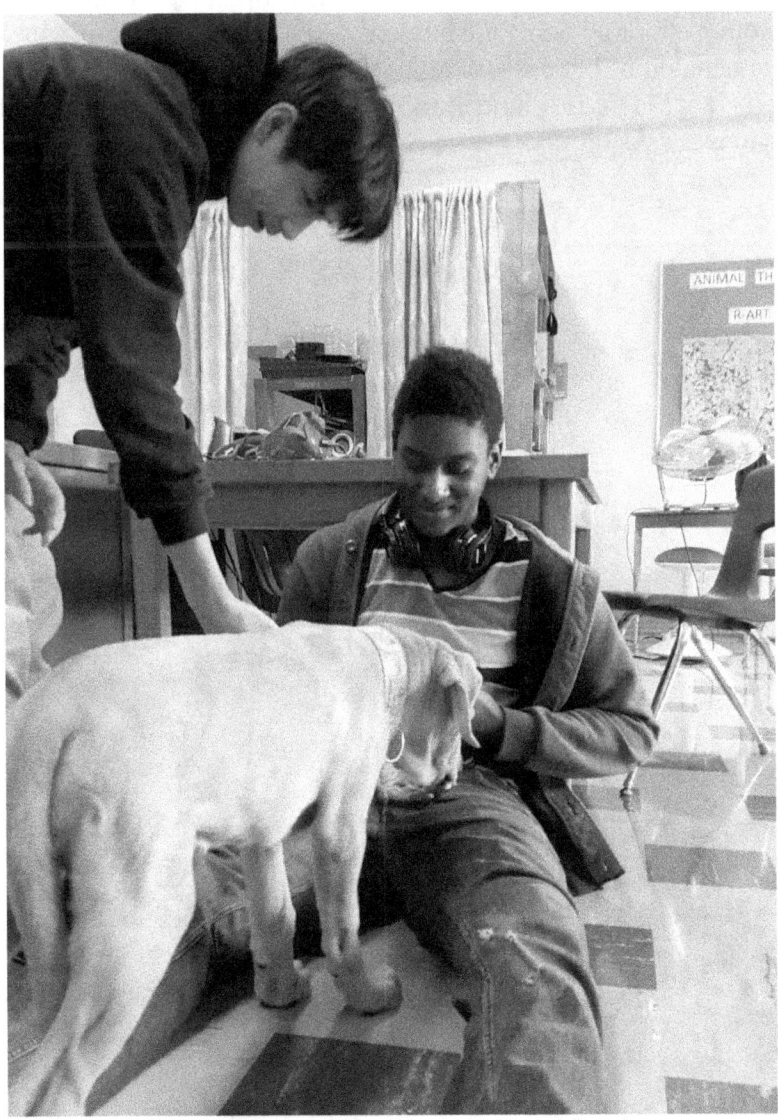

Hariette meets the AAT students for the first time.

Puppy Hariette participates in her first AAT session after recently arriving from an extended European trip. Can you tell if she is happy or not? Try to test yourself. Can you describe what you see? I upload videos to educate people about dog language. You can subscribe to the Dogue Academy YouTube channel for answers. Dog language behaviours can often be subtle to the untrained eye. Our student asks George, the dog, to *touch* his hand. The behaviour consists of placing the tip of his snout in the middle of the stretched-out hand. George executes the behaviour, but can you tell if George is happy, compliant, or reluctant? Here is a hint: I trained George to *touch* the hand of whoever asks him.

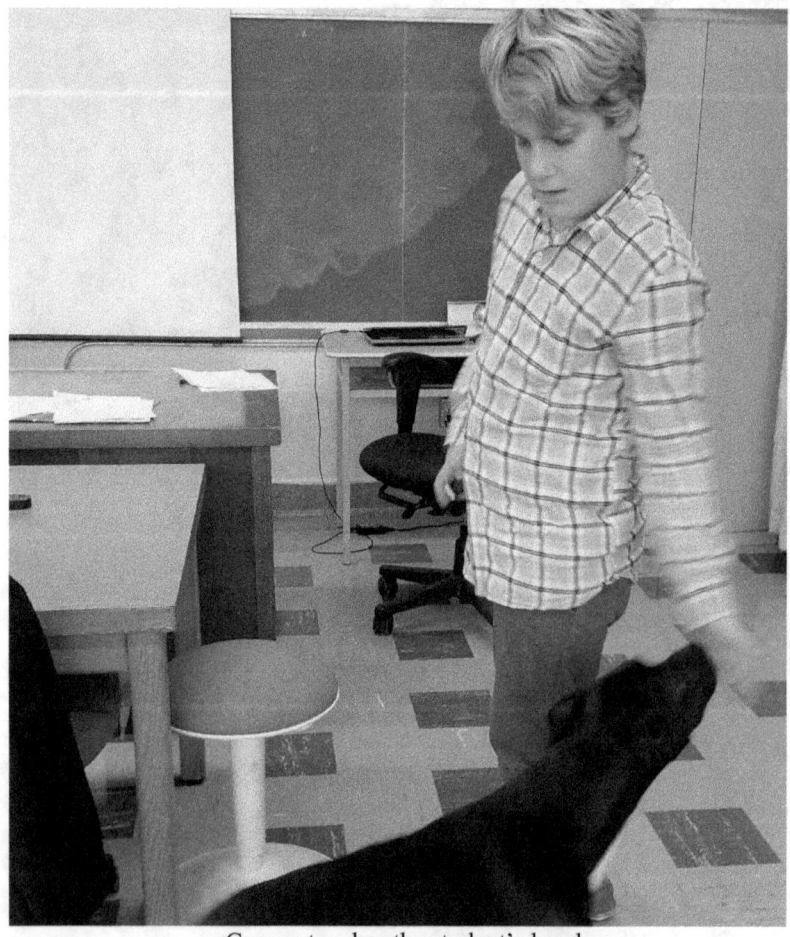

George touches the student's hand.

In many cases, you will see a photo of students wearing gloves. The program does not force students to do something they are against or dislike; however, we can and do insist by adapting to their needs. It is all about negotiating. Teens are remarkable because they work through their conditions when animals are involved, and we get to compromise. For various reasons, some teenagers find the idea of manipulating a rat to be overwhelming. Movies and television have transformed rats into vicious predators that blatantly kill humans. It is important to remember that these are nothing more than myths. Rats are clean and kind animals.

Students train a rat for agility.

In the following image, Mandu, the dachshund and the student work to perfect the dog's husbandry[5] behaviours. As a long and short-haired mixed Dachshund, Mandu often gets nasty mats in his fur; consequently, we brush him regularly. Furthermore, because he is low to the ground, objects like

---

[5] Husbandry behaviour refers behavioural procedures trained for the sole purpose of managing the animal's general or veterinary healthcare.

branches, leaves, rocks, or gum get stuck on his body. In winter, Mandu turns into a giant snowball. Although this might look funny, Mandu must be watered down with warm water to remove those snowballs from his body. We must consider each dog's needs when we go outside with the dogs. Short and long-haired dogs do not sustain cold weather the same way.

Mandu is covered with snowballs.

Husbandry training allows us to care for animals, reducing their stress load. Snowman Mandu is a testament to a well-trained dog. He lets me slowly melt the snow from his coat in the tub without a fight. He even enjoys the warm water after a cold outing. I always say the animal can refuse to execute a behaviour; however, I am permitted to insist it performs the task.

Can you tell if Mandu is happy, frustrated, scared, excited, or trying to avoid the situation? Taighe and I trained Mandu to accept grooming, but what do you see from his body language? He turned his head because Taighe was combing his ear; still, you can observe his closed mouth, breaking eye contact, and resting on his shoulder blade, which means he is tense. These are normal behaviours under the circumstances. Zootherapy animals are the ones who, in my professional opinion, suffer the most. Their stress level can increase when environmental changes occur (Ng et al., 2014). Ng et al. (2014) and Kelly &

Cozzolino (2017) state that AAI animals need extra care and constant physical and mental healthcare evaluation. AAA professionals are better suited for the job than zootherapy practitioners because of their profound understanding of animal behaviour and training. They have spent countless hours and financial resources on their education and utilize their knowledge to prevent burnout or physical and emotional injuries. I teach animal-assisted therapy to practitioners; therefore, I can attest to their training.

> "An appropriately trained handler can influence the dog's perception of the environment and minimize the stress response by facilitating controlled and predictable interactions."
> —Ng et al., 2014, p. 80

Research in the English language very rarely, if ever, discusses zootherapy as a profession. I have over a thousand research papers in my Mendeley software, and only one French study mentions zootherapy. This book is no exception. From here on, when I discuss animal-related programs, zootherapy is considered excluded from AAIs. The separation between zootherapy and AAT establishes that our profession is not a volunteer position. It is crucial to make this distinction, especially regarding safety and insurance policies. I train AAI practitioners to identify risks versus a volunteer with no formal training in assessing dog language; this poses a high risk to our profession. It only takes one bite to render our jobs obsolete.

The divide between professional and non-professionals is more valid for the following term: emotional support animal (ESA or ESD/dog). I receive daily messages from people asking me to train or certify their dogs as ESA. People want to bring their animals everywhere, which is not feasible or safe. I have witnessed many fake ESDs lash out, bark, growl, or even snap at people; their behaviour is highly unacceptable and dangerous.

Emotional support dog

Emotional support dogs, support dogs, support animals, therapy dogs, and other terms referring to human emotional management animals are synonymous with ESDs. In their research, Nagasawa et al. (2013) and Guo et al. (2018) concluded that dogs connect with human emotions based on the left lateralization gaze. Consequently, dogs seem to react to the emotional display or the biochemicals released by the body people express when they are anxious, stressed, sad, angry, or panicked. Consequently, dogs do not provide therapy; they naturally soothe their human partner because of a shared emotional attachment. Many scientists studied the effects of petting or interacting with a robot dog covered with plush fur and found similar results compared to sentient dog interactions (Edwards, 2022; Jøranson et al., 2015; Foerder & Royer, 2021) (Preston Foerder, 2021).

Emotional support dogs do not provide services, nor do they conduct therapy. Animal trainers rarely train ESD animals; however, when they are, the training plan reinforces dogs' naturally occurring behaviour. The terms emotional support and service animal are often confused because dogs assist people. I have witnessed aggressive ESD and zootherapy animals in the community. Because of a lack of regulation, bystanders are highly likely to get bit by poorly adapted and trained animals. The lack of regulation has opened the door to people who want to bring their animals everywhere. Fake service and emotional support dogs pose a serious problem to those genuinely disabled.

> *"A clear distinction should be made between emotional response to animals, that is, their recreational use, and therapy. It should not be concluded that any event that is enjoyed by the patients is a kind of therapy."*
> —Beck and Katcher, 1984

People might be upset by the harsh explanation. Yet, my objective is to discuss and clarify terms to avoid banishing all working animals because of the high risk of bite incidents to clients. A psychiatrist should diagnose people who receive ESDs for their condition. The dog trainer and the client agree on which behaviours to train that discriminate a pet from a working dog. ESDs should never display agonistic behaviour towards humans or other animals.

Finally, I believe an ESD and service dog registrar is needed to identify genuine working animals. Self-diagnosis to justify bringing a pet everywhere because it makes the person feel good is not a service or working animal. A fake ESD or service animal poses severe problems for a needy population, especially AAI practitioners. Presenting fake working dogs should be illegal and should be punished with hefty fines. If a person feels the need to bring their pet everywhere, there is an underlying condition that they should address. Furthermore, constantly exposing a dog to highly distracting and overstimulating environments harms the animal's mental health.

Service dogs

Service animals are trained animals that perform specific behaviours that facilitate a person's life because of a disability. Without their service animal, people could not function autonomously. There are two service dog categories: physical and psychological impairments. Physical conditions are visually impaired, wheelchair-bound, mobility dog chronic pain, vertigo, limb amputation, and other physical disabilities. A psychiatrist diagnoses psychological conditions such as autism, borderline, schizophrenia, depression, obsessive-compulsive disorder (OCD), post-traumatic stress disorder (PTSD), attention deficit hyperactive disorder (ADHD), phobias, and so forth. Physical service animals are often easily identifiable, such as visual assistance, mobility assistance[6] or amputees; conversely, psychological disabilities are often invisible to people. I have fibromyalgia, yet you would not know if I did not tell you. In either case, service animals are identifiable and have documentation that helps them access public services and businesses. If the animal is in a carry-on or stroller, most likely, this dog is not providing a service. The mascarade of a service animal should be governed by law and managed by an organization such as the Canadian Kennel Club (CKC).

> *"While the use of a service animal may provide some psychological benefits to its handler (e.g., decreased feelings of loneliness and isolation, or increased socialization), and not withstanding the nascent use of psychiatric service dogs (Psychiatric Service Dog Society, 2003), service animals are typically viewed as tools rather than treatments and thus do not constitute an animal-assisted intervention as we define the term."*
> —*Kruger & Serpell, 2010*

Service animals should be evaluated and registered at the resident's municipal animal management council. A unique tag given to the person could identify a service from a non-service dog. In the United States, *"The role of the service animal, as*

---

[6] A mobility dog serves as a solid base upon which a person can lean, stand, or be accompanied to walk short distances, or be pulled. Normally this group of dogs also provide other services to their owner.

defined by the ADA [Americans with Disabilities Act], is to perform some of the functions and tasks that the individual cannot perform as a result of their disability." (Fine, 2006).

In Canada, federal and provincial laws, as we have seen above, fail to protect people with disabilities as clearly as the United States ADA. Awareness and education destigmatize mental illnesses. No one should be ashamed of suffering; however, some conditions remain invisible to the naked or untrained eye, opening the door to fake service dogs. I believe pretending to own a service dog is a terrible crime because it places the burden of false representation on the person who has a disability.

When regular people bring their untrained dogs into establishments and the dog bites or causes damage to the business', disabled people pay the price of non-entry into those same establishments. I have seen a *fake service* dog enter a bus and bark almost non-stop. I called the lady out on her charade, and she disembarked the bus. I fully intended the pun to lighten the mood. Guide, signal, and assistance dogs provide a service to their human. They usually wear identifiable gear that states *do not touch* or other terms such as *dog at work, working dog,* or *do not pet* on their harness.

If you do come across a service dog, do not touch them. Your interference might cause serious harm to the owner. If you are uncertain about what a service dog looks like, ask the owner. Should you see a person and their service dog heading towards a disastrous outcome, advise and ask the owner if they need extra help. For example, corner streets can become overly complicated to cross because of unexpected incidents, thus informing a visually impaired person of the possible outcome of crossing the street. The next step would be to offer your help to facilitate the process. This interaction is the proper way to address a human with their service dog.

DAAT – HAAT – RAAT – WAAT

I designed the following AAT programs with the program

plan outline to facilitate training once we start working; consequently, I combined them into one section for this book. The animals in the programs are different, but they are social animals that require social interactions to thrive. The animals presented in this book are all trained similarly to avoid undesirable behaviours. The following chapter discusses training and working with an AAT partner.

In the eight years since I started AAT, I did not reject an animal from the program. Chapter 2 will describe a typical socialization week during puppyhood. The focus will be on dogs, but rats and wolves undergo a similar process. Dog Animal-Assisted Therapy is the most common program we conduct in high schools and is the focus of this book. The design of the dog program starts with selecting the puppies before they are twelve weeks old. I do this through group puppy classes. Once I identify a possible candidate, I inform the owner, and we have a meeting to discuss the potential future of the dog.

The program starts with a safety and norms session. The overall goals are ultimately the same, with variations depending on the species we are working with. Dogs allow the participants to develop more complex skills. In contrast, rats are better suited for creating a secure attachment and managing emotions. I trained the rodents to massage the skin with their little hands, stimulating reciprocity. I train rats (*Rattus norvegicus*) to exhibit particular behaviours because they thrive on social contact. People are often surprised when I say that because they view rats as pests and vermin. These little rodents are hypersocial and function both as a predator and prey. Rat behaviours are remarkable for establishing a secure attachment with troubled adolescents.

Horses and wolves are also unique species for building attachments. Unfortunately, they do not travel well and bring them to the city. The fact is that horses are too big to conduct physical contact exercises safely within the confines of a school gymnasium. Wolves are too destructive when presented with novel stimuli. That does not mean they do not contribute to the process. In reality, they expand the secure attachment further. When a teen is ready for the experience of physical contact, I bring in the rat colony. We work our way to larger and more challenging animals. Working with exotic and larger domestic animals is a privilege our teens must earn.

Once the adolescent has experienced and accepted touch as a positive experience, we move on to equids. Horses are excellent at teaching social boundaries, self-awareness, and special recognition. Social boundaries are lessons on where I end, and you begin. Self-awareness includes acknowledging emotional and cognitive states. We acknowledge our teens' success by recognizing where they are physically, mentally, and emotionally. The size of a horse can be overwhelming when you have never seen one up close. Equids command presence and respect because people realize that this enormous animal could kill them if it wanted to. Teens who think of themselves as badass instantly change their stance when the animal walks toward them unafraid. Some teens cry, some are scared, and some are overjoyed. The reaction is normal and subsides quickly.

Finally, the wolves complete the process. They help us teach that patience, clear communication, and perseverance are social skills we need to interact together effectively. Wolves teach people that building a relationship takes time and requires much trust. You cannot simply walk over to a wolf and start petting it; the same goes for humans. As I always say, *Wolves are socialized and trained, but not with you.*

The relationship starts from zero when I introduce an adolescent to the wolves. The difference between trained and non-trained animals is that the WAAT canids can allow the relationship to form much faster. Non-trained wolves can take weeks, if not months, to form bonds with strangers. Non-socialized wolves could take years, if at all, to come into contact with humans. Bringing teens to visit untrained and non-socialized wolves would be dangerous and foolish. Training a wolf is not like training a dog. They are exotic animals, and we constantly refer to them as such. Canids are not fur kids or fur babies, thinking they put everyone at risk of serious injury. If someone calls a wolf a dog, I correct them immediately. I do not want that seed planted in a person's mind. Period. Wolves are not dogs, and vice versa. If a person treated a wolf as they did a dog, their life would be cut short.

I must emphasize a point: anthropomorphism has no place in AAIs. I know people will argue that it serves the human-animal bond. The only ethical way to use anthropomorphism is to mirror back a projection; otherwise, it leads to animal behaviour problems and burnout. When a student says my dog looks angry, I ask the student how he came to that conclusion.

Baby Kenai and I are playing.

The teen is projecting onto the animal, anthropomorphizing it; therefore, I must return the anger to the student to address it. The same goes for positive emotions because misidentifying a behaviour could lead to a bite. Again, safety is our top priority; consequently, we plan to avoid accidents by directly including prevention and management in the program-planing phase. There's no room for error when we work with animals and people, especially youth.

The future of AAI

When I teach animal training to future AAI professionals, much time is devoted to safe practices and developing safety measures for our clients. Furthermore, suppose people reported bites associated with AAI; insurance companies could either increase their fees or refuse to insure us together. That would be devastating for all, especially our clients and profession.

Research into AAI is helping us to identify potential risk factors, develop preventative healthcare measures for AAI animals, and design better programs for our clients. Science has recently acknowledged that animals have a tremendous impact on human wellness (Friedmann, Katcher, Lynch & Thomas, 1980; Friedmann et al., 1983; Barker & Dawson, 1998; Sentoo, 2003; Burgon, 2011), which professionalizes so to speak, our industry. Research into AAI is indirectly weaning out voluntary, untrained practitioners who place an enormous risk on our profession. If you are a professional, reading this book should prompt the following: *Do I want to potentially lose my job? Do I want to create a safe haven for all professionals to thrive, including me?* I will let you answer that. My answer is no! I want to make a secure environment for those who work with animals within their practice.

The AAI field is expanding exponentially; witnessing its disappearance would be tremendously sad. Thus, we set the stage; all professional practitioners must offer their clients risk-free services. In other words, we are ambassadors to our profession; let us make it a safe and enjoyable journey for all. As I always say, *Let's set ourselves up for success!* We begin this process by scientifically training our animals to perform specific behaviours within predetermined circumstances. We do not overlook problematic situations for the thrill of encountering an exotic or large domestic animal.

"As animal-assisted applications [therapy] expand to address a widening range of participant-specific goals it will be imperative to develop clear, measurable performance objectives for the handlers and animals engaged in this work. Effective selection procedures will require more than value judgments."
—Fine, 2010

Chapter 2
Training an AAT animal

A working-class animal

AAI animals should not be considered pets or companions. They are working-class animals, also known as pet partners. Consequently, I consider my partner's selection, socialization, training, and management different from a pet. There is a recipe for making the perfect AAT animal. This chapter will discuss the steps to creating such a superhero. Before we delve into the topic, a working dog, rat, horse, or wolf is an animal that displays breed-specific and trained behaviours that allow professionals to fulfil their goals.

We should view AAI animals as making a living by helping clients reach their full psychological or physical potential and autonomy. Every animal has something to offer the world, but some subjects are better suited for a given task. We can teach a rat to retrieve, but training a Labrador to accomplish the same job is far easier and faster. On the other hand, rats are exceptional at forming secure attachments with clients. In this case, each species is ideal for performing and reaching our goals for the teens. One must expand one's beliefs that all animal species can help modify human behaviour; one's creativity is the cornerstone of success.

Some examples of animal species found in AAT programs are dogs, horses, rats, guinea pigs, cats, and other domestic animals. I like to be creative in my exotic AAT animal choices; I have worked with snakes, wolves, quails, horses, and mice. Trained behaviours vary based on the type of AAI. Therefore, I select animals based on a few factors, such as clientele age, gender, psychological, physical, or medical health issues. Working with one or multiple animals depends on your budget, training time availability, and housing options. The more animals one has, the longer it takes to care for them; finally, you must consider your finances when acquiring multiple species.

The following section will discuss the selection of an animal partner, emphasizing the dog.

Selection

Before selecting a species or individual animal, you need to write your AAI program plan. In it, you will identify your target clientele, the age group, the area where clients live, and their mental or physical health issues. The commonality between criteria is the choice of species, specifically, the selection of an individual animal.

For example, you decided your clients are five- and ten-year-old girls living in a large city and experiencing fine motor disabilities. You have selected the cat as your work partner. Your goal is to refine their motor skills development through grooming exercises. Your client selection might seem like a good choice; however, pairing felines with young children who will comb or brush a cat might not be the best choice. It would be best to acquire the cat during its imprinting period to establish safety precautions and avoid undesirable behaviours. You should simultaneously train the cat and practice with the target clientele before the sessions start. That is copious work in a brief amount of time.

I select animals based on specific socialization protocols, regardless of the species. The procedure remains the same across species; the only change relates to the critical period of social development of the species. People use the terms imprinting and socializing interchangeably. In the critical development period, animals learn to recognize their parents or substitute parents and recognize random objects as non-threatening. (Lorenz, 1937; Timbergen, 1951). This exposure is vital for AAI animals because it ensures they will be familiar with and not afraid of novel situations, people, and other animals.

The first step in my selection process is straightforward; a social animal should be social and, thus, be attracted to people. Consequently, I chose an animal that likes approaching people without being overly excited or fearful. I assess each behaviour on a scale of one to ten, with a five as the desired outcome. I test dogs at five, six, and seven weeks; rats undergo this evaluation at two and three weeks old. I calibrate the point scale where zero equals extreme fear, and ten equals extreme aggression. Five is the midpoint, where social behaviour balances between the two endpoints. A social animal can display fear if the situation calls for it and express anger when necessary. The extremes are what we need to avoid. I reject animals that score four and lower or six and higher. This evaluation applies to all the social animals I evaluate for AAT, whether they are mine or a client's animal.

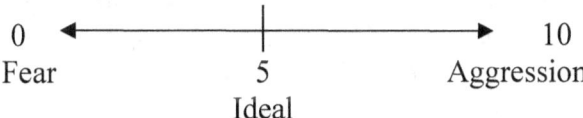

Research in evaluation processes, be it SAFER, B.A.R.Q. or Assess-A-Pet, all boil down to the same results, which is guessing. Your guess is as good as mine when assessing shelter animals for behavioural issues. As professionals, we cannot risk exposing our clients to such high bite risks. AAT practitioners should not rescue pets from shelters because of the guesswork in assessing relinquished animals. Rescued dogs often present behaviour problems after the rehoming phase. Furthermore, once you save a dog, it takes up to three months to adjust to its new environment and social group. This adjustment period is a lengthy and costly endeavour should the dog not be suitable for AAT. If you remember, I previously wrote that all animals have something to offer our clients; aggression is the exception.

The second step is taking the new pup home. In dogs, the ideal age is seven weeks, one week short of when the critical period of social development starts to close (Scott, 1958; Fuller & Scott, 1965). During this week, the dog will learn to bond with its human caregiver and discover its new work environment. The goal for the puppy's first week is to be introduced once or twice to its future work environment. Veterinarians often recommend keeping the dog home because it is not fully inoculated; however, behaviour does not wait for vaccination. According to standard vaccination protocols, your puppy will receive his first vaccine at two months; thus, it will have protection. Suppose you wait until the vaccination protocol is complete. In that case, the puppy will be four months old and have spent its entire socialization period isolated. Unsocialized animals are often insecure and either fearful or aggressive.

> *"From 3 to 7 weeks the puppy is in an extremely interesting stage in which its sense organs and cerebral cortex are not yet completely developed but in which it has extremely sensitive emotional reactions and is capable of making associations. This is the time when primary socialization normally takes place and during which it is easiest for a dog owner to establish a strong social bond."*
> —Scott, 1958, p.52

The final step is to start socializing and training the new work partner. A training schedule might seem premature, but it is quite the opposite. We must expose an animal to its future life during the critical period of social development for it to be well-adjusted later. It will be easier for the AAT dog to habituate to sounds, sights, smells, and touch at a young age; the same goes for rats and horses. Our rats come with their mother to our sessions once their eyes and ears are open; I start their training when they are a day old. All our animals are clicker-loaded; we will get back to this in the training section, and doing so before their ears open facilitates the process. When the ears are closed, they muffle sounds, making noises less scary. Once the neonatal phase is over, the socialization process to the outer world can begin.

The social phase is such a critical brain developmental phase that we devote two months of training to it. Without this exposure, dogs fare poorly in human society. I will repeat this fact to convince you that a social creature deprived of contact during brain development is detrimental to the entire lifespan of the animal. Behaviour should override vaccination protocols. Positive social experiences are fundamental for AAI animals to live and thrive in their workplace.

AAT socialization

Socialization is a process by which animals learn who their parental figure is. Animals also learn how to communicate with parents and siblings. Dogs then apply the proper behaviours to satisfy inner and outer needs (Scott & Fuller, 1965). Between the fourth and eighth weeks of life, a critical period of social development allows animals to bond with littermates. This initial socialization period is followed by a subsequent period, within the same timeframe, between the eighth and twelfth week. During this period, dogs learn to bond with people. I will refer to this second sub-period between eight and twelve weeks throughout this section unless otherwise mentioned when discussing socialization.

An AAT animal needs to be socialized and habituated to all possible stimuli encountered during future work sessions. Additionally, professionals must create a list of behaviours they will train their work partners to accomplish. Some examples are touch, take, sit, down, bring, give, a hug, and turn. We will talk about training further on. For now, let us focus on the socialization process. The process described below applies to our resident rat mischief[7]; we adapt the protocol to their species-specific needs. Non-social animals still require lengthy exposure to other animals through habituation.

Baby rats are called pups; therefore, you can substitute the word dog pup with rat pup, and you will get the gist of our rat protocol. Fine (2010) emphasizes animal wellness when he writes, *"The greater the degree of contact between animal and participant, the greater the demand for clear definitions of optimum animal behavioral and skill capacities."* (p.118). To set clear boundaries, we must establish a clear, standardized definition of behavioural wellness and needs for AAI dogs. That

---

[7] A colony of rats.

is one of the reasons I constantly evaluate and give value to our AAT dogs' umwelt. When we assess the experiencers' experience, creating, modifying, or ceasing their involvement in AA becomes feasible. Wellness is the primary reason we pick puppies, not adult dogs, for our AAT work partners.

Before I describe the first seven days of our socialization protocol, please consider enrolling your puppy in a science-based group class. A properly designed program emphasizes socialization, cognition, and habituation. Make sure at least one well-adjusted adult dog is in your class. Puppies cannot learn from other puppies how to behave as adults; they need an adult to teach them proper dog manners. I highly recommend our group classes if you are in Montreal. My colleagues teach the program I created, which indirectly schools puppies on the foundations of future AAT work. If the dog does not become an AAT partner, it will become a great pet. If you enroll your puppy in a group class, do NOT train or socialize your puppy on that day. The group class will be enough learning for the next twenty-four hours. Sleep is vital to understanding; do not overdo training.

Socialization Day One:

When the puppy arrives home, allow it to acclimatize to its new environment. Set up the crate, dining area, and outside toilet space, and observe your puppy evolve in its new dwelling. Do not plan for visits yet; the pup will be tired from the trip. Bring it outside to relieve itself after each activity: eating, drinking, sleeping, playing, or napping.

The first night in the crate is the critical one. The dog will cry, possibly at length too, but if you are patient and let them cry it out, the dog will learn that the crate is for sleep. In the worst case, this will last three days with a significant decrease each night. If you open the crate door and start shouting at the puppy verbally or taking it to bed with you, this process will be more complicated.

Socialization Day Two:

Take the seven-week-old pup to work with its crate, food, and toys on the second day. After a few hours, invite your co-workers to get down on the floor to pet your puppy. Do NOT pick the puppy up. The dog will learn that life occurs on the floor and can retreat to its crate should it need to. When the dog comes forward, ask the people to pet it for six seconds, stop, and give the pup a treat to reinforce (R+) it. Repeat the process until the puppy decides to leave or ten minutes have passed, whichever comes first. Let the pup decide whether to play, eat, nap, or sleep. Do NOT force the puppy to stay and interact.

Lack of sleep affects growth and behaviour. A fatigued dog will present heightened agonistic behaviours such as snarling, growling, snapping, or biting. Since they are mouthing during this time, biting is prevalent at this age; consequently, fatigue will increase the bite frequency and intensity. The cute puppy turns into a shark, which is highly problematic for the future pet partner.

Socialization Day Three:

Day three is a rest day. Practice Step One or leave the puppy in the crate for a part of the day. Organizing a midday outing might be a good idea. The same rules apply if you plan on bringing the puppy to work. Do not allow visitors to interact with Fido; let the puppy explore the environment stress-free. Once home, apply Step One. By now, the puppy should be able to sleep most of the night in silence. Suppose it does not; simply be patient. If the neighbours' peace of mind is at risk, reassure them that your future work partner is learning the ropes, which should end soon. Patience is a virtue, but so are excellent communication skills.

Socialization Day Four:

Bring the puppy to work; this time, add one strange object in the room for the first part of the day. The object can be an open umbrella, a chair, a large box, a baby stroller, or any other unusual thing the pup has never encountered. R+ the puppy when it looks at the object, goes to investigate it, or decides to make contact with it. Do Not force the pup to explore or interact with the situation or thing. This step teaches the puppy to problem-solve and understand that there can be positive outcomes to life's many challenges.

Forcing the pup will teach it to fear strange objects, which would be counter-productive. We take a little walk during lunch and let the puppy discover the outside work environment. The second part of the day is all about the downtime. Allow your dog to be on its own and quietly drop treats to the ground whenever it lies. You will soon have a dog that loves sleeping for a living. Call it a day and head home.

Socialization Day Five:

Day five is veterinarian day. We schedule an appointment for your puppy for his first vaccination, check-up, feces sample, and a few yummy treats when it meets the doctor. When your puppy meets Dr. X, ask them to give your dog a few treats. The environment can be overwhelming for some dogs; thus, special treats can help facilitate the first visit. Right before the veterinarian does a procedure on your dog, pet it very hard and R+ for its excellent cooperation. After your visit, start to plan day six.

Socialization Day Six:

Plan to take the puppy to see family or friends on this day. We want the dog to associate outings and good times, not just that visits equal needles in the rear end. The day's first order is to pass the puppy[8] between people and ask each person to R+ the pup to make contact. The second game consists of people dropping treats next to themselves to teach the puppy that people are amazing.

The third exercise involves asking your family or friends to play gently with the puppy and its toys. Again, make sure your pup can retreat if it wishes to. Overwhelming the puppy will be counterproductive. On that note, the placement of the crate should be visible and accessible to the puppy should it decide to

---

[8] Pass the puppy is a socialization exercise in our group class program. Puppies are passed from person to person all the while receiving treats. The puppies are never forced to interact during this activity.

cease the activity. The outer bathroom should also have been predetermined, for preventing accidents from happening is much easier than picking up after them.

Socialization Day Seven:
Congratulations on your first week with your new pup and AAT partner-to-be. Today is a celebration and a rest day. Do something special, like get a dog specialty birthday cake, walk somewhere peaceful, or relax and go through the motions slower. After one week of experience, review your training plan and make adjustments. Do not forget to treat yourself, too; you certainly deserve it. Writing an entire socialization protocol in a book is impossible because the period lasts four months. Hopefully, the first seven days will give you an idea of what to expect regarding social exposure for your newly arrived pet partner.

My first-week celebration with Albear was tragic and thus memorable. Our apartment building burned from the fifth to the seventeenth floor; as a result, we needed to relocate ASAP. We ended up staying at the house on the family-owned zoo property. Yes, you read that right: an actual full-scale zoo. Although I did not know if I could return to my home, it was the most fantastic time ever because we lived with exotic animals that Albear got to meet. From alpaca to zebra, he met them all. I could not resist sharing this picture. Albear wakes up to the lions roaring and tunes in to their cries.

In the image to the left, Albear meets the Alpacas on his first morning at our new temporary emergency home. I accustomed him immediately to a work vest to teach him the difference between leisure and work. In the image on the right, Albear is searching for a place to urinate when he hears the lions starting to roar. He stopped and actively listened to them for their entire morning vocalization. Most people do not have zoo access to desensitize their dogs to different species, but the overall goal is the same. Introduce the puppy to cats, rats, rabbits, or as many species as possible. The socialization process will ensure that your adult dog can function in the presence of smaller creatures.

Albear meets Alpacas.   Albear listens to lions.

The point of my story is to use whatever the environment throws your way to socialize and habituate your puppy. If your location is void of stimuli, seek new and stimulating places. Socialization only occurs once, so make the best of it. Go to schoolyards during recess, parks on a busy day, another busier town, or a shopping mall. Pet stores, train stations, and other businesses that allow pets are excellent, especially for dogs born in late fall and early winter. Puppies born during this period will experience Canadian winter isolation; the lack of socialization dramatically increases fear or aggressive behaviour later.

Hariette is a nearly five-year-old AAT dog, and I am still refining her skills. She loves people, sometimes a little too much; thus, she has earned herself the nickname Broholmersor, or Dinosaur for short. Mastiffs are people-loving dogs, and Hariette is no exception to the rule. I researched long and hard for the perfect AAT dog, and her breed shines within my program. It took me twenty years to import the first Broholmers to Canada, but one man had a vision. For that, I am incredibly thankful. Hariette has worked in AAT for many years, and her future looks promising.

Once the dog reaches adolescence, socialization refers to how an animal applies its behaviour to various situations and records its outcome. If the behaviour generated a negative result, that pairing is less likely to occur again. Conversely, if the event's impact was positive, that association will likely happen again. Socialization helps determine who's whom to avoid conflicts or form friendships. Social behaviours also serve to minimize collateral damages should conflicts be unavoidable. Dogs learn about one another through rudimentary interactions such as play. However, a call to compromise precedes play. The play bow signals the dog's intention to test the behaviours that come after it; therefore, the other individual dog should not take them seriously. Once both dogs have communicated their likes and dislikes, they might engage in actual play.

You will eventually realize that adult dogs typically answer the *Do you want to play?* with a clear *No!* statement. Some dogs play well into adulthood, but it is not the vast majority. In wild canids, adults seldom play. Adults pass the entertainment task to yearling members of the group. The young aunties and uncles will enjoy an excellent play session with pups, but it might not be a daily affair. We do not define adult and puppy socialization as the same. During the critical period of social development, pups learn to talk; adolescent dogs learn when to speak, and adult dogs communicate when needed.

Adults teach those valuable life lessons to their younger offspring. Canine communication is the essence of socialization. When dogs are out on a walk, they are adulting. They teach the above behaviours to dogs that have not yet learned specific lessons. When you walk and cross the neighbour's kids who have just thrown a water balloon at a cat, do you say a) nothing, b) all is good, carry on, c) that is unacceptable, d) chase them away, yelling profanity? Take this example and replace human adults with dogs and kids with puppies. Your answers will still represent typical adult dog reactions, yet that is not socialization but adults teaching young dogs. Socialization refers to acquiring and understanding social behaviours. Knowing their language allows a species to communicate its thoughts and emotions when they choose to. Being social should never be imposed; socialization is a choice. The AAT animal has to be able to make that choice. Imposed social interactions will burn out your work partner.

My approach to socializing AAT dogs is to keep exposing

a dog to stimuli while training the desired behaviours we want to use later in life. Conversely, training a behaviour might take a long time if the trainer does not expose the dog to various stimuli. Unfortunately, teaching socialization skills past the critical period of social development will remain a cognitive decision. The dog must think about using the skill versus reacting instinctively. The idiom: *You snooze, you lose!* It accurately describes social interactions, cognition, training, and brain development. Socializing and training a dog is comparable to building a house. It would help to have the right tools, knowledge, and physical skills. As the AAT students say, *"Halfassing it won't work 'cause you'll have to do it again! That's just a waste of time."* How wise they are.

AAT Training

Training an AAT dog is not for the faint of heart. It requires a lot of work and dedication. Working dogs typically have a list of trained behaviours that serve a specific type of AAT. The list varies greatly, but a dog that does not exhibit any behaviour or does not react to stimuli is not an ideal work partner. Dogs should be able to make decisions in the therapeutic process, not just be bystanders. Using dogs that don't react to stimuli is a significant safety problem in our field. Dogs that internalize their reactions are ticking time bombs. The general public and the Canadian Kennel Club assess a therapy dog based on its lack of responsiveness. The following criteria are from the CKC website.

> *"What is a Therapy Dog? It is a dog and their owner/handler who are evaluated and tested via the Therapy Dog Organization and if successful, volunteer their time and visit people in hospital and community facilities. These dog teams promote emotional support for both short and long-term patients as well as the elderly, disabled, children in a variety of hospitals,*

homes and schools."

—*CKC, 2019*

The CKC statement might sound noble; unfortunately, with their 2019 changes, the CKC decreased its certification standard. The organization recommends passing the Canine Good Neighbour (CGN) test. Still, the CKC no longer requires the CGN for AAT certification. The kennel club delegated the AAT certification process to CKC-recognized organizations. The human-dog team must fulfill a certain number of visiting hours, complete the CKC application form, and pay the necessary fees to obtain an AAT title. Unfortunately, only pure-breed dogs can be certified. The therapy titles a dog can receive are: Therapy Dog Novice (THDN) – 10 Visits, Therapy Dog Title (THD) – 50 Visits, Therapy Dog Advanced Title (THDA) – 100 Visits, Therapy Dog Excellent Title (THDX) – 200 Visits, and Therapy Dog Distinguished Title (THDD) – 500 Visits.

> *"The CKC will record titles earned by approved Therapy Dog Organizations. The owner may submit this completed application along with a copy of the certificate from the approved organization or a record of visits form (found on www.ckc.ca forms-Therapy Dogs Record Form) title certificate plus the fee as per the CKC Schedule of Fees and CKC will place the title on the dog's record and produce a certificate. Applying for the CKC title and certificate is at the discretion of the owner."*
>
> —*CKC TD Title Application, 2019*

The CGN test, on the other hand, requires the dog to complete the twelve-step evaluation from a CKC-certified evaluator. On the other hand, the CKC does not require any form of human assessment. The dog is certified as a Canine Good Neighbour if it passes all twelve steps. Below is a summary of the twelve steps required for AAT certification should you add a title to your dog's pedigree.

1. Accepting A Friendly Strange
2. Politely Accepts Petting
3. Appearance and Grooming
4. Out For A Walk
5. Walking Through A Crowd
6. Sit/Down On Command and Stay In Place
7. Come When Called
8. Praise/Interaction
9. Reaction To A Passing Dog
10. Reaction To Distractions
11. Supervised Isolation
12. Walking Through A Door/Gate

As you can see, the test is relatively basic and misrepresents AAT dogs. My dogs possess many skills but do not master steps one, two, five, and eleven. The later steps are the most disturbing. There are no practical reasons for AAT dogs to accept being taken away from their owners and subjected to *supervised isolation.* The relationship between an AAT dog and its human partner relies on a secure attachment, safety, and direction to develop positively in our work. In steps one and two, dogs must learn the difference between work and leisure outings. I do not accept the first and second criteria during my walks because meeting random people and dealing with their lack of respect regarding working dogs is overwhelming.

Conversely, overexposing AAT dogs to forced social encounters can create behaviour problems in our partners. A dog that no longer desires to help people is a sad state of affairs that is avoidable. Human and dog training can prevent pet partner burnout, notably if the person receives science-based training. For the remainder of this section, I will assume that the human did receive an education based on valid learning theories, behaviour modification, behaviour management, healthcare, and safety requirements.

> *"While the specific details of the performance outcomes will vary with the specific setting, defining such task expectations enables the handler and professional to determine whether*

or not the task can be managed."
—Fine, 2010

AAT animals do not need to pass the CGN test because their skillset overrides compliant behaviours based solely on social attraction and lack of responsiveness. Why someone would want a carpet[9] dog baffles me. Practitioners should train AAT dogs to think cognitively, problem-solve, and generate new outcome expectancies. This kind of training might sound utopic, but it is nonetheless accurate. A dog can learn how to learn, and there is a process by which you can achieve it. I created the perfect dog program and will eventually write it for everyone. In the meantime, if you follow our working dogs on social media, you will witness them behaving similarly. One particular learning theory that allows us to achieve our goal is the social-cognitive learning theory (SCT).

Unfortunately, I cannot write the entire learning protocol of an AAT dog; therefore, I will write a one-week sample from an AAT dog's life. We will take Hariette, my Broholmer puppy, also affectionately known as Broholmersor, dinosaur or hootchie mama. At one year old, Hariette is still a teenage molosser who has not fully matured physically. When writing this book, Hariette is twenty-nine inches at the withers and tips the scale at one-hundred-seventeen pounds. She is a big dog; consequently, her training is essential for safety measures. The risk of accidents in AAT sessions is higher because of her size. Should Hariette be overly excited and jump on people, she can knock them down and injure them. We will start Hariette's typical training week on a Monday and continue throughout the following Sunday. The week will give you an idea of how much training is required to educate an AAT dog fully. This protocol has been tested over the last eight years and yields excellent results.

---

[9] A dog that does not display any response towards stimuli.

Training Day One:
The day starts with revisiting simple behaviours such as *touch* and *sit*, then introducing new or more complex behaviours. On Mondays, I practice the two behaviours because they are easy to execute and are the foundation of our behaviour repertoire. Think of it as a warmup before your training routine.

Hariette, the first Canadian Broholmer, at one-year-old.

- *Touch* consists of placing one hand out, with the thumb extended upward, and then asking the dog about the behaviour. I R+ Hariette for proper execution. I repeated the process ten times.

- *Sit/Stay* This is self-explanatory behaviour. I asked Hariette for the behaviour and R+ for proper execution. I repeated the process ten times; this released overexcitement.

- *Roll Ball* The game is a more complex behaviour to train; therefore, I start the exercise after our little *touch* and *sit* warm-up. I started the session with classical conditioning (CC) of the ball to her nose approximately twenty times. I then quickly moved the ball to the floor through small successive approximations at the time. When Hariette touches the ball on the floor, I R+. I repeated this process approximately ten times, then withheld R+ to see if she would move the ball with her nose in anticipation. I R+ her if she moved the ball.

After our last training session, Hariette can play, relax, or do as she pleases. Weather permitting, we go for our long walk/run on the mountain in the afternoon. Hariette is training to run with me, but for now, she chooses to run, trot, or walk. When we return, we play a Brain Game and call it a day. She often plays with Albear after dinner and sleeps throughout the rest of the day. I do not bring Albear on the mountain because his arthritic knee does not allow him to walk for such a long period. Plus, he enjoys some time away from the overly enthusiastic dinosaur. Hariette gets to hang around with her friends: George, Mandu, Penny, and Marley, the Staffordshire Terrier.

Training Day Two:
Tuesday is the most challenging day of the week. I start with a few Brain Game rounds. The first game is at a novice level and ends with an advanced puzzle. Each game is timed and recorded. We take short pauses in between our work sessions. Hariette is allowed to play or rest during our breaks. At the Dogue Shop, we encourage dogs to think for themselves.

- *Brain Game level 1* We make these games with recycling objects in your recycling box. I use hand towels and toilet paper rolls, egg or milk cartons, and a plastic container. I placed all the recyclables in a larger box and presented them to Hariette.

I sit with Hariette as we play to give her feedback and help her when she finds the puzzle difficult. I do not solve the problem for her; I demonstrate how to solve it and allow her to devise a solution. In the social cognitive learning theory, the dog is encouraged to problem-solve, a mandatory behaviour in AAT. Dogs can and do come up with novel ways of solving problems.

Watching dogs or rats improvise a new behaviour better suited to solve the problem they face is fascinating. I enjoy watching her devise new solutions. Her mind works in intriguing ways. She can follow my game directions and quickly solves it, even if it is a puzzle she has never seen before.

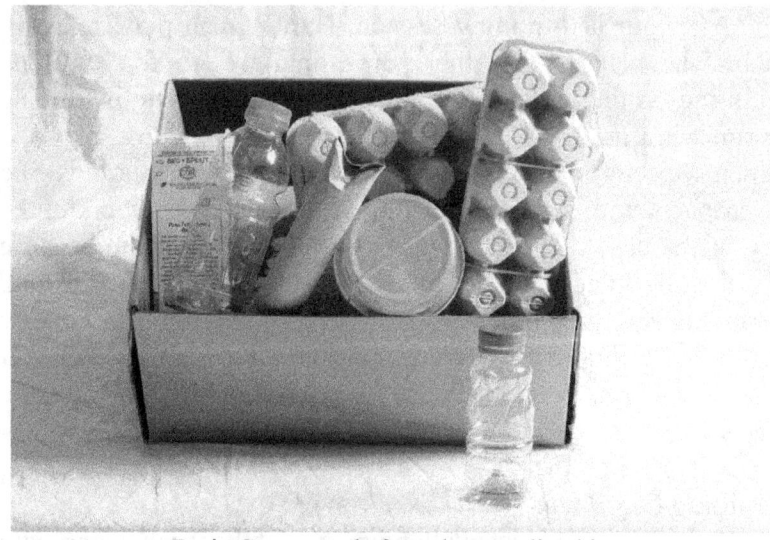

Brain Games made from the recycling bin.

- *Brain Game level 2* I accomplished this level with the help of commercially made toys. My favourites are the Nina Ottosson original Brain Games. The plastic was of better quality and more complex to solve. It could take a dog thirty to forty-five minutes to solve a game. Unfortunately, the newer versions are easier to solve.

In the following image, Hippo, one of our senior Animal Behaviour Apprenticeship (ABA) dog students, demonstrates how we play with the Nina Ottosson Finder game the SCT way. It requires dedication and patience from the trainer, but the results are excellent. Animals forge attachments much faster when working together with humans. Guidance and determination subsequently build trust, comprehension, and a heightened sense of confidence and self for the human. The SCT is a system that establishes and sustains itself. The human-animal bond solely exists based on trust; without it, animal interactions are limited and sometimes dangerous. I cannot stress enough how valuable a trust-based relationship is for AAIs. I can confirm that AAT does take trust away, but we replace it.

🐕 *Brain Game level 3* This game is the most challenging level of all. We refer to this type of training as *object recognition*. The dog must first learn to recognize familiar objects amongst ten to fifty other things. Then, we ask the dog which object it must touch with its nose. If it bites the object or knocks it down with a paw, there is no R+, and we restart with a new object name.

Hippo is working on Nina Ottosson's Finder puzzle.

We consider the behaviour learned when the dogs reach an accuracy rate between eighty and one hundred percent. This session lasted approximately thirty minutes because we conducted two previous levels of Brain Games before this session. Some dogs can accomplish this task through object discrimination, but thank god, not too many dogos can pull that off. Albear is talented at object recognition and could work for about one hour, with an average of forty-five minutes. Still, comparing him to Boreal, my Einstein dog pupil, is a piece of cake.

Boreal could sustain a consistent work ethic with a ninety to one-hundred percent accuracy rate for nearly two hours. I do not know about you, but training a dog for two hours every day is exhausting. Hariette has talent, but thank goodness she is not an Einstein dog. I say that jokingly, but at the same time, I cannot devote two hours of training per dog every day. If I did, I could not do anything around the Dogue Shop or at home. Too much of a good thing can be bad, intelligence included.

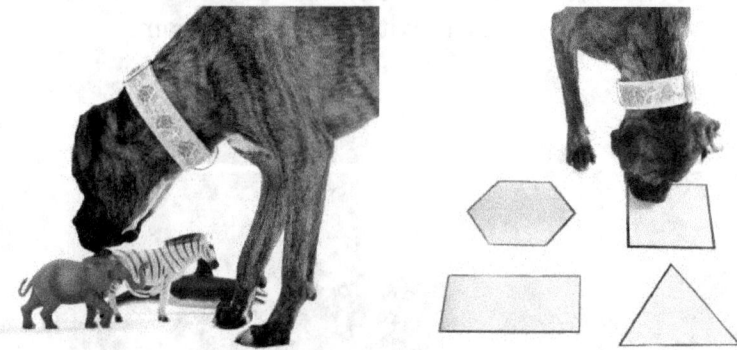

Albear demonstrates object recognition.

We train more challenging behaviours in the afternoon for two to three sessions. The first behaviour is one of the easiest for Hariette because she thinks we are playing instead of working. Harder behaviours require concentration; thus, we introduce complex behaviours and keep the most challenging ones for the end of the sessions. We use this strategy to release overexcitement. Hariette requires approximately fifteen minutes to release her emotions and gain access to her cognitive abilities.

- 🐕 *Toys in Box* The behaviour consists of picking up a toy by name, bringing it over, and dropping it in a box. We repeat this process until there are no more toys on the floor. Each attempt is R+ through successive approximations. We are at the *drop* phase of the behaviours at the moment. Thus, I R+ each attempt that closely resembles the actual *drop-in-the-box* behaviour. Sometimes, the toy falls in; other times, it lands on the edge of the box. When it lands directly in the box, it is R+ with a double reward: food and water. We repeated the training session twice more with small breaks between sessions.

I end the day with a short walk that involves training small behaviours such as *touch*, *sit*, *left paw*, *right paw*, and *kiss*; it makes for a very dynamic walk. This type of walk might seem complicated for the average pet caregiver because it requires high concentration and motivation; it is simple and entertaining for our dogs. When Hariette loses focus, we stop, allow the stimulus to pass us and resume where we left off. Changes in the environment are impossible to control when we are outside. We return our focus to simple behaviours before we move on. Allowing dogs to experience the world and work through its many challenges creates perfect AAT animals. Dogs learn to think, process information, and make decisions based on human feedback. AAT dogs feel they have control, which is one of the most important characteristics to possess. Imagine having your life one hundred percent controlled by another organism. I suspect it would not bode well.

Training Day Three:
We conduct our AAT sessions in various high schools during the school year. Some days, we visit two schools, but generally, we attend only one school daily because our animals need to rest. Dogs are not people; they need a longer recuperation time because teens project their emotions onto the animals. We must make sure dogs release the stress associated with AAT work. If we overwork dogs, they burn out fast. Workdays differ during the summer because we do not attend school; consequently, I will describe a typical school day.

- *Play Time!* Mandu, the dachshund, arrives at nine o'clock and plays with Albear and Hariette. This way, they can release their excess joy and excitement before we leave for AAT.

- *Toy in Box* We arrive at the first school at ten-thirty and start our first AAT session. The session begins with the pairing of the student and their dog. The students greet their dogs, tell us how they feel, and begin to train. Students work with clickers and treats. The teens R+ the dogs for proper behaviour and reward accordingly.

Each student and dog team has an adult appointed to supervise, give feedback, and ensure the group remains functional. When challenges arise, we discuss the problem as a group and try to problem-solve our way through it. Teens are remarkable at brainstorming new outcomes for their classmates and canine companions. For example, if a dog or rat fails to perform the behaviour, students discuss solutions they tried. Consequently, individual and group communication skills dramatically improve because everyone wants to see the animal succeed. If the conversation is fruitful, we allow for the process to reach its end. Conversely, if students change the topic, we will let them chat or redirect them to the animal's behaviour and try to apply the solution. If we have time, we will return to the discussion and conclude it. The session stops at eleven o'clock.

- *Toilet Duty* Students, dogs, and staff go outside for toilet duty. We remain outside between ten and twenty minutes, depending on the weather.

- *Attachment* The second session starts at eleven-twenty and lasts another twenty minutes. Goals and objectives dictate how the session will continue. We often change species for this session and bring out the rats. The aim can be for attachment purposes, or we can work on social skills by pairing two students with one rat. Cooperation, creativity, patience, role reversals, and communication are encouraged during this exchange.

The day ends with school number one. We then travel to school number two and start a similar process. The structure will be very similar from school to school; however, because people and animals constantly change, sessions are modified to adjust to individual and group dynamics. The group's development can be in different stages from one week to another. According to Tuckman (1965), groups develop according to specific settings, which he referred to as *stages of group development*. Our groups evolve through the five stages: forming, storming, norming, performing, and adjourning. My AAT sessions adapt to the different stages our group goes through based on student behaviour. We often move between the storming, norming, and performing phases weekly. We frequently experience all three stages in the same session.

Training Day Four:

Day four corresponds to Thursday. During this day, I practice husbandry behaviours for veterinary visits. Husbandry means caring for and managing animals. AAT animals visit the veterinarian regularly; therefore, we must train care behaviours to maintain their function between veterinary visits. I do a mock veterinary exam to check for bumps, bites, ticks and flees. I proceed with the mouth, teeth, ears, eyes, toes, fur condition, nail trimming, and practice releasing their belly when we visit the veterinarian for an exam.

- *Husbandry* Every body part goes through visual inspection. I reinforced the dog for cooperative responses. Husbandry allows me to spot problems before they even get a chance to evolve into something worse. I know what comes in, what comes out, and if my animals have abnormalities.

- *Physical Exercise* Only physical activities are allowed for the dogs during their respite. Play, walking, or running is generally on the agenda; however, we do not solicit a specific exercise. Dogs let us know what they prefer. Albear loves leisure walks at .001/mph, while Hariette wants to go two hundred mph. Sometimes, we compromise, and I take the dogs out individually.

Training Day Five:

We reserve Fridays for private AAT cases. Each person comes with different issues; consequently, we try to achieve our goals with a dog, rat or a combination of both. I like to ask my clients what goals they wish to achieve, and we make a plan together. After that, I program-plan the goals and objectives for our sessions. Private sessions are more intimate, which nourishes the attachment further. Some clients are high school students; thus, they progress faster than if we only saw each other once a week.

- *Private Sessions* Clients typically train their animals; thus, we do not conduct formal training sessions outside these sessions. Overall, we get the client to perform certain behaviours they set up and R+. An example is a teen with severe social anxiety who visits Hariette after school. He trains her to walk outside; therefore, we work on his social anxiety by building a secure attachment and inter-species social affiliation (Duranton & Gaunet, 2018).
- *ABA School* Dogs and rats also participate in the animal behaviour apprenticeship (ABA) levels one and two programs. In this curriculum, future dog trainers and animal behaviour consultants work directly with our dogs and resident rats. The dogs do not work every Friday; therefore, they get a reprieve from work on most nights. Our other AAT dogs also take part in this education training format. We regularly request our pet partners to teach them new behaviours.

Training Day Six:

Saturday, the Dogue Academy's ABA students work with the Dogue Shop's AAT animals. Depending on the curriculum, they practice with experienced or novice animals. Because the program is hands-on, the students learn to train in a highly distracting environment. Some stress is good during the learning phase, allowing the animal to improvise solutions. You could say we reinforce decision-making, not accurate behaviours. Rewarding problem-solving and decision-making are vital in AAIs because animals learn to intervene of their own free will.

- *Simple Behaviours* The training starts with simple

behaviours such as *touch* or *target*. As the program advances, the students are required to train complex behaviours. Fetting and dropping a toy in the box is tricky for teenagers; consequently, learning can be more challenging for the animals.

- *Complex Behaviours* An example of a complicated behaviour could be opening the refrigerator door, taking an object, closing the door, bringing me the thing, and dropping the object in my hand. A green dog could not perform the long behaviour series at the program's beginning. The AAT dogs step in and demonstrate their skills to our young, eager minds.

The day concludes, and the exhausted dogs go home. Typically, I ask our AAT dog caregivers to allow for a full recovery day. This work schedule is fantastic for AAT dogs because it will enable us to fine-tune behaviours when necessary. We place behaviours in maintenance, and once we return to school, the dogs have a working concept of the behaviours we ask them to accomplish. That said, the animal has to learn all the new cues the participant is demonstrating, which is difficult to sort out for the animals.

Training Day Seven:
Sunday is devoted to rest. There is nothing on the agenda for the dogs, not even a long walk. We concentrate on basic needs and care for ourselves. AAT is an emotional journey that requires releasing other people's projections; we include the dog in this process. We must guarantee our mental health remains strong and positive, and so too for the animals.

- In AAT, people burn out, too; consequently, our profession, by definition, means we always bring homework home. The constant training translates to: I live with my work partner, I work with my work partner, I feed my work partner, I bring my work partner to the bathroom, and I take my work partner on walks.

🐕 The list of everyday chores regarding caring for animals is endless, and most of those actions directly or indirectly involve our animals. Therefore, we must set time aside for ourselves, away from the dogs, and treat ourSelves to human luxuries: a shopping mall trip, coffee with a best friend, a movie or museum, a romantic dinner, or a solo run.

We repeat the schedule every week with different goals and objectives. Training exercises change, and people come and go. However, one truth remains: there is an immense quantity of training and behaviour management in our lives. If I did not teach the ABA programs, I would train at home because we must maintain dog behaviours if we need to use them at some point. In other words, there is no off button when you are an AAT professional. To stay mentally healthy, one must consider how to offload the emotions that do not belong to us. I recommend yoga, not only the asanas but the entire philosophy.

The work-life combination can become overwhelming very quickly because of the non-stop process of caring for our work partners. I live in an area where out-of-control dogs run off-leash, and this lack of control poses a problem since not all dogs are friendly or obedient. My dogs are relaxed on walks and mind their business, but Albear will not tolerate an impolite greeting. Albear will tell dogs the *jump—in—your—face—and—let's—go—play* or the *bark—in—your—face—while—I—run—your—way* behaviours are rude and, thus, will not be tolerated. Once you have trained all the behaviours required for your AAT practice, you must plan a behaviour maintenance schedule. We all need to readjust certain behaviours as we evolve in AAT programs.

Behaviour maintenance and management

I want to open a small parenthesis before I continue with this section. People often ask me how I control the dogs' weight with all the daily treats they consume. The answer is simple: I plan. When we leave for AAT, I prep all the food and divide it by the number of dogs present; then, I portion it out to size in individual containers. I adjust my dogs' nightly diets based on the number of treats left in each container. Some days, my dogs do not get a conventional *meal in a bowl*; they rarely do. The dogs will eat from a slow feeder or Brain Game. I also tell my clients if their dog will require a night meal.

Dogs love to work for their food. Emphasize the word work. Research by Schultz (2004 & 2007) and Sapolsky (2017) demonstrates that executing an action is reinforcing for dogs, especially when they know a reward is possible. In reality, the dog releases dopamine during the work phase. Working is what motivates animals. We could say that work is reinforcing, and cookies are rewarding.

Combining reinforcement and reward via variable reinforcement ratios and intervals is highly motivating for animals. If you are unfamiliar with reinforcement schedules, they are the quintessence of motivation. Konrad Lorenz proposed the psychohydraulic model of instinctive behaviour in the mid-nineteen hundreds (Lorenz, 1950).

The following image summarizes the schedules with variable and fixed options. The Y-axis refers to the outcome of the behaviour, and the X-axis relates to behaviour change over time. You can see that both variable schedules produce a high and constant rate of behaviour change. Motivation decreases over time; consequently, we must revisit behaviours regularly to avoid breakdown.

We train to keep the animal's motivation high to exhibit a specific behaviour at a relatively consistent level of performance. In human psychology, these schedules tend to elicit compulsive behaviours (Berridge, 2003; Schultz, 2004 & 2007; Salamone & Correa, 2012; Sapolsky, 2017).

High motivation levels allow professionals to keep behaviours functional without devoting excessive time to training. The team and I use reinforcement schedules for touch, come, sit, down, toy, and toutou behaviours. Placing the *touch* behaviour in maintenance would require planning a variable ratio and interval schedule and training it according to the predetermined sequence.

The session equals asking for ten behaviours, and it should minimally take thirty-eight seconds to execute the series. It would take longer to conduct the session because dogs require time to process their reinforcement, and people must complete their training plans. Albear likes to take his precious time to eat a treat; therefore, conducting this session might take five minutes. We plan each behaviour; thus, a regular training session takes five to ten minutes. Short sessions are less demanding of attention and allow us to conduct multiple micro-sessions throughout the day.

Schedules	Variable Ratio	Variable Interval	Sec.
Touch	1,3,2,4,1,1,3	2,1,3,1,1,4,3	38
Come	3,2,3,1,3,4,2	6,1,1,1,3,2,3	60
Sit	4,2,1,3,1,2,5	1,1,1,2,1,3,1	43
Down	2,1,2,2,3,2,1	3,2,3,6,2,1,6,5	63

Reinforcement schedule during a training session.

In the previous table, I planned four training sessions throughout the day. You could conduct them in succession; however, the dog will become exhausted and sleep for the rest of the day. Completing a long training session versus small, more frequent training bursts depends on your time, the dog's concentration, learning skills, and motivation. When a dog lacks motivation, one possesses other processes to increase responses. The Premack Principle and the Hydraulic Model of Motivation (Lorenz, 1974) allow us to train when motivation decreases. The model also applies to humans; consequently, we use it with our teens when their drive is low.

Konrad Lorenz hydraulic model of motivation

The Premack Principle, by David Premack, explains how we can increase and tap into stored energy by using a high probability behaviour to reinforce a low probability behaviour. The hydraulic model of motivation, by Konrad Lorenz (1950), focuses on preventing the release of stored energy into fixed action patterns (FAP) to increase motivation. Furthermore, it forces the stowed energy into a predetermined sequence of behaviours. An example of the hydraulic model occurs when a person steps on the agility rink, puts their dog in a sit-stay and tells it *Are you ready? Are you ready? Go!* The dog takes off like a bullet, running full speed onto the obstacle course.

You probably do this when you play fetch or tug of war with your dog. Right before you throw the ball, you say *Do you want it? Do you want it?* You pretend to throw the ball, only to repeat this sequence a few times before the dog explodes to chase the ball you threw. The *run-over* obstacles replace the pursuit of a prey sequence. The handler prevents the dog from performing the chase behaviour to make sure the dog runs the entire series of hurdles. In turn, it motivates the dog and gives it momentum. Whenever you tell yourself *you shouldn't eat cake,* you set yourself up to fail and undoubtedly eat cake.

57

In AAT, we motivate our dogs using the same process. I could use the hydraulic model if my work partner became confused and lost motivation. We do not allow such stressful situations; however, teens often deviate from the session and start chatting with one another, forgetting to reinforce the animal. Should a dog stop working because of frustration, I set the hydraulic mechanism up and conduct one last behaviour to end on a success. We call this process setting the dog up for success. Behaviour breakdown is one of the reasons why we train our dogs to tolerate frustration. I never want to leave a situation with our dogs experiencing failure because that would eventually burn them out. As I mentioned, it is easy to make a dog dislike work; therefore, we must constantly remain attuned to their language and needs. The maintenance of trained behaviours should include a management plan.

A behaviour management plan refers to managing animals when training is not feasible. For instance, when we take the dogs outside with our students, they must place the leash around their wrists and loop it around their hands. The technique is to avoid dropping the leash and losing a dog. We will similarly instruct adults and school staff because the leash management strategy also falls under our safety protocols. No exceptions. You will read in chapter four how a student understood the hard way and the importance of leash management requests.

To the right, the following image shows a double loop around the hand. It is not an actual double loop. Our hands-free leashes are open-ended; consequently, the hand holds both sides of the leash simultaneously, making it appear wrapped twice. Imagine putting a close-ended string around your wrist. You inevitably end up with the left and right sides of the rope in your hand. As I previously mentioned, safety is our priority; therefore, students must safely hold the dog's leash to avoid a dog from running away.

We use training leashes because they are incredibly adjustable and practical. Each student learns how to wrap the leash properly, and when they forget, we gently remind them and make no fuss over it. I like to call out their name and point to my wrist with a smile. It works every time. You will also need a management strategy that includes safety measures while you are out and about, for work or leisure, with your AAT work partner. I planned out veterinarians, drugstores, water sources, safe places, and other contingencies to ensure our animals remain secure in the case of an emergency.

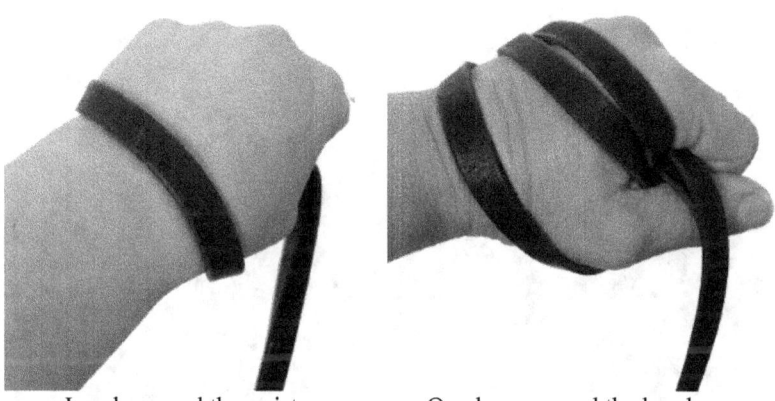

Leash around the wrist.   One loop around the hand.

In schools, I have identified emergency exits, placed the first-aid kits in the open, and where we can shelter our dogs if necessary. We often have access to a smaller room within the school, just in case. I have never needed to use a safety, first-aid, or emergency plan, but as the saying goes, *It's better to be safe than sorry!* Hopefully, it will remain as such. In the following image, Kris demonstrates (on the next page) how to hold the leash. Hariette is a scarce breed, one of only two in Canada. We trust the teens, and knowing how unique and rare the Broholmer is, Kris assured me he would not lose her. If we want to build trust, we have to start somewhere.

Giving teens responsibilities teaches them accountability, respect, self-awareness, and confidence. Walking a stranger's dog is the best place to begin the long process of trustworthiness. Rain or shine, we show up for AAT. We show up even when it snows, and half of the teachers stay home. Students are quick to point out that we came while no one else would. If anything, our presence tells them we care enough to battle the elements to be with them and work with dogs. To the teens, our presence is a form of unconditional love many have never experienced.

If my school had offered an AAT program, teachers might

have recognized my dyslexia before my twenty-fourth birthday. I pay great attention to how students write and read. The AAT team and I try to address as many struggles as possible, but it all starts with trust and safety. Once we have the students' confidence, we nourish it.

Karlo demonstrates the proper way to hold a leash.

One of my favourite management strategies to further a trusting relationship is to ask for more intimate questions as the program evolves. For example, as I hand the dog's leash to the teens on week three, I might ask what they did during the weekend. On week twenty-eight, my question might be, has your father taken you out recently? By May, my questions are personal. In private, I once asked a student if his father had physically assaulted him recently. Safety is not just about preventing physical harm; it includes mental protection. I can then relay the information through the proper channels within our multidisciplinary team.

I usually do not talk about my private life with the AAT teens, but on rare occasions, it is relevant that I do. When dogs are present, teens learn to divulge their personalities and allow themselves to be unconditionally loved. We avoid using the word appreciation because we purposefully demonstrate what love looks and feels like. Attachment, motivation, trust, and work increase when teenagers realize someone is willing to physically and mentally protect them. Before I conclude this chapter, let me discuss the word love and why every human should overuse it.

Humans are social animals and thrive when we are united and strong. We also require touch for our physical and mental health. Without love in our lives, we quickly deteriorate. Our mental health is the first to change, followed by physical illness and the *dis* conditions: disease, distress, dislike, disappointment, disillusionment, and dysregulation. The more we renounce expressing our emotions and feelings, the closer we get to becoming mentally and physically dysfunctional. The word love has become taboo, and society demonstrates the consequences of our emotional disconnect.

Words like appreciate or value communicate an underlying sense of separation from one another; love unites us. I often tell students I appreciate the inorganic and love the living; it is a simple yet powerful lesson. Your brain immediately feels better when someone tells you they love you. In their paper, Schwartz and Olds wrote, *"Brain areas associated with reward and pleasure are still activated as loving relationships proceed, but the constant craving and desire that are inherent in romantic love often lessen."* (2015).

> *"We know that primitive areas of the brain are involved in romantic love and that these areas*

light up on brain scans when talking about a loved one."

—Olds, 2015

Did humanity lose its soul, or has it fallen out of love with itself? Those are good questions to ask teenagers; their answers might surprise you. I know they surprise me.

Chapter 3
Adolescent issues in AAT

Common conditions

Montreal has an average waiting time of six months to a year to consult with a psychologist. The wait is two years to consult a psychiatrist if a hospital emergency room does not admit a person. AAI professionals have even longer wait times. My team is growing; unfortunately, I do not have enough personnel to fulfill all the requests we receive from schools and universities. I have to turn people away because the animals cannot work eight hours per day, every day. In my experience, teens have the least available services, especially regarding AAT. The lack of resources is one of the reasons I specialized in working with adolescents.

I designed the adolescent animal-assisted program to tackle mild to moderate behaviour issues. Schools often request services for at-risk youth because their probability of dropping out is high, and so is choosing a life of self-destruction, or sometimes both. Student issues vary greatly, but they all have one thing in common: animals. The dogs and rats participating in AAT programs were socialized and trained for this clientele. Most animals grew up in the AAT program as part of our socialization protocol.

According to the Diagnostics and Statistical Manual number five (DSM-5), the medical profession groups conditions into the following categories. Some mental disorders are a subsection of more extensive DSM-5 illnesses. To simplify the process, I have selected the issues most commonly found within the adolescent population in the AAT programs. I grouped the following conditions into smaller subcategories; if not, that would take tremendous space within this book. Since this is an AAT book, not a diagnostics manual, I will refer to the issues presented in the medical manual here in alphabetical order. A description of the condition will follow. Note that some teens have more than one diagnosed disorder; case studies in Chapter 4 will reflect this reality.

1. Aggressive behaviour
2. Anxiety Disorders
3. Attention-Deficit/Hyperactivity Disorder (ADHD)
4. Autism Spectrum Disorder (ASD)
5. Body Dysmorphia Disorder
6. Depression
7. Learning disabilities
8. Obsessive-Compulsive Disorders (OCD)
9. Post-Traumatic Stress Disorder (PTSD)
10. Substance abuse and addiction

The textbook-type definitions of the issues listed above will come first. I will follow with a Layman term description to shift the focus from conventional scientific terminology to a more humane definition. The teens in this book are not statistics or diagnostic labels; they are living, breathing, and feeling individuals with dreams, desires, wishes, and aspirations. Adolescents in AAT are consciously aware of their conditions and surroundings. If anything, the prevalence of teen and young adult anxiety disorders results from the lack of guidance on managing one's emotions. The state of the world also contributes, via social media, to their situation. Yet, teens have endless imaginations filled with exceptional solutions to life's many problems. My team and I adore listening to their ideologies and approaches to problem-solving; I find it refreshing, peaceful, helpful and hopeful. To validate teenagers, we must listen and accept that their ideas might be better than ours.

Aggressive behaviour

The DSM-5 introduces various new aggressive behaviour labels. The Virginia Commission on Youth (2017) defines how to diagnose aggressive behaviours: *"Diagnosis requires a failure to control aggressive impulses manifested by either Verbal aggression like temper tantrums, tirades, arguments or fights; or physical aggression toward people, animals, or property."* According to the DSM-5, the categories are as follows:

- Oppositional defiant disorder
- Intermittent explosive disorder
- Conduct disorder
- Pyromania
- Kleptomania
- Unspecified disruptive, impulse-control, or conduct disorder

The participants in the AAT program occasionally display aggressive behaviours, but to say they are aggressive is an untruth. Most of their responses are because they feel frustrated. Lack of communication is often part of a teen's experience; they feel caught between childhood and adulthood and find it difficult to express themselves. Furthermore, girls and boys communicate differently. Females like to discuss their feelings and emotions, while male adolescents tend to chat about actions or lack thereof. Boys want to be respected, and girls wish to be loved. To get a teen boy to talk, he usually has to be doing something, and the conversation starts with what he is working on. I used to chat with my son when we washed dishes.

Most of the displays we experience in AAT are verbal. In my seven years of practice, physical displays of aggressive behaviours are rare. I interjected only three times in a raised fist conflict. In both instances, I prevented the escalation of the exchange. The dogs are convincing in managing teen behaviour, especially aggression. The frustration we experience revolves around rewards and perceived values. Cookies, for example, are valued as a high reward because teens have no access to sweat. The same goes for other food, toys, and privileges.

I understand their plight; consequently, I invite them to negotiate. Teens are excellent at solving problems if we let them. Teens want adults to listen, not impose their values, views, or beliefs. I approach parenting as a guidance job. Our role is to help a person navigate through the intricacies of life by example.

When parents tell their kids, *Do what I say, not what I do,'* they genuinely tell children that behaviour overrides communication. Consequently, a parent's words mean nothing. In our AAT sessions, we strive to change that belief by pairing what we declare with what we do, with no exceptions. We brave the elements, odds, and Murphy's law to build a secure attachment; I am adamant about this truth.

We do not tolerate aggressive language; thus, we establish proper communication channels when we establish group norms during our first session. We tell teens their voices have equal value, and they can express themselves without condescending, derogatory, or aggressive words. I further add that they can ask to talk privately if they wish. Our participants do take advantage of these rules. You would be surprised at how they open up when a safe space is available to chat. Students ask for help with school or in their personal lives. I relay the information to the multidisciplinary team, and we find a solution.

I prefer to address a teen's aggressive behaviour by looking at the root cause. Once we identify what is causing the frustration and anger, we can help the person change their responses. If we modify the emotion, we effectively transform the behaviour. We achieve this through negotiations because we address the feeling, not the behaviour.

Anxiety disorders

Anxiety Disorders are growing at an alarming rate. According to the statistics from the Public Health Agency of Canada, *"In 2012, an estimated 700 000 (2.5%) Canadians aged 15 years and older reported symptoms compatible with a generalized anxiety disorder (GAD) in the previous 12 months."* (Pelletier, O'Donnell, McRae, & Grenier, 2017, p.54). The following year, the same agency reported: *"In 2013, an estimated 3 million Canadians (11.6%) aged 18 years or older reported that they had a mood and anxiety disorder."*

The numbers vary from one agency to another. According to Statistics Canada (2019), in 2017, 6.8% of the "Population aged 12 and over reported perceiving their mental health status as being fair or poor." (Table 13-10-0096-03). The following year, the number increased to 7.4%. Although the numbers represent people who evaluated their mental health, statistics still portray GAD as prevalent within the Canadian population of all ages and continues to increase yearly. As parents, teachers, or AAI practitioners, we need to be concerned about these numbers as they affect youth at a younger age, and symptoms last longer. General Anxiety Disorder falls under the umbrella term Anxiety Disorders within the DSM-5. The following definition relates to the Umbrella terms: generalized anxiety disorder, agoraphobia, social anxiety disorder, specific phobias, panic disorder, and separation anxiety disorder.

> *"Anxiety disorders are those that are characterized by excessive and persistent fear, worry, anxiety and related behavioral disturbances.[5] Fear involves an emotional response to a threat, whether that threat is real or perceived. Anxiety involves the anticipation that a future threat may arise."*
> —Cherry, 2019

In our classes, adolescents can have combined anxieties. Most often, we see social, panic, and separation disorders. The students do not like to talk about their conditions, so we do not instigate conversations about anxiety unless they start the discussion. My role is to establish and nourish communication; consequently, when the situation presents itself, I direct the group chat by making parallels between dog and human behaviour. For example, Mandu reacts to something bigger than himself by putting his tail between his legs and barking once. A student points out the behaviour, and I immediately direct the discussion toward insecurity and anxiety.

I would say something along the lines of, *"Mandu is afraid the big object will fall on him and injure him. Some dogs can start generalizing their fear and become highly anxious about big things. Some dogs might even refuse to go outside. This problem can happen to people, too."* Then, continue the discussion. Typically, the conversation starts, and the target student adds information about their condition. Suppose the goal is to reach a specific objective. In that case, I will direct the conversation without making the student uncomfortable. Suppose a classmate does make a comment that generates an anxious response. In that case, I bring the conversation back to the dog and try to find solutions to the problem as a group. I might parallel the resolution to people, but only as a general solution. I do not conduct psychotherapy in AAT.

Psychologists, psychiatrists, or social workers privately conduct their sessions with students. However, we work with other mental health professionals to match our goals and objectives with theirs. Initially, we did perform our sessions with a mental health professional present. However, students would not participate or bond with the animals, so we stopped. Most of our classes are conducted without psychologists because students feel more comfortable without them present.

One of the issues our participants with anxiety disorders repeatedly mention is how relaxed they feel when they are in the presence of our animals. This calm is why rats are so successful as AAT work partners. At the Dogue Shop, we joke about training rats as massage therapists. One day, one of the students came up with the same idea. The pulse of their little hands on the skin is the perfect pressure to solicit the nervous system without overloading it. Consequently, the gesture brings your focus to the here and now, places your attention on your body, and clears your mind of emotional and mental residual chatter.

For people suffering from an anxiety disorder, simply thinking of the rats' gentle messages can momentarily clear their anxiety symptoms. When you have anxiety, you feel the world is against you, and threats and danger lurk behind every corner. The body overreacts in a fight or flight response, and this extreme stress response feels like it never goes away. Panic attacks can follow high anxiety or a stressful situation. In either case, a panic attack includes shortness of breath, cold sweat, chest pain, and heart palpitations. When people experience their first panic attack, they often feel like they are dying. The fear of death increases the symptoms, and a vicious cycle begins.

Although it can feel like dying, the chances of actual death are unlikely. I have had one such panic attack, and I, too, felt like it would end me. My training as a yogi came in handy that day. I sat and tried to meditate. It took a while, but I slowed my heart and breathing while releasing the tension in my body. When teens talk about panic attacks, I can relate and give them exercises to try. Meditations and pranayamas are excellent tools to combat anxiety disorders. In my first book, Dog in the Mirror is God: A Scientifically Spiritual Approach to Treating Human and Animal Behaviour Problems (Dufresne-Cyr, 2018), I offer exercises to tackle various conditions.

My cousin once told me she thought she was having a heart attack when she first experienced a panic attack. She did not know what was happening. She added that the fear of dying she experienced that day makes her *"avoid life in general"* now. I have been with my cousin during a panic attack, which is unnerving. I know the true horror of losing control over one's body; saying it is horrible is an understatement.

My cousin knows what is happening now and will tell me. However, the feeling exponentiates for some younger teens or children who do not have the adequate words to express what is happening to them. Some people will come to avoid the unpleasant feeling at all costs and evade going to school, work, or socially interacting.

The following is one of my favourite quotes for anxiety sufferers. It is a challenge every day when you have anxiety, but every day does not have to be a challenge. Find the closest AAT animal in your area and plan a visit. Please seek help; you must not live with generalized anxiety or stress. Once you find an AAT practitioner, be accessible for at least one hour a week. That will total fifty-two hours without the anxiety or stress; it adds up over time and gives you tools to feel in control. AAT animal trainers are excellent at reflecting on the source of the anxiety or stress; thus, we can provide adequate services and support. When I attended the pain clinic, the head doctor told us we did not have to suffer.

> *"Anxiety was born in the very same moment as mankind. And since we will never be able to master it, we will have to learn to live with it—*

just as we have learned to live with storms."
—*Paulo Coelho*

Attention deficit & hyperactivity disorder

Another common condition in the animal-assisted therapy program is attention-deficit with or without hyperactivity disorder (AD/ADHD). Many of my friends were diagnosed with ADHD when they were older. Unfortunately, ADHD diagnosis was not very common back in the day. My grandmother used to say I had ants in my pants; that diagnosis was just as good as any. Humour aside, the following is the definition of ADHD from the Verywell Mind website.

> *"Attention-deficit hyperactivity disorder is characterized by a persistent pattern of hyperactivity-impulsivity and/or inattention that interferes with functioning and presents itself in two or more settings such as at home, work, school, and social situations."*
> —*Cherry, 2019*

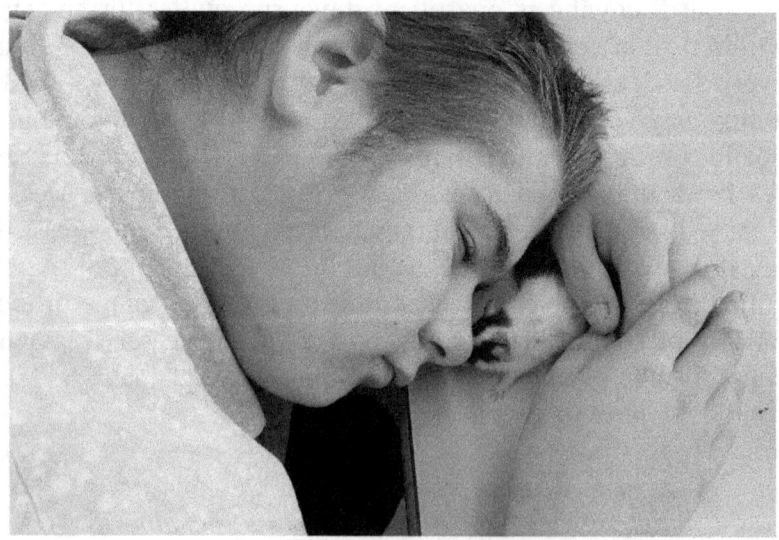

Student relaxing with a baby rat.

We tend to see more ADHD cases in our groups because teens without impulse control are more disruptive to their classmates. In our groups, hyperactive teens fit perfectly. Dogs love to work and are relentless, so when students focus on the training part of our program, they succeed exceptionally well. Kids focus on the task, but since the dog keeps moving, the movement keeps the students focused. You can think of the process as a positive vicious cycle and a cycle within a cycle. The sessions look like the Tasmanian devil from the Looney Tunes television show; the dog continuously moves around the student. The training session becomes a creative dance segment since the human tries to stay with the dog. The students tell us they like this fast-paced motion because it keeps their minds busy, and they stop thinking about unimportant things.

I take the students out for dog toilet duty, which turns into a running around session. Running with a dog requires focus and attention; consequently, doing the activity with a pet partner is very different from running alone. Our human-dog teams love a high-paced run, and I love watching them. Kids love being kids; adults are the ones who push the developmental stages too far too soon. In reality, all they want is to run around and have fun.

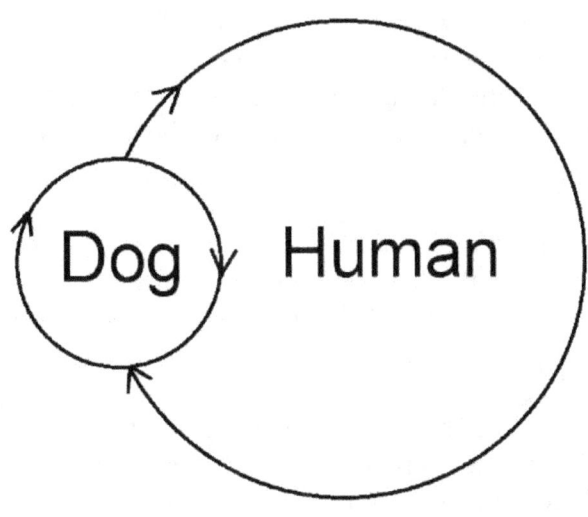

Working with a dog cycle.

Nothing is better than watching a teen playing outside with a dog and enjoying being a kid. Teens can be carefree, worry-free, socially free, phone-free, and rule-free for twenty minutes. I know they relish play sessions because they ask for them. The students come outside with us because being with their canine companions means *that whatever we do, we stick together, regardless of whether it is plus or* minus twenty degrees Celcius. ADHD is like owning a fragmented mind. Like a computer with too many open programs, the intellect has no direction because it simultaneously tries to collect information from all the available programs. We often refer to this process as *going down a rabbit hole*. Retrieving pertinent information becomes an arduous task. Imagine trying to answer questions with ants in your pants, as Ralph Wiggum from the Simpsons would say, *Unpossible!*

> *"You have a treasure within you that is infinitely greater than anything the world can offer."*
> —Eckhart Tolle

An ADHA student once told me that he and the dog were the same, and he felt for Jasmine. He based his reflection on the dog's constant arousal and difficulty in learning new tasks. It took him weeks to push through, but I told him to keep trying because all dogs succeed. He asked me if some animals had ever failed; without hesitating, I said no, it is just a matter of time. Ultimately, he taught the dog to retrieve the mail, which was an accomplishment.

The challenge of working with this particular animal taught him multiple things about ADHD and himself. People with ADHD do not find their condition pleasant or amusing. They desperately try to control themselves but cannot control their impulses. Impulse control is difficult for someone with ADHA. The mind becomes distracted by all the stimuli in the environment, and the person cannot focus their attention. It is taxing when the nervous system does not cooperate. Distractions inevitably lead down a rabbit hole.

If you walked into our group classes and I asked you to pinpoint students with ADHD, you would not be successful.

You would not know we are a distinct unit within the school if not for the animals. When I was young, my grandmother hated animals but said, *"Never underestimate the power of a dog; it spreads joy like honey bees spread pollen."* I never understood that until I was much older, and she was right. Animals have the intrinsic ability to make humans feel love from an extraordinary dimension: unity. People strive to gap the bridge between animal species to understand one another. Animals help us be human and humane. Animals teach empathy.

In AAT, students flourish from that concept. It is not rare for a student with ADHD to exclaim *Ahhhh, I get it now!* They reach their goals through persistence, patience, acceptance, openness, and consistency. We do not need to teach the rules of patience to students because animals allow the lesson to manifest itself within the student. It just takes time. I love how Virginia Satir (1988) explains our interconnectedness through our ability to communicate and function in groups. She refers to human groups as open or closed.

> *"In a closed system, the parts* [people] *are rigidly connected or disconnected altogether. In either case, information does not flow between parts or from the outside in and inside out. An open system is one in which the parts interconnect, are responsive and sensitive to one another, and allow information to flow between the internal and external environments."*
>
> —Satir, p.131-132

By integrating animals into human intervention systems, we are reconnecting parts that allow communication to flow anew in all directions. Without forcing function, AAT animals prevent system failures and dysfunctional parts within the broken system to generate more damage. Once we mend all aspects of the system, communication is possible again. This past spring, an ADHD student summarized our entire year's work in a sentence. She struggled to stay still long enough to communicate with us, but she tried her hardest. She said, *"I can't stop my body from moving; I just want it to end."* Then came a rat. These little furry creatures most people hate are a blessing when working with adolescents. Bear with me; I will explain.

A baby rat named Momo allowed her to stop her mind and body momentarily and be at peace with herself in our organized, chaotic environment. While usual chaos was occurring in the classroom, magic happened. I always leave space for wonders to occur because they are the most healing and peaceful moments. For a few minutes, ADHD ceased, and joy manifested itself. After taking the following picture, I gazed at her momentarily, sharing her happiness. The image is one of my favourites from the 2018-2019 school year because it demonstrates how much power the smallest animal can have on a human. In AAT, size does not matter.

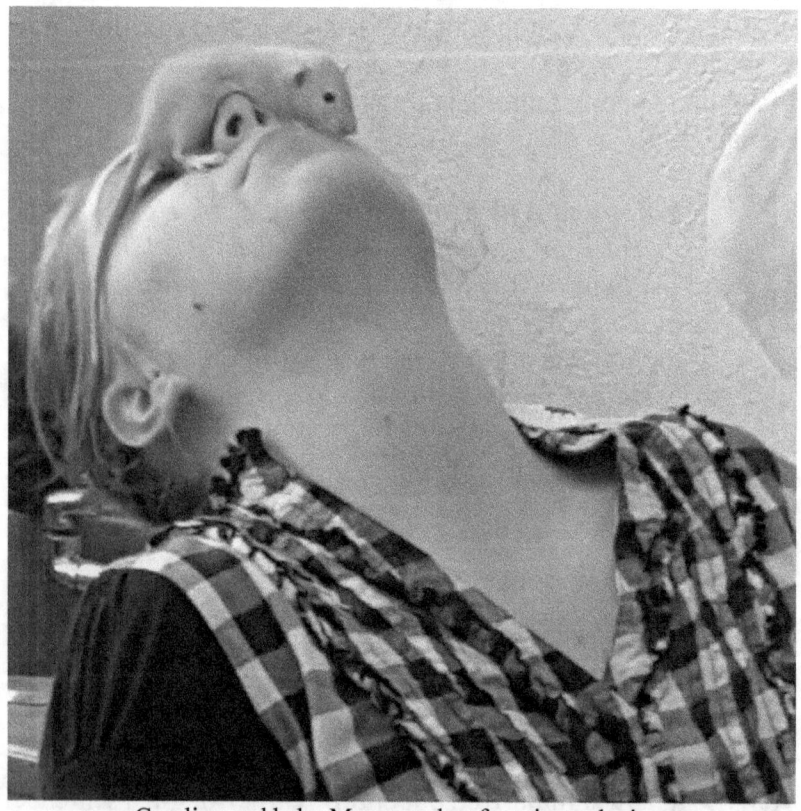

Carolina and baby Momo on her face, just relaxing.

When Carolina came out of her meditative stance, she said

There's nothing better than a rat on your face. We all laughed. The other students thought they should have all done the same thing. But then again, not all teens have ADHD. All I can tell is that she was smiling, and so, too, were her classmates. Emotions are contagious, and happiness is an emotion. We were all happy with and for her. In my groups, judgment is not allowed. We all carry a psychological bad of negative experiences and do not require someone to point it out; we know. We do not tolerate bullying, discrimination, or negative attitudes or behaviours toward other people or animals. The AAT classroom is a physically and psychologically safe place. Always.

One of my favourite animal trainers is Steve Martin; no, not the actor. He describes trust as the currency between humans and non-human animals. He explains that we need to deposit trust in the trust bank before we can ever try to withdraw. I have lived this truth for decades. Building trust is hard; destroying it is easy. Even the most minor trust withdrawal can have an enormous impact. Once we take trust out, we must deposit as soon as possible, or the relationship will deteriorate rapidly. Let me end this section with another quote from Virginia Satir (1988). Trust is the foundation of all social animal contact; without it, we lose ourselves in emotional limbo.

> *"It* [honesty] *is actually the only basis for trust. Teenagers will not be honest with adults who are not honest with them. In this case, it is emotional honesty that counts most."*
> —Satir, 1988, p.319

Autism spectrum disorder

When people think of autism, many images come to their minds; unfortunately, some ideas are negative and judgmental. Hopefully, this section will demystify and change perceptions surrounding autism. On that note, I would like to dispel a myth about autism. Vaccination does NOT cause autism. Science has confirmed this claim in a longitudinal study of 657 461 Danish children from 1999 to 2010 (Hviid et al., 2019). Please vaccinate your children; vaccines are imperative to their health and have been studied and tested for decades.

> *"Autism spectrum disorder is characterized by persistent deficits in social interaction and communication in multiple life areas as well as restricted and repetitive patterns of behaviours. The DSM specifies that symptoms of autism spectrum disorder must be present during the early developmental period and that these symptoms must cause significant impairment in important areas of life, including social and occupational functioning."*
> —Cherry, 2019

Most participants in AAT who are on the autism spectrum disorder (ASD) experience the milder end of the scale. They have a social awkwardness that might be imperceivable to the average person but not to the family and friends surrounding them. Unsuspecting or misinformed adults might label autistic kids as *strange* or *weird*. I find our teens perfect as they are. They are funny, intelligent, direct, determined, collaborative, and precise. *What you see is what you get!* And it suits my team perfectly. Autistic teens have impeccable clicker timing and observational skills. Autistic kids can call out animal behaviours faster than anybody else. The dogs love the attention and the endless affection they receive from their socially perfect work partner.

One of my favourite pictures is of a young lad who felt socially awkward until he met Hariette. Hariette, aka the dinosaur, loves to receive hugs from her favourite accomplice, Seymour. Every week, she falls in love all over again. Hariette knows that when her human partner sits on the ground, it is hug time. She lays on her side and welcomes the embrace. I trained to receive hugs, but she accepted them with great anticipation, joy, and trust for a few select teens. When working with animals, we are depositing trust in an emotional bank. Still, sometimes, we have to make a withdrawal. The wonderful thing about trust credit is that animals accept the expense and will continue to work. Dog hugs function under the same process. We train them (debit) and sometimes ask them to give one even if they are slightly uncomfortable (credit). The equation balances itself because we immediately make another deposit. Reinforcement is a deposit at the trust bank. Without trust equity, humans would be unable to work with animals, especially exotic species. Wolves are unforgiving to humans who do not abide by their social rules. Invading a wolf's critical space without their acceptance will land you, at best, in the hospital or, worse, in the cemetery.

In the AAT program, we sometimes play games designed to help specific teens flourish alongside their peers. These games usually serve as a social catalyst between teens and adults, facilitating attachment. Because a secure attachment is an AAT goal, the bond between the dog and the participant needs room to grow. It can be a sensitive process for many professionals since the owner-dog relationship needs to cease momentarily and develop between a stranger and the animal. I love watching the attachment form; it is my reinforcement for a well-done job. Autistic participants in our groups also have a unique insight into animal behaviour. In her 2005 book Animals in Translation, Temple Grandin describes how being autistic gives her a cutting-edge approach as an animal behaviourist. She states that autism allows her to relate to animals.

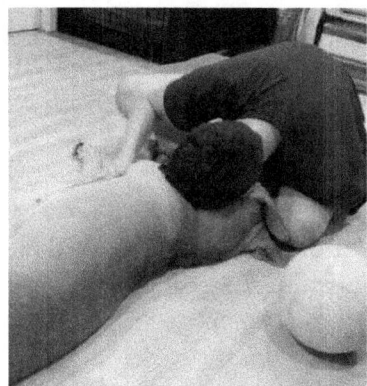 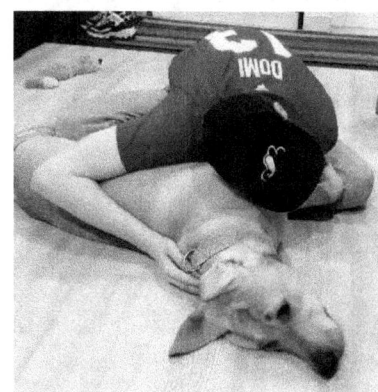

Hariette works with Seymour.

Grandin (2005) says, *"And it wasn't until I was in my forties that I finally realized I had one big advantage over the feedlot owners who were hiring me to manage their animals: being autistic."* (p.1). She makes many comparisons between autism and animals. I can certainly see how it comes to be that our clients with ASD connect with our animal partners without seemingly any effort whatsoever. Their natural affinity resides in the type of relationship they form with animals. Young people with autism closely resemble a dog's cognitive and emotional interaction experiences. I am not comparing humans to dogs, but rather their responses to emotions via their limbic system. Teens are smart, but they become overburdened when emotions hijack their responses.

> *"Since I'd noticed so many similarities between animals and autistics people in my career, the fact that Nancy Minshew [neurologist] was finding a connection between autism and an orientation to detail gave me another reason to think I was right about animals."*
> —Grandin, 2005, p.33

Being in a state of emotional arousal for extended periods creates havoc on the body. Repetitive behaviours or self-harm changes their focus, shifting the emotional pain from inside to outside. The first thing we do when our AAT teens with autism express negative emotions is to offer them a break. I suggest they step into the makeshift isolation room within the class to partake in self-management. Accompanied by their dog, they can relax and reduce their overwhelming emotional state by engaging in ritualized behaviours. One such dog ritualized behaviour is to ask their pet partner to touch their hand, followed by the cue to lay next to them for comfort. Students process their emotions faster when the dog is there and people step away. The relaxing session never lasts long, and the students return to their team.

My favourite moment was seeing a student curl onto Hariette. The young boy started talking with her as if she understood. It was as though he could perceive Hariette talking back to him. Hariette closed the gap between faces and gently licked the student. He whispered *I love you, dinosaur*, stood up and asked if he could train a different behaviour. We chatted about what he wanted to do and shifted from one training plan to another. Nothing is stuck in stone when working with adolescents and animals. Another reason I adore this clientele is that they never run out of solutions. I believe parents forget to teach their children the concept of locus of control. Teenagers must learn they have some control over their lives, bodies, minds, and emotions; if not, they fare poorly in adulthood.

The main difference between generations is our ability to manage ourselves and problem-solve. Parents who gave their children responsibilities learned how to cope with life later on. Granted, most parents still believed in corporal punishment and used it to control their kids. We are past the stage of physically punishing children. Unfortunately, younger generations tossed consequences out with the baby water.

My son and I established punishments together for specific unwanted behaviours. Here is the key to success: implement the consequence. I'm not talking about physical punishment; I am referring to a predetermined cause-consequence rule. For example, my family sat together and discussed what we would do if our son hit someone. The predetermined consequence would be a timeout from playing outside. I would return to my friend and her children only to release my son after a set time. He hit his friend, or anybody else for that matter, once.

Life is full of adverse outcomes, and if we don't prepare our kids for the real world, they will struggle their entire adult life. I see so much anxiety around us, yet it is part of the human condition; therefore, it begs the question, what is normal anxiety? In AAT, we strive to give teens the tools they need to face life. Norms serve that purpose. I strongly recommend that parents establish consequences for undesirable behaviours before they occur. That way, the child will know what is coming and accept it because they have pre-agreed to the outcome. We define outcome expectancies as anticipated positive or negative consequences resulting from engaging in a behaviour (Reesor, 2017). Life has aftermaths, and children are disadvantaged if they have no control over them and no way to solve their problems. Children need rules and boundaries to thrive.

According to Ofner et al. (2018), authors of the Public Health Agency Canada's Autism Spectrum Disorder Among Children and Youth, approximately two percent of Canadian children aged between five and seventeen years old were diagnosed with Autism in 2015, with a higher prevalence amongst males. The statistic draws our attention to the need for human science programs to develop AAT curricula, which future professionals could integrate into their practice. AAT programs could be highly beneficial in the context of autism education and intervention. AAT could also benefit pre-existing infrastructures and other institutions that educate populations or support families. Human relationships are complex, but autism is even more challenging for children and teenagers. Animals facilitate connections and pull kids out of their heightened emotional state, even for a moment. I believe it is our professional call of duty to offer such possibilities.

> *"Many Canadians living with ASD need appropriate supports to reach their full potential, while family and caregiver quality of life can also be improved if timely and appropriate support services are offered throughout the lifespan."*
> —*Ofner et al., 2018*

Body dysmorphia and gender dysphoria

According to the Substance Abuse and Mental Health Services of the National Health Services (NHS) in the United Kingdom, a person cannot perceive their body as it presents itself and try to attain an unrealistic physique to compensate for the distorted view. In other words, the limbic system tricks the mind into believing the body looks a certain way. When the visual representation does not align with beliefs, the person tries to rectify what they think instead of what they feel. People will see themselves as overweight and feel bad, so they stop eating to feel good. In reality, it is the bad feeling of oneself that needs healing. Once the person no longer thinks or feels bad about their body, the dysmorphia vanishes, for lack of a better word. The distortion can be about one part or the entire body.

> *"Body dysmorphic disorder (BDD), or body dysmorphia, is a mental health condition where a person spends a lot of time worrying about flaws in their appearance. These flaws are often unnoticeable to others. People of any age can have BDD, but it's most common in teenagers and young adults. It affects both men and women."*
>
> —BDD, 2021.

The Diagnostic and Statistical Manual of Mental Disorders (DSM-5) in North America adds that a component of obsessive-compulsive disorder exists within the BDD and Gender Dysmorphia (GD) diagnosis. The DSM-5 classifies body dysmorphia within the Obsessive-Compulsive and Related Disorders category. I am a science person but generally highly critical of the DSM. The American Psychological Association (APA) removed homosexuality from the DSM-3 manual as a disorder in 1974, and *"Distress over one's sexual orientation remained in the manual, under different names, until the DSM-5 in 2013."* (Rubenstein, 1995).

> *"Preoccupation with one or more perceived defects or flaws in physical appearance that are not observable or appear slight to others. At some point during the course of the disorder, the individual has performed repetitive behaviors (e.g., mirror checking, excessive grooming, skin picking, reassurance seeking) or mental acts (e.g., comparing his or her appearance with that of others) in response to the appearance concerns."*
>
> —DSM-5, 2016.

Homosexuality was not a disorder; adding new labels does

not guarantee that every new condition is a disability, disease, or disorder. Dyslexia, for example, is considered a learning disability, yet 15 to 20% of people share this condition (Dyslexia Canada, 2023). With a large portion of the population displaying reading and writing limitations, dyslexia may be an evolutionary strategy, not a disability. Since the condition is prevalent among men, thinking in 3D might be valuable. Dyslexic folks solve problems in a very efficient way. Men who could visualize how to catch food were more successful hunters. Similarly, what if distorted body image was part of the adolescent development phase?

Body dysmorphia is predominantly a condition found in adolescence. The disorder affects roughly 2% to 3% of the general population —about 1 in 50 people (Phillips, 2022). BDD strangely coincides with Erikson's adolescence period of development. The parallel begs the question, is the condition a direct cause of Erikson's Identity vs. Role Confusion conflict, or is BDD a consequence of an inappropriately solved dilemma? According to Erikson, people without a clear identity perception will undoubtedly suffer from role confusion (Erikson, 1959). Conversely, the other extreme yields a rigid identity and does not allow flexibility or adaptability. Solving the dilemma should reside somewhere in the middle.

Identity ◄───────────┼───────────► Role confusion

Healthcare professionals should systematically refer to Erik Erikson's stages of development when assessing a teenager to avoid emotional, physical, and mental confusion. Parents and school personnel should never push gender affirmation onto children and teenagers until they resolve their psychological dilemmas and have matured into adulthood. With inappropriate guidance or lack thereof, people with BDD and gender dysphoria (GD) patients suffer enormously emotionally.

The DSM-5 describes GD as a psychological condition stemming from a conflict between identity and sex. According to the National Healthcare System (NHS) in the United Kingdom, *"Gender Dysphoria is a term that describes a sense of unease that a person may have because of a mismatch between their biological sex and their gender identity. This sense of unease or dissatisfaction may be so intense it can lead to depression and anxiety and have a harmful impact on daily life."* (Gender dysphoria, 2017). The National Library of Medicine website explains the disorder as a *"marked incongruence between their experienced or expressed gender and the one they were assigned at birth."* (Garg et al., 2022). Note how definitions still refer to gender and sex as the same.

Hariette in here incognito costume.

The lack of longitudinal research creates false data; however, studies that address a person's condition after their transition report increased suicidal tendencies (Dhejne et al.,

2011; Madisson et al., 2016; Wiepjes et al., 2020). Madisson (2016) states, *"By parent report, children with gender dysphoria show an increased rate of self-harm/suicidality as they get older."* In his book When Harry Became Sally: Responding to the Transgender Movement, Ryan Anderson, Ph.D., states the following.

> *"The medical evidence suggests that sex reassignment does not adequately address the psychosocial difficulties faced by people who identify as transgender. Even when the procedures are successful technically and cosmetically, and even in cultures that are relatively 'trans-friendly,' transitioners still face poor outcomes."*
>
> —Anderson, 2019

People must question their identity and sexual orientation; introspection is fundamental to good mental health. Conversely, adults must support children and teenagers, not force them into a given role. *"In fact, people who have had transition surgery are nineteen times more likely than average to die by suicide."* (Anderson, When Harry Became Sally: Responding to the Transgender Moment, 2019). Transgender activists admit that 80 to 95% of children with GD will eventually identify with their birth sex if adults allow them to develop according to researched and documented stages of development (Anderson, 2023). I know some will disagree with such statements. However, the underlying disorder is not a physical one. Changing one's body part will not achieve the desired outcome without solving the psychological discord.

Depression

Because depression is a category in the DSM-5, it has to stand alone as a section in this book. However, depression and anxiety are teens' top three mental health issues in our AAT programs. Because the students in our groups are at-risk teens, one gathers that life is not easy for them. Many life events can lead to depression: divorce, moving, changing school, losing friends, accidents, physical ailments, disease, death, break-up, or reconstituted family. Life has many stressors; some are within our control, while others do not. Furthermore, some forms of depression are clinical, while others are temporary. The former is a lifelong battle; the latter is a transient condition brought on by a stressful situation; one does not diminish the other. Both forms can be equally emotionally painful.

> *"Depressive disorders are a type of mood disorder that include a number of conditions. They are all characterized by the presence of sad, empty, or irritable moods accompanied by physical and cognitive symptoms. They differ in terms of duration, timing, or presumed etiology."*
> *—Cherry, 2019*

The depressive conditions stated in the DSM-5 are disruptive mood dysregulation disorder, major depressive disorder, persistent depressive disorder, other or unspecified depressive disorder, premenstrual dysphoric disorder, substance or medication-induced depressive disorder, and depressive disorder due to another medical condition. To simplify the text, I will refer to all conditions as one general category.

Over the years, one depressive state can emerge with another. Take divorce, for example; children and teenagers tend to blame themselves for the situation and start to experience a variety of symptoms. Different age groups react differently, but depression affects them in one form or another. Children of all ages believe separation or divorce directly results from their behaviour. Blaming themselves generates a vicious cycle of disorderly conduct and escalation of parental conflict.

In other words, children blame themselves; thus, they act out. Parents get mad at their children, which validates the child's deviant behaviour. Kruk (2013) discusses how children experience divorce regardless of age differences in his book The Equal Parent Presumption, Social Justice in the Legal

Determination of Parenting After Divorce. He states the following.

> *"The form and severity of children's reactions depend on factors such as age, gender, and particular circumstances, and although some disagreement exists as to which age group tends to show which symptoms, studies continue to show that children of divorced families frequently exhibit behavioural difficulties, poor self-esteem, depression, and poor school performance."*
>
> —Kruk, 2013, p.89-90

I remember going through those same emotions when my parents divorced. Kruk (2013) continues with a simple yet powerful explanation of how teens feel when he writes, *"Adolescents show continuing anger, sadness, a sense of loss and betrayal, shame and embarrassment, and a concern about their own future marriages and relationships."* (p.92). These are the teens we work with within our AAT programs. Participants experience anger and sadness simultaneously, which results in conflicting emotional states. If our teens are in a relationship, we might share their first breakup. Albear was the best AAT pet partner for these situations. He allowed the person to cry their emotions out, however long it took.

I remember asking a student why he was so angry at his pet partner dog; then I saw his white face when he looked at me. He was dumbfounded. The student was not expecting someone to call him out on his projection. He did not answer me, and he did not have to. It was an *I know what you know* moment, and I left him to reflect for the remainder of the session. We did talk about it afterwards, and the student confirmed the source of the anger. I mentioned that it was okay to feel angry but to remember that the dog did not know why and did not deserve the aggressive response. The student apologized and hugged the dog; we both knew he was genuinely hugging himself. Dogs allow us to forgive ourselves; in that sense, they are genuine superheroes.

Our depressive students vary in emotional intensity from

the beginning to the end of the day. Anger, sadness, frustration, joy, lack of motivation, confusion, and back to rage is common during a session. Overall, the organized chaos sessions run smoothly and enjoyably. Human behavioural changes do not matter to the AAT dogs because we trained them to think and problem-solve through emotional changes during sessions. The following images show a student (left) feeling depressed and shut down because of family and other personal issues. He was in the AAT class for weeks before he started to engage and interact with the dogs. By the end of the school year, he was still highly unresponsive but more engaged. He began to interact when I actively took on his case with Albear.

The student (left) was disengaged for months.

By the end of the year, the student started talking to and interacting with the AAT team. I kept teasing him by telling him I would get a nice photo of him smiling and interacting with a dog. He kept telling or brushing me off. Anger is powerful, but not even the most formidable defence mechanism can resist puppy cuteness. I did get my picture on the last day of school. You will read more about him and the other students in Chapter 4. Depression is not easy to live with; these students suffer greatly and need all the help they can get.

Each moment we toil with the teens yields a positive outcome, for they leave happier than when they arrived. My team and I perceive their challenges and try to change each individual's experience. Hopefully, we can change their perceptions about themselves and their place in the world. I celebrate every little victory with them because we care. Animal-assisted therapy is not letting strangers pet a dog for one hour. AAT is about changing deep-rooted beliefs. When children have not experienced unconditional love and empathy from an animal, it is harder for them to adjust to life later. Children and adolescents require non-human relationships to practice their emotional skills.

Learning disabilities

According to Statistics Canada (Morris et al., 2019), specific learning disabilities, classified as Neurodevelopmental Disorders in the DSM-5, affect 3.9% of the population above fifteen years old. Unfortunately, this statistic refers to diagnosed cases. The actual number might not reflect the percentage of people with a learning disability. The statistic might not sound imposing; however, the number reveals that most people get diagnosed during later adolescence and early adulthood. I find this statistic alarming since young children would benefit from resources early on in their academic lives.

I received my diagnosis at twenty-two years old. I profited immensely from the education center at my college. Still, had I been diagnosed earlier, my scores would have been different, thus offering more possibilities. I firmly believe that high schools should mandate a learning disability profile for all students leaving grade school. High school is a fundamental academic level for future teens. College profiles often require specific prerequisites obtained during high school.

Specific colleges and universities operate the learning center; unfortunately, the diagnosis process remains the student's responsibility. Consequently, if a person does not know they have a learning disability as I did, the likelihood of a person seeking help is improbable. As the saying goes, one cannot fix what one does not know is broken. If your instinct about your child tells you something's wrong, pursue the venture because you will most likely be correct. Fortunately, one of my teachers caught on only because I had the same writing problem as her daughter.

> *"DSM-5 considers SLD [Specific Learning Disabilities] to be a type of Neurodevelopmental Disorder that impedes the ability to learn or use specific academic skills (e.g., reading, writing, or arithmetic), which are the foundation for other academic learning. The learning difficulties are 'unexpected' in that other aspects of development seem to be okay."*
> —Tannock, 2019

Many students in our AAT groups have recently been diagnosed with a learning disability. Reactions are different from one person to the next. Still, I distinctly remember thinking and eventually saying, *"I'm not dumb after all!"* My diagnosis made me feel confused. I was happy I finally knew what had been wrong with me all those years. However, I simultaneously felt angry that no one had realized something was wrong. When students share their learning disability, especially with a long face and sad look, I tell them, *"It's OK; so do I, but you must know we have superpowers others don't!"* Typically, their face changes because they see it is not a limitation; if anything, it can be a rise to success. Who would not want to think visually in 3D and easily solve problems?

Most dyslexics I know can take any object or situation, render a perfect 3D model in their mind and reverse engineer it. The organization Made by Dyslexia wants to change the stigma behind the misunderstood disability, making people with dyslexia a vital asset to businesses. When I talk about dyslexia, I always tell people that if Elon Musk were to describe how to build a rocket, I could visualize it in 3D and reverse engineer it to solve his problem, all the while knowing nothing about how rockets work. Another example is the ability to hold in one's mind a 3D map of the human body, inside and out. Imagine having a CT scan or MRI in your mind and accessing it at will;

that is a superpower.

A student once told me he would prefer to quit school because it was pointless; he would be dumb his whole life. I pointed to the dog he was working with and said, *"You know, when you started working with this dog, you both knew nothing. Still, you both succeeded with patience, trust, and confidence. You are responsible for her learning, and that is remarkable. Remember that!"* Dogs allow so much room to grow when you look at things differently. Learning disabilities are emotionally draining because they are persistent. On particular days, things run smoothly; the next seems insurmountable. Understanding one's dyslexic brain is a full-time occupation.

Teenagers' discouragement is palpable. When I perceive student disappointment, we train a behaviour the teen and the dog have not done in a while. The training session reminds them that things were once complicated but will improve. Positive achievements help teens push through hard days. We often bring human reinforcement for the teens to reward their behaviour. By behaviour, I mean their accomplishments, not good or bad conduct. The team and I always try to devise various ways to reward them. On such an occasion, I printed a photo of their best accomplishment and gave it to them.

When I get visually distracted and forget to reward students, it is not uncommon for them to ask in my ear. I apologize, wink, and give them two rewards. I do so because students know they are successful and deserve reinforcement. I treasure those moments because the adolescents also dared to ask; the lesson they learned was self-worth. Teens learn to celebrate small victories. Through systematic desensitization, we teach kids that their voice has the same weight as anybody else.

Some people have a distorted view of their value. The ego has its plan for managing one's behaviour, thus confusing the mind and generating conflicting emotions. Living in a conflicted state is highly uncomfortable to experience. In the animal behaviour apprenticeship classes at the Dogue Academy, I wrote *Trust the Process* on the wall. The quote summarizes a chant I keep telling my students, *"It's all about small victories; baby steps!"* I try to remind students that AAT is a process.

In the movie What About Bob (1991), with Bill Murray and

Richard Dreyfuss, Bob (Murray) learns to break down life challenges into smaller steps, which his psychologist, Dr. Leo Marvin (Dreyfuss), calls *Baby Step!* In animal training, we call those steps successive approximations. Students recognize the breakdown of behaviour because they use it in their training sessions with the AAT animals. Consequently, it is easy for me to parallel the two. The same learning theories govern human and animal behaviour. Therefore, students come to understand that animal and human training processes are identical; hence, *Trust the Process*. Once people make the parallel, they can reinforce their behaviour.

Next to the previous quote, I wrote *Pick Your Battles*. Another motto students often hear from me. Academic results are very stressful for teens with learning disabilities; some days, they feel they are losing the war. I remind them that war comprises small victories, so wisely picking their battles is essential. Pouring energy into challenges they think are the most important is what they should focus on. The struggles can be discouraging at times, but persistence is what defines people with learning disabilities. With time and diagnosis, it becomes easier as we age. I try to teach students that a disability can also be a superpower, another quote I repeat often.

My famous quotes at the Dogue Academy.

At the learning centre at Dawson College, my instructor, Rose, described how people with learning disabilities, especially dyslexia, process information from one perspective. For me, that was, and still is, animal behaviour. One student in my group is a history genius, especially political history. He can learn anything and everything if he can process the information from a historical perspective. Here is an example. When I learned advanced math in college, I would replace the numbers with visual representations of dog breeds. It was easier to process the information instead of figuring out which number I saw in the first place. As the semester concludes for our AAT participants and exams start, I can see their nervousness increase. We pay extra attention to our students and encourage them as much as possible. We have occasionally allowed the dog to assist the student during his exam.

After a challenging test, we celebrate the grade regardless of the number or letter they achieved. Reinforcing achievements is equivalent to reinforcing animal behaviour. Because students relate to their animals, they acknowledge they are worth the reward. It might sound crude, but it is nonetheless truthful. In her book Don't Shoot the Dog, Karen Prior (1984) discusses how people can use learning theories to change undesirable behaviours into desirable behaviours by reinforcing others, even ourselves, through multiple successive approximations, aka *Baby Steps!* I strongly recommend that students watch The Big Bang Theory episode (Prady, 2009) when Sheldon trains Penny using operant conditioning. Sheldon's humouristic explanation accurately represents how we, and animals, learn.

> *"One possible application of reinforcement training is reinforcing yourself. This is something we often neglect to do, partly because it doesn't occur to us, and partly because we tend to demand a lot more of ourselves than we would of others."*
>
> —Prior, 1984, p.18

Obsessive-compulsive disorders

People often joke about having an obsessive-compulsive disorder (OCD) when they organize their work station or need to make their research paper perfect. Still, a significant difference exists between experiencing a genuine disorder and striving for perfection. Perfectionism is a symptom of the OCD diagnosis but is not a cause. We all have impulses, but most humans control them. The chemicals in your body activate and inhibit neural activity; we refer to these chemicals as excitatory or inhibitory. The DSM-5 is clear about the definition of this mental health disorder.

> *"The diagnostic criteria in the DSM-5 specify that in order to be diagnosed with obsessive-compulsive disorder, a person must experience obsessions, compulsions, or both.*
>
> *Obsessions are defined as recurrent, persistent thoughts, impulses, and urges that lead to distress or anxiety.*
>
> *Compulsions are repetitive and excessive behaviors that the individual feels that they must perform. These actions are performed to reduce anxiety or to prevent some dreaded outcome from occurring."*
>
> —Cherry, 2019

According to Statistics Canada (2019), 7.2% of Canadians above fifteen years old suffer from mental health disorders or disabilities. The Canadian government has not released data from 2021 to this date (May 2023). Obsessive-compulsive disorder lies within the emotional structures of the brain within the limbic system and regions in the pre-frontal cortex. In principle, OCDs are reciprocal control circuits known as feedback loops. In other words, repetitive behaviours release the emotional charge, which sustains the obsessive and compulsive aspects of the anxiety disorder.

Sarah-Nicole Bostan (2018), in her article Brain Signature of Obsessive-Compulsive Disorder, explains the discrepancy between emotions and expression. She states, *"Thus, OCD can be better understood to be characterized by both intense emotional arousal and problems with executive functioning, which contribute to maintaining the OCD cycle."* (2018). Furthermore, people with OCD will tell you they cognitively know performing repetitive behaviours has no specific value. Yet, they cannot stop performing the said behaviours because it *makes them feel better*. In AAT, OCDs tend to disappear because teens focus on objectives that require one hundred percent of their attention and concentration. Training an animal allows our students to place their emotions onto the rat or dog. For the entire length of the AAT session, students can be symptom-free.

Mental health awareness sheds light on conditions that we once thought to be the devil's work or punishment from god. Thankfully, science has led us out of the middle-age. However, the awareness needs to take another step forward and stop minimizing mental health and all its symptoms. People with OCDs suffer, and individuals diagnosed with mental disorders do not enjoy belittlement. You would think it is an obvious statement, yet people with mental disorders still feel stigmatized because of their conditions.

Our AAT participants are often victims of emotional bullying and condescending remarks. We hear it from other students and strangers when we are outside with the dogs. In those circumstances, I remind the teen that some people suffer from other conditions, such as ignorance and lack of moral ethics. In those instances, I focus the teen's attention on the dog because our students are excellent at caring for our animals and fundamentally understand that dogs do not judge.

A student once told me dogs are like god; animals love unconditionally. To which I always answer, *Yes, yes, they do! Excellent observation!* and carry on with our day. Teenagers do not appreciate it when people tell them how they are or not; they know what is wrong with them. After all, the adolescence phase of development is called Identity vs. Role Confusion (Erikson, 1980) for a reason. Parents and other caregivers like teachers should remember this, especially when someone questions their sexual identity. It is important not to confuse Body Dysmorphia with the natural perplexity of adolescent development.

Post-traumatic stress disorder

You could think that children with Post-Traumatic Stress Disorder (PTSD) at such a young age is impossible, yet you would be mistaken. From abuse to war zones, PTSD affects between 1.7% and 8% of Canadians fifteen years and older (Statistics Canada, 2022). That said, accurate numbers are hard to obtain since PTSD is a new field of research, globally speaking. To illustrate my point further, Ontario held its first PTSD awareness day on June 27, 2019. Less than two months after the event, I still cannot find accurate statistics on PTSD.

> *"Trauma- and stressor-related disorders involve exposure to a stressful or traumatic event. These were previously grouped with anxiety disorders but are now considered a distinct category of disorders."*
> —Cherry, 2019

In their 2008 research, Van Ameringen, Mancini, Patterson, and Boyle stated that 1.3% to 37.4% of Canadians experience PTSD. The paper adds, *"Traumatic exposure to at least one event sufficient to cause PTSD was reported by 76.1% of respondents."* (Van Ameringen et al., 2008). There were three thousand respondents in the research aged eighteen years old and above. I am not surprised the numbers are this high. PTSD is not exclusive to war zones—trauma results from assault crimes, natural disasters, deaths, accidents, injuries, and illnesses.

Furthermore, witnessing violence, natural disasters, deaths, accidents, and serious injuries can similarly cause traumatic responses. One student saw his brother get killed and watched as his parents tried to commit suicide twice. This teen had

PTSD. He had lost his sense of self and was shutdown. He looked dead inside, and the observation would not be false. I recognized that stare in a second. My father was a military man, and he returned home one day after a long absence, and his eyes were dead. Thus, speaking from experience, PTSD is a complex problem that, like other conditions, affects sufferers' entire families, friends, and work networks— if they can work.

> *"If you have no internal sense of security, it is difficult to distinguish between safety and danger. If you feel chronically numbed out, potentially dangerous situations may make you feel alive."*
>
> —Van Der Kolk, 2014, p.121

Teens with PTSD might experience some or all of the following: episodes of reliving or re-experiencing the event, avoiding things that remind the individual about the incident, such as anxiety, negative thoughts, nightmares, flashbacks, anger bursts, difficulty concentrating, exaggerated startle response, and difficulty remembering aspects of the event (Cherry, 2019). Some students share vivid images from their nightmares and tell me how fearful they are of sleeping. Teens often add that they cannot wait to reach adulthood to acquire a large guard dog that will keep them safe. If only I could provide them with such a request; regrettably, that will have to wait.

Insomnia translates to unruly behaviour such as frustration, anger, and grumpiness. Interrupted rest can become chronic or fully transform into a sleep disorder. In such cases, students are moody and do not want to participate. I call a time-out to allow the kids to nap with their dog. Teens with PTSD do not smile often or exchange with my team. They follow our instructions and achieve what they intended, eventually breaking the sleep deprivation cycle. It takes months, if not years, to see changes in their behaviour, but once we do, *It's all uphill from there*. Thankfully, we do not encounter many teens with PTSD. It is a good thing because it means teenagers are resilient.

It might not seem like a fruitful session to let kids sleep in class, but a rested teen is a happy one. Teachers are grateful when students can resume learning with a relaxed face and a clear mind. Remember, *There's nothing better than a rat on your face*. We spend a lot of time ensuring that our participants leave in a better emotional state than when they initially arrived in class, which is why we use assessment numbers. Parents are likelier to continue the process after witnessing behaviour changes firsthand.

> *"The conclusion is clear: Children who are fortunate enough to have an attuned and attentive parent are not going to develop this genetically related problem [PTSD]."*
> —Van Der Kolk, 2014, p.156

I lived with a PTSD parent and can confirm that animals have immense healing powers. When we train dogs to signal their handler that they are about to lose control, their handler automatically benefits from a boost in confidence. They know the dog will execute the behaviour, which reassures them that they will be able to cope with life's constant reminders. People living with PTSD are more social and stop fearing the outside world. Their quality of life improves because the dog serves as a catalyst between reality and their memories.

Substance abuse and addiction

The use of recreational drugs is a common occurrence during adolescence. The baby-boomer generation explored LSD and other hallucinogenic drugs combined with hashish and alcohol. Millennials and Centennials prefer prescription drugs, ecstasy (MDMA or Methylenedioxymethamphetamine), also referred to as the *love drug*, and cannabis over harder drugs like cocaine, methamphetamines (crystal meth), heroin, and more recently, fentanyl. Although more prevalent in western Canada, the drug has arrived in Quebec.

Most teens, however, are looking for cheap pills; therefore, the parental medicine cabinet has become a place to raid. For example, suppose a person does not have ADHD and takes Ritalin. In that case, the medication will have the opposite effect. It will act as a stimulant in a normal functioning brain. In essence, Ritalin acts like a speed.

> *"These changes in brain chemistry were associated with serious concerns such as risk-taking behaviors, disruptions in the sleep/wake cycle and problematic weight loss, as well as resulting in increased activity and anti-anxiety and antidepressive effects. Dr. Thanos said."*
> —Toich, 2017

In our high school AAT population, the use of stimulants is very trendy, and according to Lakhan and Kirchgessner (2012), students who take stimulants are misusing their prescription to induce a heightened sense of cognitive function, or in the words of Lakhan and Kirchgessner, *"Moreover, students without ADHD misuse stimulants to improve performance or to induce euphoria."* (2012, p.665) The team can identify if students are high because their behaviour directly affects the dogs. One student came to class, displaying outgoing behaviours, and socially interacted with his classmates. These actions were uncharacteristic of his personality. Unfortunately, I had to escort him out of the AAT class.

Drinking is still prevalent among young adults. Statistics Canada (2018) states that people aged between eighteen and thirty-four represent 28.7% of the adult population. High school students between twelve and seventeen only represent 3.4% of the drinking population. The numbers represent provincial legislation, which places the legal drinking age in Quebec at eighteen. I have never had a student drink alcohol in AAT. If we did, I would have removed the person from the program for the day.

With prescription medications lies a complication. Unless we know students well, assessing if a student is high on prescription drugs is almost impossible. The norms we establish at the beginning include consequences for specific actions. The teens and I discuss possible outcomes and verbally agree to them.

We trust the AAT students to make wise choices. They already know the consequences when they break the rules since they agreed to the outcome. We do not need to explain what will happen. Thus, we apply the punishment, making students less likely to repeat their mistakes. We have used this strategy twice in nine years. One, stated above, was a minor offence; the other opened the door to dangerous actions. Thus, we removed the student from the AAT program.

> *"Substance-related disorders are those that involve the use and abuse of different substances such as cocaine, methamphetamine, opiates, and alcohol. These disorders may include substance-induced conditions that can result in many associated diagnoses including intoxication, withdrawal, the emergence of psychosis, anxiety, and delirium."*
> —Cherry, 2019

Substance abuse is either a cause or a consequence of the environment. Physical abuse, neglect, violence, and trauma can trigger substance abuse. The mind wants to avoid emotional turmoil and, in some instances, physical pain. Whatever the reason, drugs and other substance abuse are problematic, and we see many cases in the AAT program. Substance abuse is often the consequence of a much larger, deep-rooted problem. Other disorders can lead to substance abuse or occur in combination with different mental health issue categories.

The students often feel guilty and beat themselves down for abandoning their pet partners. When they return to class, we tell them that from the dogs' and our human point of view, they are perfect regardless of their actions. The sheer fact that they showed up again constitutes motivation and dedication. We do not judge or condemn teens for their actions as long as they abide by the safety rules. Sometimes, life gets in the way; thus, we forgive and carry on. One of my favourite quotes sums it up.

> *"You can pretend to care, but you can't pretend*

> *to show up!"*
>
> —*Unknown*

Adolescence is one of the most demanding phases we go through as humans. Puberty includes life-changing events that generate intense introspection, emotional uproar, cognitive discoveries, and biological changes. The fact that we emerge from adolescence as functional adults sometimes makes me scratch my head. That said, AAT generates results because of the teens themselves; they might struggle with disorders or experience all of the above, but they show up, which is reason enough to celebrate their successes. A small series of victories led to massive accomplishments. Animals ultimately do not care if teens are labelled this or that; the only thing dogs and other animals care about is their human training partner showing up.

Adolescents might drink or take drugs to forget their pain; animals remind them who they are and heal their pain. I will never repeat that enough: Animals do not care for labels or emotions; they care that you are here now. That is where the power of AAT lies. The energy that unconditionally bonds a teen and a dog is unconditional love. The connection is so strong that it can pull the inner child out of the most brutal humans and make them act like they were three years old again.

I have seen this countless times during the AAT programs or private consultations. Substance abuse seems to toughen the soul, but it does not. Inside each person, there is a version of themselves wishing to express itSelf. Animals allow the voice to take the front stage and communicate its needs. In that sense, animals are liberating. Research demonstrates that children who have grown up with animals fare better in life (Purewal, Christley, Kordas, Joinson, Meints, Gee and Westgarth, 2017; Herzog, 2017).

> *"In summary, current evidence suggests that overall, pet ownership may be beneficial to child and adolescent emotional, cognitive, behavioural, educational and social development. Although the majority of studies performed to date had methodological*

weaknesses, the pattern of findings among sub-populations and age groups suggests that companion animals have the potential to promote and contribute to healthy child and adolescent development."
—Purewal et al., 2017

Animals are necessary for human development, so dogs and people have become symbiotic partners. Animals stimulate our observation and introspection abilities, which allow us to appreciate our place in the world. One could say animals teach humans how to become humane. When trust in humanity is severed, teens learn empathy through animal interaction. Social media presenting animal encounters is staggering because people feel deprived of basic human needs such as touch, affection, love, and companionship; thus, they seek it in other animal species.

Every human science discipline, such as teachers, psychologists, social workers, or professional therapists, cannot offer physical contact, say a hug, to their clients. Associations only allow verbal reinforcement, which is insufficient when a person struggles through a complex crisis. Humans revoked humanity from the human sciences; how ironic. There is a need for safety protocols, and I agree with the measures. However, extremes are never good. Instead, I elect to film sessions rather than avoid hugging a distressed student. If anything, animal-assisted therapy puts humanity back into humans. As a result, teenagers learn to become a better version of themselves regardless of their labels. The positive energy created between humans and animals is where the magic lives.

Chapter 4
Changing Lives with Animals

AAT adolescents

The AAT program has grown and seen over one hundred teens in the last five years. Unfortunately, I cannot write about everyone; therefore, I chose cases that impacted my team and me and our legacy for an emerging generation. That said, not every story has a happy ending. The passage of specific individuals has led us to tears, but joy cannot emerge without sorrow. Some teens make poor judgment calls, while others are victims of their circumstances.

High school is frequently an adolescent's last opportunity to realize that adults care about them and that they can effectively choose a better outcome for themselves. Dropping out and crime are often inevitable choices when a person has only experienced such possibilities. With nurturing and care, animals teach humans to live in the moment and appreciate, enjoy, and even love what is happening to them.

Each individual comes with various physical, cognitive, and emotional challenges, yet when they walk through the door, labels are left behind, along with our egos. I forbid judgment calls and speech suppression in AAT, for each individual is allowed to speak their mind. I enable the teens to share opinions, desires, ideas, frustrations, and disbelief in a safe environment. Through discussions, we establish cooperation.

We get to know one another and bond through the animals. Teens go at their own pace, and we demonstrate respect by accepting that we are all unique yet connected by animals. Some students have ceased the program yet still acknowledge the group and visit. Animals, indeed, are woven into the fabric of human relationships.

Finally, I wrote the cases in the past tense to keep the writing consistent; however, please know that some students are still in our classes to this day. Some teens have been in our program since it started; therefore, I will only present certain parts of their AAT journey to you. I cannot tell the entirety of their story within this book. I hope you can appreciate the complexities of writing about individuals who have gone within a group while others remain.

Alexander

Alexander, 13, was diagnosed with Autism, specifically on the Asperger Spectrum, when he was younger. Alex found social interactions and certain academic subjects difficult. He mostly kept to himself and rarely exchanged with other students. Alex was a tall lad with short dark brown hair. His view of life was genuine and straightforward. He was an intelligent lad with an interesting outlook on life. If I had to describe him using only one word, my choice would be *just*. Alex disliked inequities and would call them out when he saw them.

The first time I met Alexander, with dogs present in class, he focused solely on the animals. I remember asking him if he had a dog at home; he swung his head from left to right and said he had a rabbit. Alex repeated how much he loved animals a few times. I saw a flicker in his eyes and knew he would enjoy this program.

I had planned to pair Alex with Albear because of his experience with people and advanced training skills. However, Alexander feared him because *he was big and scary*. I respected his wish, and Alex chose his dog in a strange twist of affairs. He decided he wanted to work with Lua, a Pug. I quickly rearranged the groups in my head and said yes. Nothing happens for nothing. Right?

At this point in the program, I asked students if they played video games; this let me know if they needed more clicker practice once we started working with the dogs. His answer was yes, but in his own words, *nothing too gruesome*. I grimaced at the idea of extreme bloodshed, death, and decapitation. He shook his head affirmatively. I paired Alexander and Lua with another boy. At the beginning of the program, he worked side by side with the young man, but they did not cooperate much as a team. Alex's partner was a shutdown boy who hid behind his hoodie. He was transitioning between schools and had just lost his friends. One day, Alexander became frustrated and needed to manage his anger.

I told him it was okay to take a moment and that we would revisit the situation shortly. Alex, his partner, and Lua took a time-out from the training session and relaxed. We individually regathered our thoughts to problem-solve our way through the situation. The issue resided in cooperation. Each boy wanted to apply his solution to the problem of getting Lua into a recycling box. Yet, progress was at a standstill, and Lua was frustrated. She started to bark and look at her owner for feedback. When this happened, I intervened to help the kids negotiate.

When we got back together, I proposed they try different solutions and decide what worked best for Lua. The boys opted for a third option. The boys suggested they combine their techniques, so I answered my usual, *Let's try and see what happens*. With a new vision and cooperation, the team finally worked together.

As you read these lines, the events unravelled quickly, yet it took weeks to get to the solution. I have the video of the moment Lua decided to jump in the box, and let me tell you, we all joyfully screamed as Mathieu clicked his clicker. At that moment, and for the first time, a face emerged from under the hoodie, boasting a giant smile. The joy on those kids' faces was worth all the gold on earth. Mathieu was ecstatic and kept jumping up and down.

We shed tears of joy for the odd pair and proclaimed them the best trainers of the day. People often forget or do not give reinforcement to other people, especially employers. Instant gratification is essential for a person to understand that what they have done is accurate and suitable. Conversely, imagine a boss always telling employees what they accomplished was wrong, terrible, awful or slow.

When this occurs, individuals are left guessing their way through life, hoping that, at some point, they will achieve what the employer requires of them to achieve. Do you remember the hot and cold game we played as children? If so, imagine playing the game, but the guide only tells you *Yes* or *No*, and there is no other feedback. It would take you hours, weeks, or even months to figure out what you had to find. Not to mention that frustration and discouragement prompted you to quit. Reinforcement is essential to all living organisms.

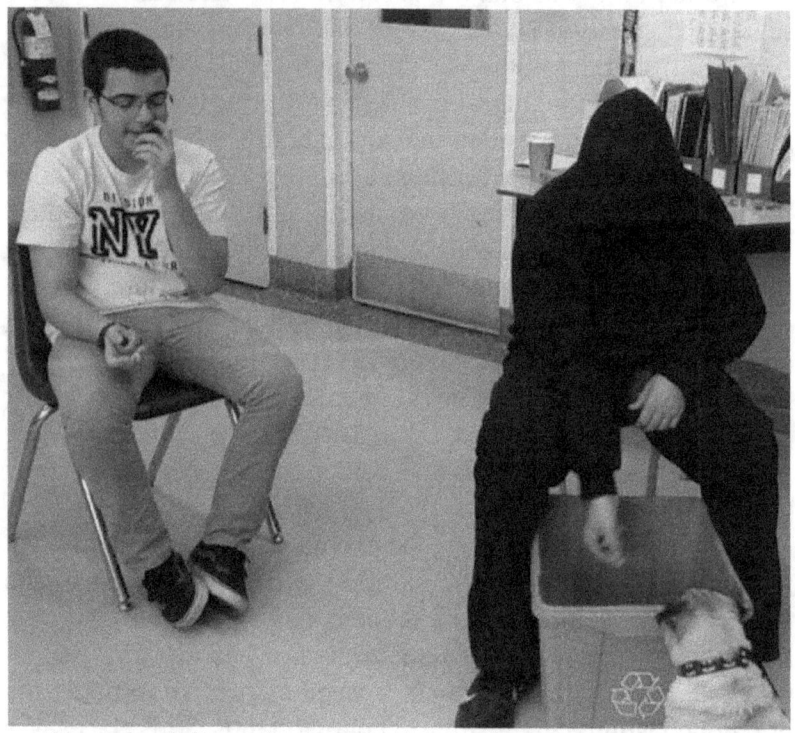

Alexander (left) was frustrated and decided to manage his emotions.

I told the boys to repeat the behaviour to ensure it was not just a coincidence. Lua repeated the behaviour, and one more round of cheers exploded; this time, the entire classroom accompanied us. Students had stopped their sessions and were now watching ours. In anticipation of their classmates' success, they waited until the click sounded and cheered along with us.

We had ten students in AAT that year and many stories, but Alexander's story flooded everyone's hearts. He was a quiet chap until he had something to express. When he did speak, it was as with the swiftness of a professional actor who had rehearsed those lines his entire life, stepped on the stage, and blown everyone's mind open with a flawless performance.

I enjoyed openness and directness in communication, and Alexander always delivered. He would tell me without sugar-coating the problem if I asked what was wrong. It saves time when we can get to the source of an issue, an aspect the animals appreciate, too. AAT dogs go to schools expecting to work. When participants deprive them of their training, they get frustrated or quit altogether. Therefore, the dogs remain happy if we promptly address a problem and work on its solution.

Lua executes the perfect recall in the schoolyard.

The concept of a dog wanting to work might seem strange, but AAT team members can attest that dogs start to cry three streets away from a school. A little fearful at the beginning of the program, Lua screamed and snorted her little heart out to get to work. She overcame her insecurity when she jumped in the recycling box; thereafter, a superstar was born. She once did a recall from across the entire schoolyard towards Alexander and his partner. It was a spectacle.

Alexander and Lua's adventures did not stop there. Because we were victims of our success, the students bonded with the dogs faster and harder than anticipated. With the year coming to an end, we needed an adjourning idea. Adjourning in group theory refers to effective and positive methods of dissolving a group because it has come to term (Tuckman, 1965; Tuckman & Jensen, 1977; Nestor, 2013).

> *"This final stage involves the disengagement of relationships between team members and a short period of recognition for the team's achievements. Sometimes, concluding the operations of a team is disturbing for members, especially if they have worked together for long periods of time."*
> —Nestor, 2013

With the school staff's help, we ended with a bang. The AAT group would present the behaviours they wholeheartedly trained throughout the year to their peers and parents. Social pressure and emotions increased for Alexander and his teammates. The presentation meant working and talking in front of a large group. Consequently, displaying the learned behaviour in front of people meant possible failure. I told him that yes, that was a possibility, but I also told him to remember that we are constantly working on animal time. I added that I would be there, and if he gave me his unique cue, scratching the top of his head, I would step in.

In any case, we would not let the animal fail. The plan was to practice in the gymnasium without viewers and build group sizes to desensitize the dogs. The last day was an amazing one. All the students came to watch their peers present the behaviour they had trained their dog to perform. We had four teams. Alexander's team went last. Lua failed three times, and I saw the cue, so I jumped in. I whispered, *Remember, I told you this could happen, so let's help Lua and set her up for success.*

I told the audience that animals could have stage fright, too, and added that they could cheer Lua on because it was relatively silent in the gym. In retrospect, our classes and training sessions were always loud and chaotic. So, I whispered to Alex *Ask Lua again, but this time, add your visual cue,* pointing to the box. Lua lined up, hesitated for about five seconds, which seemed like an hour for us, and finally jumped into the box. Mathieu screamed, and so did everybody else. Alex released a huge sigh.

Hard work always pays off. During graduation, I gave Alexander the award for best dog trainer in the AAT program. We celebrated as he basked in joyful memories.

The following year, Alex matured and better controlled his emotions. He was excited to work with Lua again. Sadly, I paired Mathieu with a Beagle named Maggie. My colleague rescued the little dog from a breeding farm. Maggie was new to the outside world and new to training. This little Beagle acted more like a puppy than a senior because everything she saw was for the first time. Alexander found her to be uncooperative and wanted to work with Lua. I explained that he and the little Pug shared many great moments, but his talents would benefit a far greater cause. Besides, Lua was with a newcomer to the program, and we both knew the new boy would profit from an experienced dog. He reluctantly agreed, and we started the year.

It did take time for Maggie and Mathieu to bond, but they eventually did. Maggie was so enamoured with the person who fed her treats each week that her devotion to Mathieu became grandiose. Nevertheless, the team was not always consistent because the human part of the trio was often highly anxious and had panic attacks. One day, we started the morning on a positive note, but Mathieu left the class because of an anxiety attack. His heart's desire to be with Lua caused him distress. He did return in time to say goodbye, only to softly whisper that his pet rabbit had died the day before. The animals made him feel good, which became overwhelming because he was also grieving. I said all was good and that we would go at his pace. I would accept his return whenever he was ready. He was here the following week.

Mathieu and his human partner had the most challenging task in the class: teach a nine-year-old Beagle to retrieve. With the help of their adult guide, Annick instructed the boys on a need-to-know basis. Maggie was easily distracted by all the treats falling on the floor from the other teams. Working with her was frustrating for the boys because of her wandering mind. Annick was sitting on the floor behind a desk when she proposed to address distractions and the setbacks they faced. Alexander looked at Maggie, sighed, and thought long and hard. The boys decided on a different course of action and set out to train.

A Beagle's job is to find things, NOT bring them back. So

Maggie would look at the ball and touch it with her nose but never pick it up. It was beautiful to watch the dog's behaviour. The mind games intertwined so seamlessly between Alex and the dog that I would lose track of who was training whom. Maggie won a few rounds, but so too did her human adversaries. Sessions often ended with nothing gained and nothing lost; it was a minor setback for both sides of the team. One crucial life lesson teenagers acquire during the program is that failure is a part of success. We do not produce behaviours; we train them. Working on new skills includes setbacks, successes, and much patience.

The success of animal-assisted therapy depends primarily on one's ability to parallel animal behaviour to humans. For example, animals must learn to trust their human to establish and maintain relationships. The same goes for people. Without trust, human relationships fare poorly. We can apply the equivalent concepts of communication, respect, honesty, and love toward animals. We call this a reciprocal relationship or a symbiotic partnership. Linking humans to animals is where the bond establishes and maintains itself.

Alexander (right) thinks about a proposed solution to their problem.

Mid-way through the program, we usually evaluate the students and the curriculum. We distribute forms via e-mail to complete with their regular teachers and hand them in at the next AAT session. We never do in-person staff meetings, so the teens cannot determine how my team assesses them. Alexander had asked to leave AAT; therefore, we decided he would be removed from the class for a few weeks for logistics reasons. He had bonded with Lua so profoundly that he no longer wanted to work with Maggie. Alexander decided to focus on academics, which is the actual goal of AAT.

Sometimes, you have to take a step back to move forward. Alexander did just that. He became overwhelmed when starting the school year with new classmates and dogs. He had managed his emotions like a champion until then. I agreed that stopping was better than blowing *a fuse*. I certainly did not want him to start hating Maggie or Lua. I told Alexander and the school staff that he could return whenever he was ready. I was confident Maggie, the groupie, would be ecstatic and greet him like a god.

Weeks passed, and Alexander was still on leave of absence from AAT. We paired Maggie with a team of three adolescents. Alexander returned to AAT shortly before Christmas but was in and out, depending on the week. He officially rejoined the group when we came back from holiday. Alexander told me that he had processed the loss of his rabbit, accepted Lua was working with other people, and that Maggie needed his help. After all, he was the senior trainer in the class, and he was right.

Alexander was the oldest and only returning member after the holidays. The school board frequently transfers students from one school to another. We had returning students from the fall, but Alexander was in AAT the year before, making him the eldest trainer in the group. The senior acknowledgement came with a condition: he could visit with Lua during breaks and train her at least once before the school year ended. I agreed to those very reasonable demands. We had a working plan and a happy Alexander. I love it when teens come up with valid arguments to solve their problems.

When Alexander returned to AAT, I decided to change the behaviour he was training because Maggie was getting frustrated. We did not want the experience to become aversive for her. A little frustration helps solve problems, whereas too much shuts the mind and body down. Frustration is an unavoidable fact of life when you do not live in an environment deprived of stimuli. For some dogs, stepping out of the front door can yield tremendous stress and frustration, while others experience mild to no stress. The critical factor to tolerating stressors resides in socialization. Dogs and humans must learn to cope in stressful situations to build resilience.

When we returned from the holidays, Mathieu resumed working with Maggie; I proposed two little activities that could be enjoyable and educational. I suggested that each group research their dog's breed or mix of breeds. The group was not excited until I gave an example. Someone suggested I explore the Staffordshire Bull Terrier, Chica, as an example. When they saw the information on the breed, they were dumbfounded. They quickly realized that social media, the news, and the internet, in general, were biased and seriously misinformed. One student asked why municipal or provincial governments introduced Breed Specific Legislation (BSL). I answered truthfully.

Maggie is excited to see her partner again.

Chica was not a pit bull, nor was she vicious or dangerous. They saw a little dog that loved to work and was not only affectionate with people; she enjoyed playing with the dogs in the classroom. Students accepted the project and began researching. As the weeks went by, and they discussed their findings with one another, solidarity arose. Students emerged from the class as advocates, favouring deeds over breeds. Animals create ambassadors.

Students started correcting their teachers and other students. One teen even said he rectified his parents' information during dinner. His father had mentioned Marco was working with a pit bull at school, and everybody shrugged. Marco had interjected and said Chica was not a pit bull because a pit bull is not a breed, and she was a Bull Terrier.

I love teenagers because society and culture have not fully conditioned their minds. Fueled by a comprehensive rationale, their individualism and creative ideas often generate new ways of thinking and experiencing life. Social media sheds light on their creative potential and some profit from their ideas. In that sense, social media becomes beneficial to their development. I always tell students they should use the internet like a library and learn to discriminate fact from fiction. As for social media, please do not believe everything you see until you thoroughly research it.

Alexander and his human partners trained Maggie to target. The target behaviour essentially boils down to the dog touching its nose to the end of a stick, pen, ruler, or whatever lies around the school. Alexander did a lot of what we call setting up the behaviour. His colleague was the clicker and treat distributor, while Annick oversaw the process and monitored human and animal frustration levels. Alexander would place the target near Maggie's nose. The other person clicked and rewarded the dog when she executed the behaviour. Team training is an excellent way to develop communication, attention, problem-solving and decision-making skills, all essential to human life as adults.

Typically, students exchange roles after ten minutes, but Alexander likes working directly with the dog. These unilateral decisions can generate conflict within the small unit, but it worked itself out. Occasionally, his partner asked to be the trainer, and Alexander accepted. The role reversal was possible because the boys agreed that, when asked, Alexander would concede his spot. The boys worked well together. Alexander wanted things to be clear beforehand, and so did his partner. Adults sometimes overcomplicate things, so we let adolescents solve their problems. Children and teenagers are not small adults; they are youth seeking understanding and guidance to fit in the adult world. Our job as parents is to teach them how to get there.

The end of the school year came too fast; it always did. We needed to prep for the final presentation in the gymnasium, and Alexander was anxious about the event. He anticipated failure and feared a repeat of what had happened with Lua the previous year. I asked Alexander, *Do you remember what I told you last time?* He did. Failure was possible, but I reassured him I would still be there if he needed a plan B. My response comforted the young man; we were in this together.

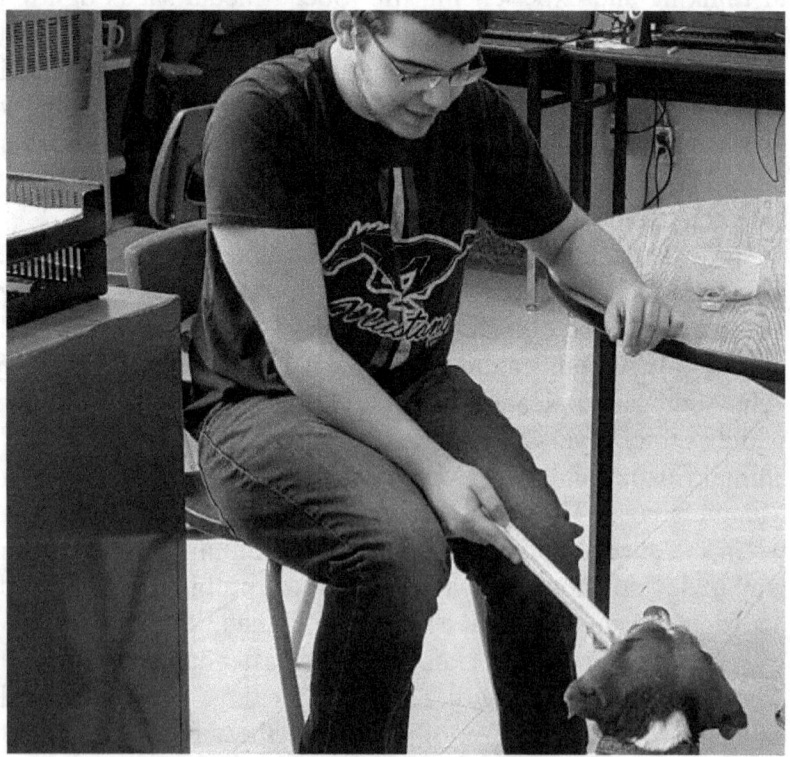
Alexander target training Maggie.

Target training from a few feet away is easy; crossing a gymnasium with many distractions was another. I decided we needed to start working in the gym again. We practiced there for four weeks before reaching the end of the year. We went to the gym on the last day of class to rehearse before the official presentation. Rehersal was perfect. All the teams performed flawlessly. I was in shock. Now, they had to do this in front of the school. I remember being as nervous and anxious as Alexander, but I kept my composure. We took our places when the school staff and a few parents arrived. I was the master of ceremony, and the kids were professionals.

I explained to our spectators what we had been doing during the year. I started the show by pointing to the table with research papers and decorated drop boxes. That year, I made Alexander go first. I figured Maggie would be less likely to run towards the other dogs for leftover treats than she was in class. Alexander told Maggie to stay, walked across the gym, and said Maggie, *Touch!* The little Beagle waddled like a duck across the gym as fast as her little legs could. She focused like a long-range ballistic missile on the target. We all screamed when the clicker went off.

Another student watches Maggie cross the gym in disbelief.

It was a fantastic moment filled with anguish and much joy. I believed Alexander would ace the behaviour because he had worked so hard. He was happy to discover we shared each other's victories or defeats. He realized that dogs allowed groups as diverse as ours to form relationships. Dogs, it seemed, could modulate our social behaviour without us knowing. The entire group shared his sentiment, although some were more reserved in their comments. I must admit, though, that a picture is truly worth a thousand words. The student in the back of the gym watching Maggie cross was priceless. My team documented each session, which immortalized the amazing moment.

My assistant, Taighe, captured the above image of another team's reaction to Alexander's success, or what I should say about it being a success. That year, Alexander shared his trainer certificate of accomplishment with another boy. What a way to end the school year. Unfortunately, as I write these words, sadness overwhelms me. Kelsey messaged me, saying it would be Lua's last summer. Our little miracle worker is terminally ill with stomach cancer. My heart grieves with Kelsey during these challenging times, and my thoughts include Alexander; his heart will break when I tell him his dog friend, Lua, passed away. Sometimes, things are more complicated than others. Sadness is such a profound motion to manage when you are an adolescent.

Alessandro

We have a very high male-to-female ratio of participants. For every ten teens, nine students are male. Alessandro was a fourteen-year-old boy diagnosed with an attention deficit hyperactivity disorder, also known as ADHD. He had poor grades, and his previous school kicked him out for clowning around. For Alessandro, academic success was challenging for two significant reasons: impulse control and distractions. The young man was a funny, humorous lad. He liked to joke around, talk a lot, and tell stories. Communication was not a significant issue for Alessandro; the opposite was true.

After meeting with the staff, we concluded that his most important goal would be to control his impulses and sort out distractions; thus, I added a physical component to the program. Because we can modify the AAT syllabus as needed, I added an objective: silence. At some point, there would be a silent training day. I love that exercise because it makes us realize how much we say in five minutes. Most animal communication is seventy-five percent non-verbal language, including humans. People speak way too much, and unnecessary chatter hinders the human-animal bond.

On the first day of the animal-assisted therapy program, Alessandro expected to start working with an animal, but he was disappointed. We conducted the first AAT session without the presence of animals because it was a meet and greet with a purpose. I assessed human and dog interactions during day one to determine which dogs naturally gravitate to which teen.

The following week, I paired the teens with the dogs I believed would help us reach our goals and objectives. I tell the students they might not work with their chosen dog. In Alessandro's case, he did not. He wanted to work with Albear, but I paired him with Jasmine, a beautiful blond mix breed rescued from a shelter. It was the perfect match, for it displayed hyperactive behaviour similar to ADHD in people. Her overly energetic persona made Jasmine the best work partner for Alessandro.

The second part of the day serves to establish rules and norms. Safety rules include non-negotiable behaviours, such as running, screaming, jumping, play fighting, and hitting the dogs or one another. When someone from my team said STOP, everybody stopped. I have used the *stop* command only once in all my years of conducting AAT sessions. Conversely, we establish favourable rules such as affectionate displays toward animals, talking, training, dog toilet duties, sharing, empathic conversations, listening, and eating together. Occasionally, a training session momentarily stops because we get caught up in a topic of discussion that we all enjoy. More frequently, smaller groups quietly converse together. Finally, we establish norms as a group. The rules typically revolve around the following list.

- No cell phones
- Allow free speech
- No disrespecting
- No discriminating

- No animal discrimination (BSL)
- Ask before giving something to the dogs
- Ask questions one person at a time
- Pick-up after the dog you take outside
- Do not click without giving the dog reinforcement
- Define the emotional scale rating

There is a final part of the first day, and it is learning about dog language. Before interacting with the dogs, we require teens to take the presentation *Decyphering the Canine Code: Understanding Biology and Behaviour*. The short presentation explains what dogs tell us and why they behave the way they do. On the first day with dogs, we recapitulated dog language as a means of communication and revisited rules and norms. We gave handouts, and I paired the dogs with their human teams. Alessandro was surprised to learn he would work with Jasmine.

The day's first order was to bond with the dog you were assigned; we encouraged the teens to play and cuddle. The second order was to learn about clicker training. Shortly after, we began training a simple behaviour. Alessandro was in the same class as Alexander; consequently, some exercises were identical, while others were not. The first behaviour Alessandro and his human partners taught Jasmine was *touch*.

That was not an easy task for Jasmine, and the boys soon realized it would take more brainpower than they had initially planned. The boys successfully trained the *touch* behaviour, and Alessandro slowly started learning to control his impulses. During the following weeks, Alessandro and his partner devoted their time to teaching the *Fetch the Mail* behaviour.

Alessandro and Kathlene chose to retrieve the mail as their behaviour because they thought it would be practical for both the dog and Kathlene. They had their work cut out for them. I remember a session that challenged Alessandro the most; he had been stuck on the same step for a few weeks but had not realized it until that moment.

Jasmine would take the mail, a folded piece of paper, and randomly walk around with it to steal treats from other teams.

Alessandro was frustrated, and his confidence took a hit; his general behaviour deteriorated. He stood and aimlessly began to walk around like Jasmine; he was lost and did not know what to do. I stepped in and asked what the problem was. He said Jasmine was not doing the behaviour because she was *out of control*. I asked him how he was feeling. Alessandro replied that he did not know what he was doing, making him anxious, frustrated, and confused. I wondered if he felt out of control, to which he answered yes. Then he looked at me perplexedly and asked *Just like Jasmine?* I nodded in the affirmative. From there, we revisited the training plan and adjusted the steps. With Kathlene's guidance, they were back on track.

The new approach included taking three deep breaths. I recommended they take one step back only to take two steps forward. Jasmine returned to her team within a few minutes and started working once more. She returned the mail to the boys and dropped it on the floor, which they considered successful.

During breaks, Alessandro loved clowning around. He would entertain the group with all kinds of shenanigans or tell jokes. His peers appreciated his sense of humour. Alessandro could talk up a storm in front of anybody. He was charismatic, charming, and somewhat debonair. He was the perfect candidate for a television news report on AAT.

In early March, CTV News contacted me to film a segment on teens and animal-assisted therapy. The AAT team and I chose Alessandro to be our spokesperson for the program; however, we decided not to tell anyone. I would only push for him, but ultimately, the television crew decided.

We were not disappointed. Caroline Van Vlaardingen and her cameraman selected Alessandro for their interview. In this case, ADHD was a positive asset. Alessandro was a natural in front of the camera. In that way, he reminded me of my son. Both young men had a talent for acting, and Alessandro exploited his fifteen minutes of glory. As suspected, Alessandro was delightful, amusing, and astute. Alessandro's energetic personality boded well on the screen. Most importantly, as he spoke to Caroline Van Vlaardingen, Alessandro realized that his condition and Jasmine's behaviour were the same. In his words to the news reporter, *She has ADHD, just like me, which means we understand each other.* Alessandro was wise beyond his years.

Caroline Van Vlaardingen, CTV News, interviewed Alessandro.

I remember a poem by Emily Dickinson that essentially says we do not know our true potential until we accomplish something we have never done before. If we remain true to ourselves along the journey, we will succeed. Being successful would be a daily occurrence if we were not scared of measuring our ego to god. The idea that god judges people is ludicrous, for the deity we think of as a person is nothing more than a fundamental energy. Dickinson might have argued that comparing ourselves to god was necessary, for its quality is unconditional love. Consequently, if we compare ourselves to a higher power and rise to the occasion life offers, we become better versions of ourselves.

> *"We never know how high we are till we are called to rise; and then if we are true to plan, our statures touch the skies. The heroism we recite would be a daily thing, did not ourselves the cubits warp for fear to be a king."*
>
> —Emily Dickinson

Society teaches us to judge ourselves harshly in a negative way. If our true self guides us, we rise above our expectations and become grandiose. Not because our egos commanded our actions but rather because of love. Young children five and above and adolescents remain true to Emily Dickinson's poem. Teens unconditioned by egocentric measures live true to their beliefs and perceptions of life. If we let teens answer the call to rise, they blow our expectations out of the field of intendment; as such, adolescents are genuinely Kings. That is the reason I love this stage of development. As we called Alessandro to rise, he did not hesitate to measure himself against what he knew he could become.

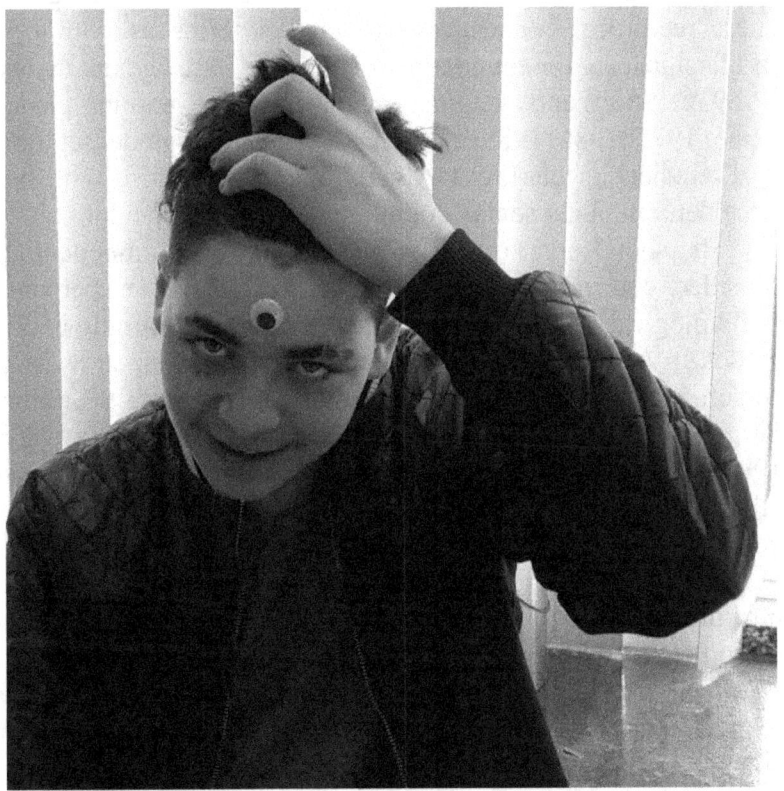

Alessandro pretends he has a third eye to read animal minds.

Alessandro had a fun personality; working with him was always a pleasure. When we returned from the holidays, he thoroughly worked on his research. We focused on his strengths and addressed his weaknesses to facilitate his learning disability. I know firsthand how frustrating it can be to have a learning disability. When Alessandro needed to write a text, I made him recite it aloud to the dog. The lack of judgment from a furry friend helps alleviate stress and fear of failure. Jasmine was surprisingly patient with Alessandro when he read her a text. She looked at him as if he was a god. The *puppy-look* on the dog's face confirmed that Alessandro was a deity to the dog. Witnessing a canine wait patiently until the reading exercise is over before it can get excited again is magical, at least to me.

Alessandro's ability to focus inward and concentrate on the reading task was beautiful. A dog looking at his human focus and understanding that now is not the time to play is magical. These reciprocal connections, which I describe as symbiotic partnerships, are the foundation for Bowlby's attachment theory (1969 & 1988b) and Bandura's social cognitive learning theory (1965; 1977; 1986; 1989 & 2001). The triangular model set forth by Canadian psychologist Albert Bandura (1986) establishes three determinants: social, cognitive, and environmental.

The social determinant is the you-and-me component. It considers your personality, biology, and other entities' personal and biological needs. Attachment theory favours learning in this model. In AAT, attachment refers to the relationship between a person and an animal. Based on Mary Ainsworth's Strange Situation Test (Ainsworth et al.,1978; Ainsworth & Bowlby, 1992), Adam Miklosi and his team tested the human-dog bond (Topál et al., 1998). They concluded that the attachment styles between dogs and humans were equivalent.

The cognitive determinant relates to how we encode information through our senses and recall it via memory. Each person and animal has different abilities when it comes to recollecting information. We observe intelligence when the dog remembers and uses learned behaviours in different contexts or situations. Biology directly influences cognition. For example, learning is almost impossible if the dog needs to urinate or eat. A famished animal is a dangerous one. Another aspect of the cognitive determinant relates to emotions. The limbic system considerably impacts education because it directly influences behaviour. When dogs reach their emotional threshold, learning stops. The same goes for people.

The final determinant refers to the environment. Where we learn affects humans and animals; however, the two parties experience the locale differently because of their senses. Criteria, such as temperature, noise, smells, sounds, and sights, influence perception, rendering the environment inhospitable for acquiring new information if stimuli are negatively perceived. Most people can suppress a sensory organ from distractions; unfortunately, it is much harder for animals. Competing cues are dogs' kryptonite. Competing cues relate to too many stimuli co-occurring, and the body does not know which one to focus on. Imagine you are outside on a hot summer day, looking at a cat chasing a mouse while sipping water.

Suddenly, your neighbour arrives, triggering the dog's loud bark; simultaneously, you smell the cake cooking in the oven. What do you do? Your mind pauses for a moment to try and figure out which stimulus you should respond to first. While you place your thoughts on hold, for a fraction of a second, your bladder screams for attention, and you run to the bathroom, looking at the oven on the way there. If there were a fire, you would attend to that situation first.

Imagine the same scenario from a dog's perspective. When the dog pauses, aka freezes, it is likelier to choose to run after the cat, even if its chances of capturing it are nil. Why did the dog neglect to urinate first? As an opportunistic predator, reacting to moving objects outweighs peeing, barking at the neighbour, or checking on a cake to ensure it is not on fire. Our senses and genetic disposition are different from dogs; therefore, the same cues are perceived differently depending on the organism and the environment in which it evolves and lives.

In the social cognitive learning theory model, determinants must connect and work reciprocally. Each determinant is, thus, by-directional.

The social cognitive approach hides another essential process: motivation. In AAT, we often use Konrad Lorenz's hydraulic system of motivation (Lorenz, 1974). Alessandro developed an attachment with Jasmine through the work they were conducting. Cognitive tasks deepen social connexions, and the social determinant further develops cognition. Learning occurs when we nurture the triangle in a conducive environment. In summary, the SCT model builds on itself, generating a secure attachment and increasing motivation. The wonderful thing about SCT learning is that we can actively change an insecure attachment style into a positive one; therein lies the success of AAT.

We are constantly building and assessing triangles in AAI programs. When the SCT fails, relationships and learning stop. The theory of small group development states that there is a perceived or actual conflict if the number of people interacting within the social determinant decreases (Tuckman, 1965; 1977). More recently, I added hugging me as an option. When students stop this behaviour, I immediately know something is wrong.

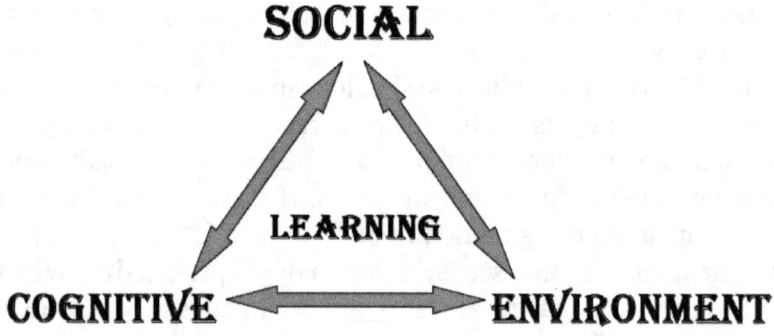

Social cognitive learning theory model.

Alessandro was far from ceasing to amaze us; his research paper was one of the most complete and accurate among the presentations. It does not take anything away from other groups. It simply means Alessandro worked very hard and went beyond the call of duty to present what he thought was a loving tribute to his dog partner. Alessandro was in the AAT program for one and a half years. In the second year, I paired him with Chica, a black Bull Terrier mixed female of approximately one-year-old. Chica was also high energy and somewhat ADHD. But this time, Alessandro had experience and was confident he could succeed in any behaviour we would ask him to train. Alessandro did not know the extent of my imagination. I asked him to teach Chica to roll a ball. It seemed straightforward, but it was far from being obvious. Alessandro's pet partner had other plans, especially regarding balls or other rolling things. It took three weeks for her to focus on the ball and gravitate toward the floor. Alessandro was struggling and needed help; I suggested we use a larger ball. The size of the ball might help Chica pay closer attention when it started rolling. I also asked Alessandro how he was doing.

The emotional scale rating tells us rapidly how a student feels. When I ask, *What number are you?* The student replies with a number from zero to ten. The scale goes from emotionless to euphoric. The number lets us know their feelings without going into a lengthy discussion. Students can nod in the door's direction if they want to talk, and so can we. Based on group norms, this action tells us that the student wants to discuss something. I comply and step outside of the class for a chat. Alessandro said five and nodded to the door. I followed him out a few seconds later and asked what was up. He said he felt behind his classmates and did not want to do this behaviour anymore. I reassured him he was not behind; he was right on target. I continued by saying that t*he fun part about AAT is not the result; it's the journey along the way.* I asked Frederick for a scale number on his overall experience with Chica. He said seven and a half. I replied that S*even point five was better than seven!* And we laughed.

Working with animals tends to push just the right button for a life-altering lesson. Confidence is often one of those teachings. Alessandro's decreased self-esteem came from his learning disability and ADHD in general. He once told me he wished he was *normal*. My reply was that *Normal is simply a person without a label. Eventually, we all get at least one: married, divorced, young, old, sick, ill, injured, name it, there's one for everybody.* I started to count my labels when he stopped me because he understood what I meant. Chica was labelled *pit bull type*, even though she was a Bull Terrier. Alessandro realized he was not ADHA; he had ADHD. Those were two very different realities.

Society conditions people to feel bad about themselves; our job is to recondition specific emotional attributes such as confidence, self-esteem, and self-efficacy. Alessandro returned to work with his pet partner, feeling better than before. The following week, Chica had a breakthrough. During the second session, she accidentally pushed the ball, and Alessandro clicked at the exact moment. I told him to give Chica a jackpot reward and cuddle her for a few seconds. Dogs, it seems, never teach a lesson without offering compensation. Chica overtly demonstrated high affection for Alessandro. The teenager's reward? Knowing Chica loved him unconditionally. Unsurprisingly, his peers saw the success and were jealously happy for Alessandro's team.

When we presented the behaviours at the end of the school year, Alessandro was confident about the outcome. He added that he did not mind if Chica failed or succeeded because he knew the truth behind the labels and that nothing could take his hard work away. The journey had been pleasant for Alessandro; in the end, he believed that if he could teach a dog to roll a ball, there were no longer any valid reasons he could not train himself. I agreed with him and gave him a big hug.

Reinforcement is not exclusive to non-human animals. Yet, our species has lost the ability to confer verbal and physical reinforcement, say a hug, when another human has successfully achieved a goal, whatever that might be. Physical and emotional contact is essential for social animal development and well-being.

Here is a little exercise. Close your eyes and summarize your day thus far. Did you receive reinforcement? Did you give it to someone? If you have teenagers, when was the last time you told them *Good job!* for an achievement other than academics? Praise and tangible rewards go a long way in an adolescent's life. I have learned from our teens that they are far more aware of what is happening around them than they let on. The Identity vs. Role confusion phase of development requires more positive reinforcement than any other age group. Teens struggle with who they are, hence the title of this period.

AAT kids feel lost, confused, inept, and hyper-self-aware. As adults, have you forgotten that adolescence is a physical and emotional tornado? I do not know about you, but I remember my adolescence and boy, it was a long-lasting nightmare. As an adult, I realized my friends were going through the same tumultuous phase. Nowadays, I tell teens that life gets easier with age.

In her book, Kids Are Worth It! Barbara Coloroso (1995) states. *"The beauty of empowering another human being is that we never lose our own power in the process."* (p.25). I would add that if you give X to others, you are simultaneously giving it to yourself. For example, if you are angry at someone, you are truly angry at yourself; if you love a person, you love yourself. Buddhist monks say you create your world through thoughts, words, and actions. I recommend to our teens to be careful about what they think. Setting ourselves up for success is imperative to a positive life outcome. Alessandro ended the school year knowing he had made a difference.

The face Alessandro made before I asked if he needed help.

During his graduation, he received many certificates attesting to his multiple achievements. The following school year, Alessandro returned to his previous high school; I was so proud of him. We missed his enthusiastic personality and wit, but he had worked hard to reach his goals. We missed him, but I knew he was happy at school with his friends, which is what truly mattered. Chica is now retired. I love to imagine she dreams about her days in AAT with the kids, receiving rewards for being the best dogo she could be.

Jamal

Jamal's presence was short-lived in the AAT program. However, it still deserves to be mentioned because of significant changes within his six-week passage. When Jamal came to the program, we were already well into October. The other teams were set and working with their dogs. The young man hid his face in his hoodie and never made eye contact. He was, by all means, shut down and barely responsive. Jamal suffered from depression and PTSD.

He was utterly catatonic and refused to speak to the school staff, students, or dogs. I gave the young man time to observe and assess the group's dynamic; this way, Jamal could determine how we operated and which team he would like to join. When I asked him which dog he preferred, he refused to answer. My response was sincere and straightforward. I would work with him and my dog.

Albear was the best animal for addressing challenging emotional situations. I trusted my dog's experience to find the best way to start training. Albear had a talent for figuring out what made a person positively interact with him; he was imaginative and intuitive. Albear was by far the best problem-solver I had ever encountered. In the third week, I met Jamal with Albear.

The tall, strong-built teen still hid behind his hoodie and remained unresponsive to my greeting. We entered the classroom and told him to pick his seat. He went to the corner of the room free of chaos and sat with his head down, isolating himself further. I let him settle in while we started our day. I aimed to make him feel at home without overwhelming him with attention.

Midway into the session, I asked Jamal if he wanted to ask Albear for a touch; he shook his head negatively. I told him he did not have to do anything but place a hand or fist on his knee, and I would instruct Albear to touch it, then click and reward the dog. Behind his hoodie, he nodded yes. The young man timidly placed his fist on his knee. Albear did not wait for the cue; he enthusiastically performed the *touch* behaviour as if his life depended on this very performance. I clicked and generously rewarded Albear. I told Jamal that Albear occasionally disobeyed commands for the good of humanity. In that sense, he was genuinely a superhero. He lifted his head, and I could see a faint smile. I screamed *VICTORY!* in my head and repeated the behaviour several times as if nothing had happened. Jamal would relax after each trial, which made Albear feel confident about his intervention.

The following image was taken in mid-November, three weeks after Jamal had joined the AAT group. By then, the hoodie was gone, and Jamal had started to exchange a few words with my team but not the school staff. Overall, he remained unresponsive. I kept encouraging Jamal for each baby step he took. I offered reinforcement, including him in discussions and congratulating him on the activities we did as a group. To my request, the other students ignored my new prodigy to prevent triggering his PTSD.

Jamal sits in the back of the class, disengaged from the group.

Jamal asks Albear to *touch*.

When we entered the school on the first week of December, the head teacher asked me in her office. She was eager to tell me that Jamal had finally started speaking to staff members after we had left the previous week. I was ecstatic. She congratulated me for this remarkable achievement, and I thanked her for believing in the AAT program. Barbara White allowed me to conduct my university internship at Perspective I High School, the only institution that had accepted my candidacy. She concluded our impromptu meeting, and I hurried back to class with increased motivation. I now had her, the principal, and the school board's approval for AAT.

When I entered the classroom, Jamal stood and walked toward me, something he had never done. I asked Jamal if he wanted to instigate the *touch* behaviour. To my surprise, the young man nodded affirmatively. I asked him if he remembered the steps, and he nodded again. I told Jamal he could ask when he was ready and that I would be his clicker partner. He stretched out his arm and opened his hand. I was puzzled but instinctively asked if he wanted the clicker. He replied yes, so I gave him the tool. I asked if he wanted to provide the treats, and he answered no. Jamal took the clicker in his fist, stretched his arm, and spoke softly to Albear; he clicked, and I gave the treats. In the next round, Jamal asked for the bowl of goodies, which I pushed in his direction. I was in shock. This young teen was stepping outside his comfort zone faster than I had ever seen. In three minutes, Jamal went from instigating the behaviour to giving reinforcement and rewards. I was flabbergasted. I asked my colleague to snap the following picture because I wanted to remember this moment for the rest of my career and life.

When the class ended, Jamal stayed seated until everyone had exited. I walked over to him to ask if he was okay. The young man softly whispered, as if this was a matter of national security, that he did not want to return to AAT. I asked him why, and he kindly said *I don't like dogs!* I burst out laughing and immediately regained my composure and asked *Did you do all of this because you thought you had to?* He nodded yes. I told Jamal I was proud of him for two reasons. The first was because he challenged himself to accomplish something he disliked. The second reason was that he stood up for himself and made a valid request.

I felt terrible that it took a month and so much effort for Jamal to feel secure; it was a well-learned lesson. Jamal won many awards during graduation, but pieces of paper are not what struck me. I remember seeing a teen confidently standing, smiling, wearing a t-shirt and boasting nicely braided hair, walking to the front of the room to receive his awards. Jamal had drastically changed so quickly that school staff remained shocked throughout the year as he progressed and reached new milestones.

Jamal was the poster child of resilience. When I congratulated him during lunch, I could not believe the young man standing before me was the same person. As I pointed to the awards, I paid my respects for a well-done job. Jamal said the AAT team allowed him to adjust at his speed and thanked me for including him regardless of his participation within the group. I replied that it was my pleasure and would not have done it any other way. Humans can make or break each other; consequently, we can never truly know our impact on someone's life unless they disclose their experiences.

Jamal could be considered an AAT failure in its true sense; however, Jamal succeeded at AAT because he chose to rise above his limitations and voiced his needs. Albear's delicateness and determination created a safe space for the teen to heal. With patience and unconditional love, people can explore their true potential. Learning what you dislike brings you closer to what you love; our job is to guide teenagers in the right direction. Working with people requires patience and perseverance; I am happy to report that our animals possess both. Jamal still had a long road, but I was confident in his ability to walk it.

Markayla

What a lovely name for a beautiful young lady. The school added Markayla to our program for fearful behaviours and impulsivity with bouts of anger. Markayla was not a tall teen, but what she lacked in height, she made up for in strength and character. Conversely, she was the most delicate person when working with animals, especially with rats. Our socialized colony is exceptionally efficient at creating secure attachments in short time frames. Similarly to dogs, our rodents are clicker trained and accept food rewards or affection by crawling into a person's pocket, hoodie, or shirt. The latter refers to the rats climbing on a person and entering their clothing for security and shelter. I designed the rat animal-assisted therapy (RAAT) program because these social creatures are excellent at teaching affection and intimacy.

We conducted the first AAT session without rats to explain rat biology and behaviour. Why did we train rats for AAT? The answer is that Norwegian rats are hypersocial animals. They live at the bottom of the food chain; consequently, rats and mice spend much of their life hidden in small, dark places such as pockets and hoods. Our pet partners love it when we carry them around suspended in a fabric pouch-like contraption similar to marsupial fur-lined sacks such as kangaroos and opossums. Our students work toward intimate skin contact as the weeks progress, and they discover their pet partner's personality.

Teens have authority over their comfort level and learn when social rewards are due. Some teens found rats tickled too much for skin contact; we consider that a good problem in AAT. We allow the teens to get acquainted with their furry friends at their own pace. At the same time, teens learn why rats are vital to the environment. When you see life from the rat's point of view, you understand why they look and behave as such.

Markayla was in her second year with us, but it was the first time she worked with rats, and she did NOT like the idea of training *"disgusting rodents."* The first day, she gagged, just looking at them. She wore two hoodies and a pair of latex gloves on her hands and still refused to touch her pet partner.

I paired Markayla with Vincent, the senior AAT male rat and sire of the colony within the program. Vincent was a big blond boy and made an impression wherever he went, but he was the most gentle male rat I had ever bred. The first session's objective was *target* training. We had special sticks made for the occasion, but Markayla was not going anywhere near Vincent.

However, Markayla got better at interacting with Vincent each week. She could see the other teams working on behaviours and succeeding; her competitive nature turned into motivation. I must admit I had never witnessed someone confront their fears and work toward resolving them the way this young lady did. She became very anxious when she was near one but soon recognized that people misunderstood these rodents; Markayla added pity as another source of inspiration.

A few weeks into the program, I threw the RAAT group a

curve ball. The teens must now start teaching the rats agility. The students look at me dumbfounded and skeptical. Still, I show them a video about Alice doing an entire agility run, and they smile— it gets them every time.

In my experience, telling teens what will happen too far in advance creates heightened anxiety because they build up the event in their minds. Consequently, they feel they have failed if the outcome does not meet their expectations. I prefer to build up momentum and then present the challenge. By then, the participants possess the necessary tools to take on the challenge and try to achieve the best result possible. For Markayla, agility represented an even more significant task because she had to manoeuvre Vincent physically. Male rats are not as energetic as females; therefore, to conserve his energy, the young woman had to move her pet partner from the end of the run back to the beginning after each trial. I knew Markayla would be successful because she was a natural nurturer.

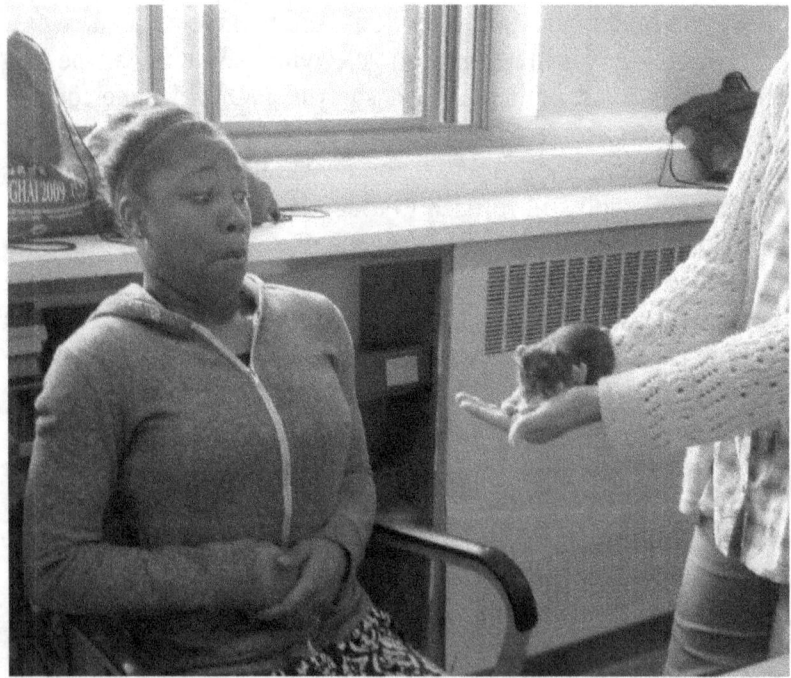

Markayla meets a rat for the first time.

Markayla said she always thought rats were dumb and

useless, but she slowly changed her perceptions about rodents and her fear of them. I kept encouraging her to explore why she feared particular objects, events, or ideas she had. One day, we had a group discussion about male rats, particularly Vinnie Barberini. Markayla never touched Vincent because she feared dropping and killing him. I explained that it was improbable, but I did not try to convince her. One day, Angie, the one-eyed female rat, slid off a table while her human trainers discussed the latest video game. Markayla saw the event and screamed at the boys, saying they had injured the rat. As the young lady expressed herself, she moved toward the team and punched one of the boys in the arm. I told her to sit and asked the boy if he was okay. He said he was. Markayla and I went into the hallway to chat. She told me she often threw punches when emotional; insecurities usually result in a fight-or-flight response.

Markayla had become the fighting type because of one event in her life. Her brother and friends pinned her to the ground in the park and threw spiders and bugs at her. She screamed at them to stop, but they did not. She freed her arm and punched one of the boys in the stomach, which made him let go. She then struck her brother and the other boy. At that moment, without knowing, Markayla's body had registered that when running away was not an option, fighting was. I understood her reaction and tried to work it out should another emotional event occur.

Conditioned emotional responses (CER) lead to defence mechanisms, a critical survival method. I monitored Markayla more closely after this incident. My goal was to teach her that other conflict resolution options existed. The objective was to replace her deviance with a healthier one. Instead of punching people, I trained her to voice a number based on the number scale. Teaching her to do this in a controlled environment would lead to generalized behaviour and allow her to function in real-world situations.

Markayla had another underlying insecurity about death. She was too young to be thinking about dying, but she did. The passing of her grandmother had traumatized her a few years prior. It was an unexpected event, and the void was unbearable since she had a profound connection with her *granma*, as she referred to her. Every little thing set her off, and punching had become a deep-rooted visceral reaction; nevertheless, Markayla made tremendous progress.

By November, she had trained Vinnie to finish two out of four obstacles in the agility run. That was remarkable because Vincent was extremely lazy; the blond rat preferred petting and eating treats over working. I was impressed by Markayla's commitment to training her pet partner, and I rewarded her profusely. She worked hard on herself, and the changes were phenomenal. Teens changed during the program, but Markayla took her experience to the next level.

On the last day we worked with rats, Markayla removed her gloves and picked up Vincent to place him in his carry-on. I told her she did not have to do this, but she wanted to prove to herself that she could overcome her fears. Markayla picked Vincent off the table and moved him to his carry-on case across the room. I was so proud of her.

Markayla demonstrates Vincent's two obstacle chain.

Moments like these make me want to cry out of joy, but I kept my composure and celebrated her victory. One day after the holidays, Markayla told me she never thought she could enjoy working with rats. She told me she had relished working with Vincent more than she thought was possible. I smiled, placed my arm around her, and squeezed slightly. Reinforcement came in various forms, affection being one of them. When I asked her if she would do it again, I received a resounding *"Oh hell, NO!"* We both laughed and high-fived one another.

Markayla was not the same person when we started working with dogs; she was excited and joyful. Her fears disappeared, and her insecurities dissipated. The bouncy teen told me she loved dogs, and we all agreed. Markayla displayed relaxed behaviours around canines, and her constant visual scanning disappeared. I paired her with a puppy named Ivy. The young dog was a rescue mix breed from the Montreal SPCA. Ivy was a beige-pink colour and had a fantastic personality. The puppy was very athletic and loved to learn. When Markayla saw Ivy for the first time, she sat on the floor and immediately cuddled the puppy. It was love at first sight; the smile proved it too.

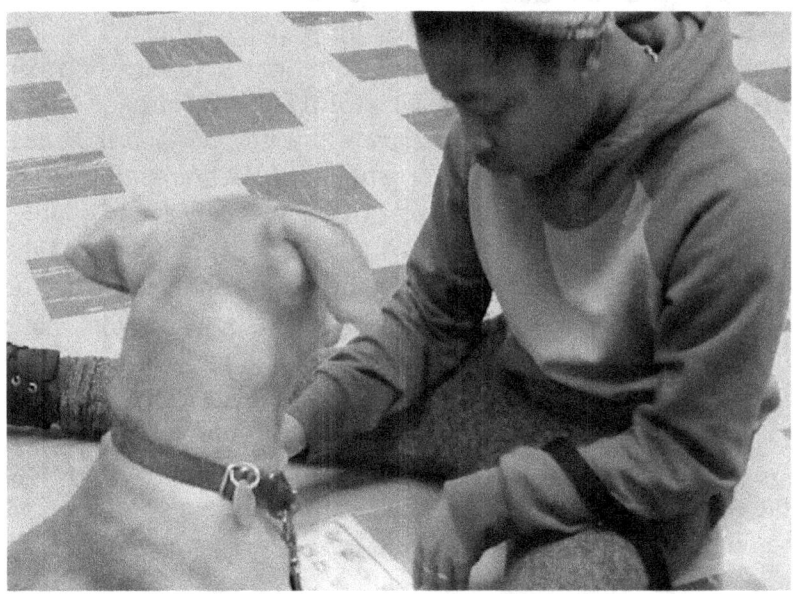

Markayla is doing her homework with Ivy.

Markayla kept joking that she would not give Ivy back at the end of the program. Her fondness for the puppy was incredible; finally, Markayla would be able to bond. And bond they did. Markayla did everything with Ivy when we were in school. She would take her to the human and dog bathrooms. She would even sit on the floor with Ivy to finish her homework from other classes. However, Markayla still needed to control her impulses and not overprotect Ivy. The pseudo-forced isolation limited the dog's socialization needs. Markayla never reacted fearfully or aggressively when we were in school. Her possessiveness of the dog eventually mellowed out, and Ivy was free to explore the world and everything in it.

Markayla's insecurities and anger would return, to a lesser degree, when my team was absent from school. Although she was learning to control her impulses with Ivy, she found it challenging to generalize her skills to other activities. On one occasion, she quarrelled with a non-AAT student who had entered our class. There was a brief argument stemming from Markayla's repeated request that the student leave our classroom. The student refused, and the conflict escalated. Markayla was threatening him with her fist in the air. I softly spoke to her, asking her to sit. Accompanied by Albear, I walked the stranger out. I placed myself in the doorway between Markayla and the student. When she lifted her other fist, I gently reminded her that she would have to hit me first and then deal with a very unhappy Albear. I pointed to the dog sitting at her feet, watching her every move. Albear was a peaceful, loving dog, but no one could mess with me; he was adamant about that.

I trained Albear as a puppy to be wayward on cue. The cue to the *Bad Albear* behaviour was closed fists. The signal made him growl, bark, and pounce like a fox on a mouse. She immediately set her eyes on my dog and realized this was a bad idea in the making. I advised her to sit and that Albear and I would handle the situation. She responded to my request, and the conflict stopped there. Albear was not an aggressive dog, but reminding Markayla that he could be was reason enough to stop anger dead in its tracks, no pun intended.

Mid-way through spring, another student joined the class, and I immediately paired him with Markayla. I will talk about Rayvon later, but for now, know he also had anger management issues, specifically Oppositional Defiant Disorder (ODD) and substance abuse. Placing these two together was a gamble, but I do not regret my decision. The reason they bonded was not anger; it was their love for puppies. One afternoon, Markayla did not want to work; she just wanted to snuggle with Ivy. I asked her if everything was okay. She shrugged at me; therefore, I assumed something was wrong.

I asked her to accompany me outside momentarily and bring Ivy along. I asked Markayla if she needed to chat or if I could do something to make the session more enjoyable. She mentioned a problem at home, but the source of the problem was her human partner. She said the young man did not want to get involved and was unresponsive to her requests. I admitted I had made the same observations. I asked if she had thought of solutions. She told me she wanted to jam the leash in his hands and force him to do the work. My reply was *that it was probably not a good idea!* But, I offered information in return. If she could ask Rayvon through the dog, he would most likely accept. The teen wanted to participate in the training but felt unwelcome in the emotionally bonded AAT group.

Markayla meets Ivy for the first time.

Markayla came up with the best strategy. She mentioned to Rayvon that she was feeling depressed and that she feared Ivy would pick up on her emotions and become depressed. Markayla added to her speech that it was unfair to Ivy and wondered if he had a solution to help the dog return to her natural, happy, wiggly self. It worked. Ray stepped in and took over the training for the rest of the session. A funny thing occurs when we tell people an animal needs help; they step in and accomplish what is required. Conversely, they often answer no if you ask someone to help you and an animal. In my thirty-five years of working with animals, training, consulting or conducting AAT sessions, this rule has never ceased functioning. It closely resembles reverse psychology and works beautifully each time.

Rayvon before Markayla spoke with him.

During a training session in early May, Markayla was experiencing frustration towards Ivy during a training session. Her behaviour was noticeable because she had not displayed this type of reaction toward dogs throughout DAAT. My inquiry confirmed my suspicion. Markayla suffered insecurity about graduation, and her fears came charging back. What if she failed high school? What if she could not get a job? The list went on. With each interrogation, her fear increased, and a vicious cycle started. Anger manifested itself with impatience and frustration during training. We took a necessary pause and sent everyone outside for dog toilet duty. That included Rayvon and Ivy. Fresh air and exercise are excellent mood stabilizers, so off we went.

The AAT team and I gave the ill-prepared teens our gloves, beanies, and scarves. Working outside in Canada requires winter gear. As they left the classroom, I realized many students did not have adequate winter equipment, so an idea came to mind. I shared it with my team, and with a resounding yes, we set forth a clothing campaign amongst the Dogue Shop's clients. We asked anyone who could upcycle winter clothing, accessories and boots that we would distribute the articles within the AAT program. Since teens are proud, we told them our clients often dropped off winter gear for our homeless program, but we had too much; some parents knitted beanies and scarves. The tradition remains. When winter is around the corner, we take note of our students' needs and distribute clothing to them.

Rayvon trains Ivy after Markayla speaks to him.

While the teens went outside, I stayed with Markayla and chatted about transformation. I explained that there was only one guarantee in life: change and death. I did not mention death to Markayla. Instead, we discussed a few strategies to minimize her fear. I reminded her how dedicated she had been to Vincent and how successful they were in agility. Markayla was a very bright young lady and excelled at finding solutions to her problems; she needed reassurance about her choices and their possible outcome. Life choice feasibility can be challenging during adolescence. Our role as adults is to say, *Let's see what happens!*

Markayla was in AAT for almost three consecutive years and navigated the process with relative ease. She became more confident each year, learned to communicate more efficiently, and was less reactive. She realized words could be impactful when she used them correctly and that picking her battles was an option. Time and energy wasted on negative situations only nourished her aggressiveness. When life calls you to rise, you should soar above the noise and judgement from people stuck in the illusion that fears generate; there is no other way to avoid negativity. Emotions are choices based on our past experiences; consequently, we can modify conditioned emotional responses that parents and society put in place during childhood. Learning a new way to respond does take time, but with the help of an animal, we dramatically shortened the process.

Rayvon

The first day I met Rayvon, Ray for short, he was sitting at the entrance waiting for us to arrive. The young man was high and talked jibberish about dogs. I kept nodding and smiling until we made it to the AAT classroom. That is when I introduced him to Markayla and Vincent, the rat. Rayvon had a substance abuse problem, Oppositional Defiance Disorder (ODD), aggressive behaviours, and an insecure avoidant attachment. If Ray was not angry at someone, he shut down. The young man would isolate himself from his peers, completely inactive and silent.

His defence mechanisms were avoidance and anger. For the first few weeks, he hid in the corner of the room or screamed in someone's face. I attempted to establish a secure attachment between Monique, Ray, and me during the following months. My goal was to connect with Ray before his classmate graduated high school. Thankfully, it worked to some extent.

AAT never forces people into human-animal relationships because that would be counter-productive. AAI programs aim to motivate teens to invest time and effort in themselves; animals serve to facilitate change, not hinder it. Most of our participants feel constantly pressured to accomplish something they perceive as futile; consequently, we try to make the sessions amusing by chatting about different topics. One of my favourites is finding a cartoon doppelganger for the participants. Ray eventually bonded with Markayla, but not before his personality shone through. The easily frustrated yet often silent character reminded me of the coyote in the Loony Tunes cartoon shows. Thus, I nicknamed Ray Willy Coyote, sometimes Wild Bill, or Billy the Kid.

Although Rayvon was slowly coming out of his shell, it took him almost four months to connect with Vincent. The Willy Coyote teen ultimately did enjoy Vinnie because he was such, in his words, a *"cool dude."* As AAT practitioners, we suggest, encourage, reinforce, and reward every *baby step* toward self-esteem, confidence, and trust. Rayvon started investing in himself when we brought a new brew of rat pups to school. True to his persona, Wild Bill began changing into an Elmer Fudd that day. He rolled his eyes when I proposed we conduct a target training session with the rat. His facial expression meant he anticipated failure, not success.

Little did he know these little critters were females and that my animal behaviour students had previously trained them. When Rayvon sat in his chair and started the exercise, he was dumbfounded by what happened. Even though the female rat he was assigned was only four weeks old, she was smart and touched Ray's stick. The teen looked at me with a seemingly confused glance and tried again. The same result occurred. When Wild Bill looked at me again, I smiled inconspicuously and nodded encouragingly. He sat straight and started to enjoy the interaction. Rayvon was highly successful during the session, and his confidence increased by four points.

Male rats were not motivated to work, but Vincent had a purpose; he helped Markayla bond. The female baby rat taught Ray to trust. The young man's communication skills improved, and we noticed a significant decrease in swearing and vulgar language. A few weeks before we introduced the dogs, I asked Rayvon why he kept describing people, animals, and things with racist and condescending terminology. The Wild Bill look he gave me replaced the *Explain yourself, woman!* I had grown accustomed. I told Ray how dogs could smell negative attitudes, creating distance between themselves and humans.

Conversely, if he could stop swearing and discriminating, people and animals would most likely enjoy interacting and working with him. I proposed we try a session together. I aimed to make him realize how often he communicated using negative words. I used my target stick inconspicuously and pocked his leg when he uttered swear words or discriminated against himself. He caught on very quickly and started to correct his vocabulary. Watching this angry human politely ask for my help was terrific. I was so proud of him. When we introduced the dogs, a new can of worms opened up.

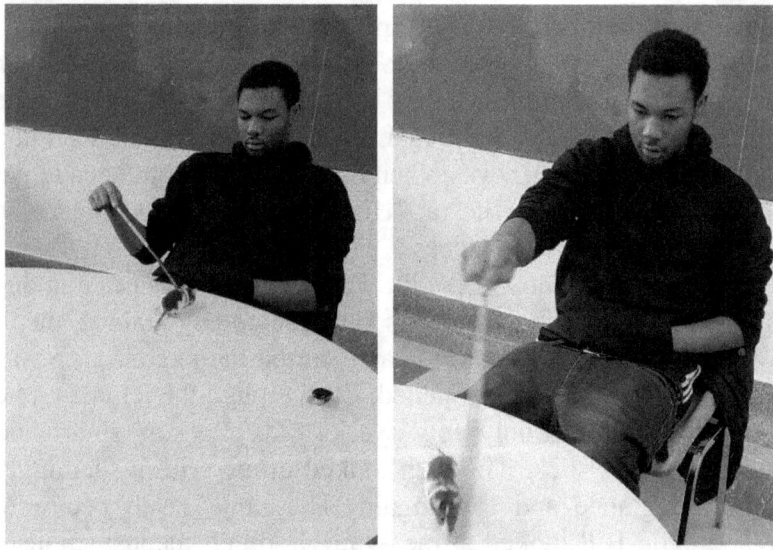

Ray straightens up and softly smiles after the baby rat targets.

I had planned to pair him with a senior AAT student in our group. My vision worked wonderfully for approximately five minutes. Rayvon did not take well to working with another male teen. His family issues came racing back to his consciousness, and a wild swear fest exploded. I quickly reminded Willy Coyote that other students were present and that his loud, foul language was scaring the dogs. Both boys immediately stopped quarrelling, and we took the conversation outside.

Rayvon was frustrated with the student because he did not do what he asked. I reminded Ray that this was a partnership, not a dictatorship. Animals acquire information in environments that predispose them to learn; the teens' arguments were counter-productive and unnecessary. We discussed solutions instead of problems and re-entered the classroom once they had devised an operational plan. The remainder of the day went well, but the following week would be a game-changer for everyone.

Rayvon's (left) reaction to my offer to work with him.

The two young men were training with results when an argument exploded. The debate concerned how they would teach the dog, and since they were working with Jasmine, the hyperactive dog, this posed a problem. The other student, DJ, disagreed with Rayvon's technique and no longer wanted to work with him. Ray was no longer sure he wanted to continue AAT. DJ added that he was interested in cooking now and wanted to leave the group to pursue his new passion. Rayvon became infuriated, and when he subconsciously realized his colleague rejected him, the furious teen screamed *Whom the* *f*** is going to work with me now?* I replied *No need to swear, I will!* Another student took pictures of the group and coincidently took the following image of Rayvon's reaction to my proposal. He was surprised. The deal closed; Rayvon and I started working with Jasmine the same day.

Rayvon had many memorable events and emotional moments during his passage in AAT. One of these occasions occurred on a random uneventful day. I was setting up the room when Rayvon walked in before class with his arms extended, reaching for a hug. I was taken off guard but pretended it was the most normal request and hugged him back. He immediately exited the class, and I looked at my colleagues in awe. They were as surprised as I was. That is how much power animals hold over us. We feel compelled to interact with dogs or rats because they help us understand our humanity. Close encounters tell our emotional brain that something bigger than ourselves loves us unconditionally. There is no argument against that fact. The only case we can make in light of the human-animal bond is that humans are emotionally helpless without animals.

This rugged, angry, recluse teenager outwardly displayed affection for the first time in over one year. I became teary-eyed but managed to keep my composure and finished setting up. When students demonstrate love, we must remain emotionally grounded. Our goal is to convey that emotions are normal. When students cry, scream, hit, or laugh, we ensure they learn to manage their feelings and reactions. Our teens want to fit in as ordinarily as possible. It was the first, but not the last, time Rayvon displayed affection toward me and my team volunteers.

The second memorable event occurred during a training session. Rayvon and Jasmine were struggling with the *retrieve* behaviour. I asked him why he was angry and wanted to quit. He said it was pointless to do this exercise. I reminded him that Jasmine came to school expecting to work, which made her joyful. In her dog's mind, it did not matter if she succeeded or not because the actual work made her happy.

I told Rayvon *I think the same of you. It does not matter to my colleagues and me if you succeed at training this behaviour; spending time with you is what makes us feel happy*. He looked at me, stood up and said *Jasmine, get your dog, but over here, we're working now!* I smiled as he took charge of the exercise. Rayvon then asked me what to do to move forward. I did not need to say much; he already had the answer but was too emotional to think it through.

When we took a break from the training session, I rested against the heating system, and Wild Bill jumped up to sit on it. My colleague asked me a question, and Rayvon made a joke without knowing, which made my colleague and I laugh; he caught on. Out of nowhere, this young man placed his arm around my shoulders as I often do to them. I made nothing of it. I could tell he was happy, and so was I. When he left that day, Rayvon hugged Kathlene and me in front of the other students. I wished him a good week and was eager to see him again. Hugs remind us that our relationships are sound and trustworthy. Rayvon tremendously changed that year, and his social worker, psychologist, teachers, and classmates agreed. He still had his moments of frustration that turned into anger. Still, overall, he was calmer and a lot more cooperative. When I look back at Rayvon's first and last-day pictures, it seems they were two different people.

Last year, Ray was in our program, and we enjoyed him tremendously. His sense of humour was refreshing and created a positive group dynamic. Gone were the N-word and all the derogatory name-calling. There were many difficult times for everyone, but Rayvon seemed to pull through unscathed, at least for the most part. My human partner was suspended from school for a week and was angry when he returned. The reason for the suspension did not occur in AAT; therefore, I will refrain from discussing the case. That said, Wild Bill was back to his old shenanigans and needed help to release his anger. The class came together for a brainstorming session and concluded that changing dogs was necessary. I paired him with Rick, a giant and highly trained German Shepherd.

Rayvon thought it would be easy since Kelsey had already taught her dog. My intuition convinced me Rick would train the young man. Highly trained dogs do not like slow trainers who have inaccurate clicker timing, are easily distracted or are overly emotional. When Rick got frustrated, the dog would bark at his trainer, the equivalent of a *Stop fooling around, get yourself together, and click!* Rayvon would relax and try the behaviour again.

Relationships normally deepen when dogs teach trainers to put their money where their mouth is. Rick worked his magic, and Ray had no choice but to upgrade his training skills. He had to stop thinking and start acting. My partner had to change from a human being to a human being. He learned to live in the present moment when he was in AAT. The following week, I paired him with Ivy, the puppy. She was young but intelligent; therefore, the young man needed to stop daydreaming or being absentminded.

When I paired him with Jasmine again, Rayvon learned another valuable lesson: trust the process. I took photos of his first and last training session with Jasmine. I recall Ray surpassing the achievements I had planned for him. I was amazed at the change. A student sitting near him could not break Rayvon's concentration, even though he was purposefully trying to. I reinforced our Wild Bill for ignoring the student. I ensured Jasmine was sitting between the two students; this way, if Rayvon became angry, Jasmine blocked him from standing. I call this approach *the emotional guard dog*.

When emotions become volatile, dogs act as psychological mediators between the mind and body. The connection between an animal and a human is so strong that it can instantly change a person's behaviour. The once shutdown and angry adolescent was now an extroverted, calm young man capable of training one of the most excited dogs in the program. Rayvon was not perfect, but he was a teen trying to make the best for himself with what he had. My best friend used to say *It takes courage to look the bull in the eye and say I can do this!* Ray certainly took to the saying.

In typical adolescent fashion, he protested about working. I never heard him complain about dogs or rats once he began training animals. I must add that Rayvon never came to class under the influence of drugs or alcohol. He took great pride in telling me each week that he was sober. I believe the animals helped him, at least once a week, to have a clear mind.

Substance abuse is common in adolescence, especially when teenagers take prescription drugs. Ritalin lasts for only a few hours in the body. Adolescents who are off medication feel vulnerable, lost, and confused. Their ability to perform mundane tasks is a battle. Some adolescents search for an alternative to the negative feelings they experience. Consequently, street prescription drugs are trendy, and now that marihuana is legal in Canada, it is easily accessible.

Nevertheless, most of the participants in AAT do come to class sober, for if they are under the influence, we ask them to leave. If they are not in our class, the principal knows why and expels the student. Compromising their participation would mean losing what makes them feel better about themselves and their role within a group that respects and accepts them for who they are. Unconditional love goes a long way for kids in the grips of a social system with too many youths in its care.

Rayvon concentrates, and Jasmine successfully targets.

Rayvon was happy he was clean during AAT and ensured I knew about it. I respected him for his honesty and openness about his substance abuse. Rayvon left our school that year, and his departure saddened me. I miss his outgoing, exuberant personality and sense of humour the most. Students may physically come and go from the AAT program, but it remains etched in my mind forever. Rayvon is one of them. He was delightful to work with, and I hope our paths cross again someday. I believe our Willy Coyote would love Hariette, and she would undoubtedly want to work with Ray.

Calvin

Calvin has been in AAT for the last five years. He came to us and kept returning each year because he loved animals, and animals loved him. Calvin was Autistic, but most people would not label him on the Autism Spectrum. Calvin was such a sweet teen and an excellent animal trainer. Not many students could get away with simultaneously training an animal and upholding a conversation, yet Calvin could do both easily. The young, intelligent, and reflective man had a fun personality; he loved books and video games. But his favourite activity was to be with the dogs and the rats. The first thing Calvin did when he entered the classroom was to seek out his pet partner. Calvin took that animal in charge if someone needed to step out or needed a break. He was a trustworthy nanny.

The first day I met Calvin, our group had sixteen students. We were trying out group sizes. In hindsight, that was way too many people to personalize our sessions. Since then, we have downgraded the number of participants to accommodate a maximum of eight teens. On the first animal day, along with the sixteen students, there were four adults, five teachers, and five rats; it was chaotic but fun. The adults enjoyed the session, which became problematic because we were there for the teens, not the teachers. So, I gently requested that the teens approach and gather around the rats for team pairing. I handed a friendly and calm little rat to Calvin and his partner. The goal for each group was to socialize and train their rat to do an agility run. Calvin would have an extra challenge to overcome: his height.

At thirteen, Calvin was already six foot one. With standard grade school-sized tables, one can imagine how difficult standing to train a small rat would be. We adapted and made it work. Calvin took the challenge to a new level; he decided he would stand to work with the rats because sitting meant his legs got in the way; they did not fit under those tiny tables. Coming from multiple generations of tall people in my family, I could relate to Calvin's predicament. I let him work in the position he best felt comfortable. Students' first order of the day is to familiarize themselves with their rat partners. Animals are sentient beings; they have good and bad days. Teens need to greet the animal before they can start a session.

The greeting procedure allowed students to pick up on the animal's emotional state of the day. As a result, they identified if the animal was joyful, sad, angry, fearful, disgusted, trusting, surprised, or vibrating with anticipation (Darwin, 1872). According to Darwin (1872), animals have basic emotions; thus, they are easily identifiable. Hypersocial animals like rats display their state of mind clearly and concisely. Alice, for example, would run around your arms, neck, and hands if she was not in the mood to work; playing was on her mind. We allowed the participants to analyze their pet partner and deduct when and how to begin the training session. Dogs experience sentiments, but social creatures have more straightforward responses to life than humans.

The difference between emotional management in people and animals is the capability to process multiple feelings simultaneously and remain below their functional threshold. Each organism comes with a pre-programmed threshold, so to speak, which determines when the organism loses its reasoning abilities and overreacts. In other words, the organism no longer acts and starts to react. The overreaction serves to disrupt cognitive skills in favour of survival responses. The limbic system, or emotional center, has taken over the body. In this state of reactivity, the animal can no longer learn.

Resilience is the ability to tolerate over-stimulation and bounce back relatively unscathed emotionally and cognitively. People and animals with high levels of resilience tend to process and manage traumatic events relatively well, often without external help from professionals or pharmaceutical therapy. We can effectively move the threshold to increase resilience with the SCT learning approach and other theories. Working under stress might seem like a good option; however, it will not raise an animal's resilience. Stress can be motivating; thus, working in an environment void of stimuli is best.

The following image represents the emotional simplicity the teens use to identify how animals and people feel at any given moment. The colours of the emotional wheel are darker and more vibrant in the inner circle; conversely, the colours become lighter and pastel in their appearance as the process expands outward. This colour variation represents emotions in terms of intensity rather than complexity. Usually, the wheel places Darwin's basic emotions as the second level within the wheel. The colours help people with limitations identify and communicate their emotional states concisely. Dogs share the inner section of the wheel. However, the general scientific consensus confirms Darwin's theory that most animals cannot process or express the outer, more complex emotions found in Plutchik's wheel (Plutchik, 2002).

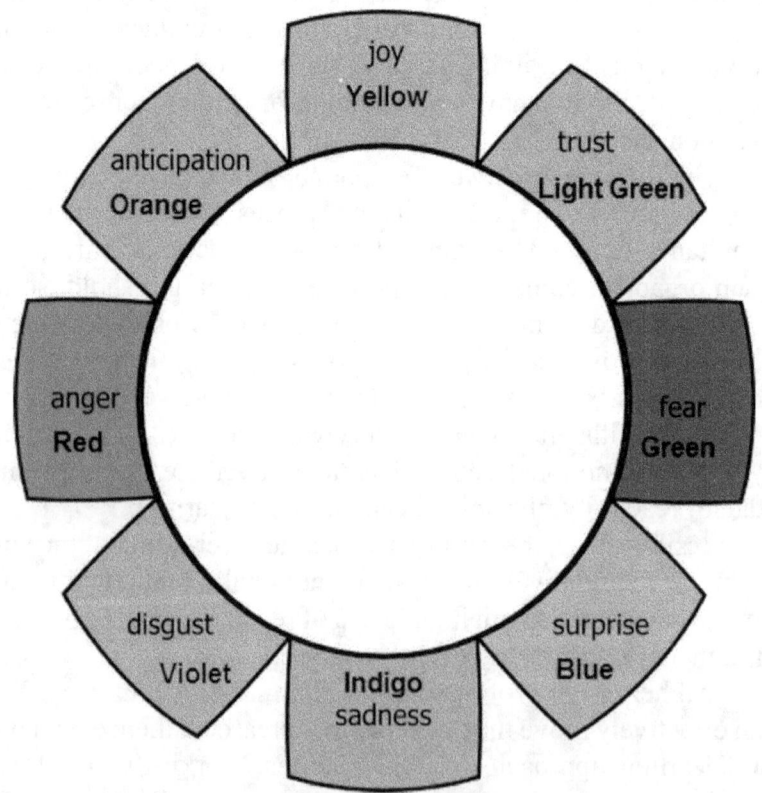

Plutchik's emotional wheel with Darwin's basic emotions.

Before we continue, I want to draw your attention to fear and anger. The opposite emotion of anger is not love; it is fear. Anger and fear are opposing emotions because the brain processes them as two distinct molecular structures. Neurons release chemicals that allow the body to respond in two ways: fight or flight. Bitting and running away are different; therefore, living organisms cannot process both outcomes simultaneously. From this understanding, we now conclude that animals cannot be fear bitters. Canines are insecure-aggressive or insecure-fearful; it is impossible to be both. I can never stress that point enough. Knowing the difference between fear and aggression is essential because we can train insecure dogs to be more confident. Conversely, training a secure, aggressive dog takes infinite financial resources and time. City officials request euthanization when a confident dog bites. Depending on the outcome of the bite, municipal canine services label such dogs as dangerous and keep track of the case.

The teenagers in our program are amazing people. They think a lot about animals and our relationship with them in ways we often would have never explored. Calvin is one of those students. One day, during the animal greeting period, Calvin asked if dogs and people could share emotions. He immediately clarified his question and asked if dogs could become sad because their human is sad. I praised his questions because I enjoy those introspective ideas and reasoning queries. My answer was yes. People and animals can and do share emotions. I believe this is the fundamental reason people have dogs.

Calvin was happy with my response. He looked at his dog and gave it a treat. I did not ask why he gave the dog a cookie; I assume he perceived his emotions in the animal and thanked it for pointing them out. Adolescents are grateful and will share their sentiments if you do not judge them or make a spectacle out of their vulnerabilities. AAT is effective because of the bond created between humans and animals. We come to share intimate lives with our teens because they feel secure about expressing their emotions. Calvin has difficulty interacting with other people, yet with the animals, he feels free to be himself. One of the norms in our groups is that *no judgment is allowed*. We leave our egos at the door and share the craziness of interacting and working with animals.

Calvin once diffused a conflict between two boys because one was teasing the other about the rat peeing and pooping on him. Calvin said *The rat peed and pooped on you because it feels comfortable enough to do so, and that's a compliment from an animal!* He then looked at me for approval. I confirmed his claim, and the teasing immediately stopped. A millisecond later, the teasing boy got peed on by his rat, and we all laughed. I remember one boy saying *Karma baby, that's how it works!* Another magical process occurs when teens and animals work together; they start to police themselves. Calvin liked to remind participants not to run in the presence of the dogs. He also enjoyed reciting facts and tidbits about the animals. His memory was phenomenal; sometimes, he amused the group by recalling the animals from the stories he read or the video games he played.

Another memorable souvenir in Calvin's long list of experiences occurred while playing a game of dog ball in the gymnasium. Everybody was running after the yoga ball when Albear body checked a Border Collie named Trillium. The sound was impressive, but to see Trilli fly off and land a few feet further was jaw-dropping. Albear prevented Trillium from scoring a point. It was a great move, but we stopped breathing momentarily and remained dumbfounded. Thank god Trillium did not sustain any injuries from that maneuver, but that noise is sketched in our minds forever. The force Albear used would have knocked any NHL or NFL player off their feet.

I had never seen anything like it before. Albear was in the moment and took the game too seriously, in my opinion. Still, the event created memories for all present that day. Calvin gave many examples of what the tackle looked like. A lion knocking over an antelope was an excellent example. None of us knew what possessed Albear to act this way, but according to the students, he did not want to lose the match.

Calvin spent his last year of high school with us, and he talked about the event a week ago. In June 2019, two years after the Trillium event, the students remembered that day as if it were yesterday; that is how impactful animals are. Every week is an adventure when we head out for AAT; I would not change that for anything. I love our experiences in *Teen Land* with our superhero animals.

Not all accounts of AAT end in joyful laughter and memorable stories; sometimes, animals die, and we must tell the teens. Rats are animals that have the unfortunate habit of dying young and unexpectedly. In 2015, the AAT team welcomed a new mischief of rat pups. Calvin was appointed a little rat with only one eye named Charlotte. This genetic defect did not limit her; she was the group's most active and curious troublemaker. Charlotte died at three of cancer right before Christmas 2018.

When Calvin asked why she was not in a class, my heart sank, but I could not lie. I told him the truth, and we took a moment of silence. He understood that death is part of life and made peace with her passing. Teens often share animal stories with new students; teenagers cope by remembering an animal's contribution to the AAT program. Charlotte's rat painting still hangs in the classroom as a reminder of the joy and love little and big critters bring into our lives.

One such adventure occurred in 2017. An idea popped into my mind: have the teens participate in a training session with the Montreal Mounted Police (MMP). One afternoon, while driving back from school, I stopped at the stables of the MMP to ask if it would be possible to bring the AAT group to participate in their training session. My goal was to reacquaint teens, via a positive experience, with the authority they despised. I planned on achieving my objective through the same training methods we used with the animals in AAT.

Therefore, the teens would recognize and relate the exercises to their experiences. The MMP accepted my request with a unanimous yes and a little skepticism. I distinguished their apprehension regarding the MMP's concerns about inappropriate behaviour around the horses. I reassured them that the boys would never inflict harm or demonstrate negative behaviours toward their animals.

The project moved forward, and I was thrilled for the teens. I could not wait to tell them. The following week, I announced we would have a memorable outing in fourteen days. We kept the event secret until we left school to prevent unnecessary anxiety. Leroy was thrilled. The other teens were also happy, but

I will tell their stories within their respective sections. The school and my team were confident that the teenagers would enjoy the experience; regardless, I planned for problems. Being overly prepared is necessary when we work with such large animals.

When we mentioned where we were going, Calvin started enumerating everything he knew about horses. From that chatter session, I could discern his happiness and excitement. Calvin often appeared calm and collected, but he was emotionally simmering inside. Overarousal is typical of people on the autism spectrum. I always allow the participants to experience the full range of their emotions unless they need help. A request for assistance might come from a look, a physical gesture, or an outright demand. When that occurs, I allow an animal to step in.

Calvin, in the background, is working with Mandu.

Calvin once tensed so rapidly that I immediately asked if he needed help. He answered, *'I just need to manage my anger; give me a minute!'* I responded, *'Take all the time you need; we're not in a rush!'* Nothing is worse than interfering in a teen's emotional state without consent. As parents, we spend much time teaching our kids to control their impulses and emotions. Therefore, we should trust their ability to manage themselves appropriately when the time comes. Our responsibility to children, in general, is one of guidance, not dictatorship. Parents do not need to take charge of their children's emotions. If not, they will rely on other people. Eventually, the future adult will view others as responsible for their emotional state.

Last year, we paired him with a dog that emulated him. When Calvin met Mandu, the mini Teckel, he laughed. Height would be a significant issue when working with this tiny little dog. However, what Mandu lacked in size, he made up for in character, and Calvin appreciated that. I could not hold myself back when Calvin came to class with his hair shaved into a Mohawk haircut. I turned around and transformed the dog's hair to match his own. I admit Mandu looked more like a unicorn, but it still made everybody laugh. After all, being different makes people enjoyable. The same goes for dogs. Mandu is different from Hariette but remains a canine, and we treat them as such. I make no exceptions to this rule. A dog is a dog, is a dog is our group.

In October, I asked the students to disguise themselves for Halloween; it was around the corner; thus, it was time to plan for the day. Most teens find it lame and refuse, but we insist and tell them we have a surprise for them if they do. On the *Day of the Dead*, we dressed the dogs into their costumes and had a blast eating food and candy while the students enjoyed the treats we brought them. We always give little gift bags filled with food and non-food goodies. The teens appreciate the thought and enjoy themselves. They even get to offer special dog treats to their canine companions.

Reinforcement goes a long way, and we strive to create a positive environment for all involved in this program. One of my favourite Halloweens was in 2018. My team dressed up all three dogs in very appropriate costumes. Mandu, the Teckel, was dressed as a hot dog; Hariette, the Broholmer, was disguised as a lion; Albear, the Boxer, wore his famous Darth Vader outfit. The teens dressed up for the occasion, and we ate, plaid, and took photos of the event for our records, but for the teens too. They love souvenirs, and we love giving them. It all works out for the best.

We have collected fond memories in photos and videos over

the years, allowing me to share them on social media and in this book. As the longest participating teen, Calvin shares many memories with the team and me. We also like to dress up the dogs for Christmas, but Calvin was not with us in 2018; he was on vacation with his family. My team does not believe in the anthropomorphic value of the costumes. Still, there are benefits to dressing animals in humanistic accoutrements. Such benefits are tension release, laughter, symptom alleviation, conversation piece, stress release, confidence boost, positive self-esteem, and spatial awareness. Dressing up dogs and rats serves a dual purpose: maintaining the animals' behaviours in working order.

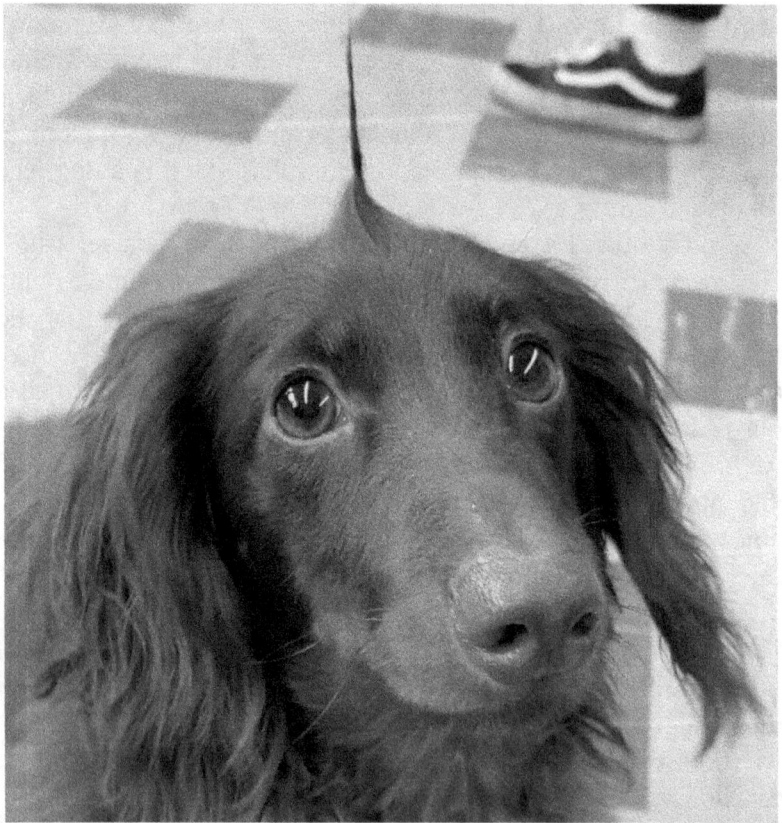

Mandu's impromptu unicorn hairdo.

Animal-assisted therapy tends to focus on animals, but that is not what should occur, at least not in my programs. The animals play a crucial role in creating secure attachments, which are reinforced via food treats and sometimes play. However, I aim to emphasize the teens' positive behaviours through positive reinforcement. I bring human reinforcements to class as often as possible, but without creating a habit. Whether we are rewarding non-human or human animals, the laws of reinforcement remain the same; therefore, I will fulfil a need my team has identified.

Rewards can be food, trinkets, gift cards, books, or clothing. Last year, I gave them candy, loves, and tuques in their Halloween gift basket because I could see a lack. Calvin was very thankful for the gesture, especially knowing the beenies were hand-knitted by the mother of my animal behaviour volunteers. Students need reinforcement for their hard work with the animals, pushing themselves, and sometimes just showing up. For at-risk teens, staying in school is challenging. The pressure to drop out can come from low self-esteem, living situations, friends, money, drugs, pregnancy, crime, mental illness, disorders or disabilities. Teens in our groups are still on the fence but barely hanging on.

For Calvin, AAT was a lifesaver, too. Autism alienates them from societies that do not understand the disorder. Societal pressure contributes to the negative emotional state of the person, isolating them further. AAI and AAT serve to demystify, normalize, and reintegrate adolescents into their communities. It is a gateway to understanding one's self and adapting to an ever-changing environment. Erik Erikson once said, *"In the social jungle of human existence, there is no feeling of being alive without a sense of identity."* (1963).

My job is to keep them coming back and hopefully tip the scale so they can invest in themselves and graduate high school. I wish there were a way to collect longitudinal data on the success rate of our AAT program. Unfortunately, many students are transients within the alternative school system. Moving from one school to the next, when their grades increase, I lose track of many students and never hear from them again. I cannot know if they finished high school unless they contact me. Social media and access to the internet are not always accessible for our participants. For example, I asked Karlo for permission to use a photo I took of him and Alice, the rat; Karlo approved.

When we give teens a training exercise, we are often

motivated by an objective within a set goal for that person. A teen's personal goal is usually compatible with group goals and objectives. Therefore, we can pass an individual exercise as a group activity, and teens will still benefit from the challenge. Sometimes, I tell my team members about the adolescent's psychological history. Other times, I keep the information to myself; it depends on the outcome expectation and biases. Because our overall goal is to bond with students, volunteers might subjectively assess the outcome of an exercise based on an unconscious expectation. The assessment should always remain objective, for science requires facts, not feelings or emotions. We are human beings; thus, knowing someone is suffering influences our critical thinking skills.

Calvin is getting acquainted with Mandu.

Calvin has had many issues, some of which the school could not share. It does not pose a problem because I see their behaviours through their struggles. An excellent example of a subjective occurrence is when students tell me they are feeling good. However, objectively, I observe hostile behaviours from the teens. Subjective interpretation means the person explains their condition, usually from an emotional perspective, without understanding what is genuinely occurring. One session brings the memory of why the objective rule is essential.

The dogs show off their Halloween costumes.

One day, Calvin was distant and removed from the group during a session. I asked what he was wrong, and he said nothing. His answer was typical for a teenager. I asked my questions differently. The second time around, I related my question to something he was comfortable talking about video games. Almost every student projects their emotions onto animals; consequently, using the dog as a mirror to reflect their feelings was more manageable than talking about them. Subsequently, I decode their explanations of how the dog feels to represent the student's emotional state. Animals are excellent mirrors of human behaviour.

My approach was to place the animal within a context the person could relate to. I pursued my interrogation with *If Albear was in a video game, which character would he be, villain or hero?* He said, *villain*. That comment conveyed Calvin felt terrible, so I continued my questioning: *You know Albear likes to dress up as Darth Vader; what's the worst thing he ever did in the video game?* Calvin answered *He killed Luke!* His answer told me the problem most likely had to do with a direct family member; I guessed his father. I then asked how Albear, AKA Darth, could make the situation right.

Calvin told me he would go back in time and not kill Luke; however, knowing Albear could not do that, I asked, *What was our next best option?* He answered, *Asking for forgiveness from Luke's family.* I agreed that was the perfect scenario, and Albear got a treat for being cute while we talked. I learned after the session that all was not well at home. I was happy I did not know beforehand because it could have clouded my questioning, judgment, and emotional response.

I have learned many things in life, but my son taught me that a parent should never give up on their teen. Keep asking questions and ask a different one if you do not receive an adequate answer. Calvin and I bonded the first year we met, more so than other students. In retrospect, the connection between teens and AAT personnel should occur over several months or years. There are essential differences between Calvin and other students: the time spent in the program. Developing a bond can happen quickly, say six to ten weeks, but the overall secure attachment style takes much longer as it grows progressively stronger each week.

Creating an emotional management strategy for the student also takes time; this is why animals are essential for our humanity. Domestic and sometimes exotic animals teach people how to cope with loss, bereavement, anger, fear, or stress. The connection, in turn, further develops our resilience toward life's challenges. We use the social cognitive learning theory model because it is bidirectional. Dogs help humans; humans help dogs; an inter-species symbiotic relationship genuinely bonds us.

When we ended the 2018 school year, Calvin had come a long way since 2014 but was not out of the woods. Summer can be difficult for adolescents who cannot work because they are too young or without experience. Furthermore, summer camp day programs typically end when kids turn thirteen. The lack of activity creates an occupational void for adolescents between thirteen and eighteen. My goal is to one day fill that void; for now, I can only hope teens return to school the following autumn to graduate high school and get their diplomas. I was confident Calvin would achieve great things because he was intelligent and resourceful. If he returned, I had a new challenge awaiting him. Our senior student would take on a leadership role in AAT and become an assistant.

I was confident Calvin would fulfil his duties with the highest professionalism he displayed in class. He never screamed or swore at anyone and conducted himself with diplomacy. Overall, Calvin showed all the characteristics of a trustworthy assistant; he needed the opportunity to express his leadership skills. People with ASD can flourish when they find their niche.

Kathlene took over Calvin's group that year, but since she had been an AAT team member since 2014, I knew Calvin would have no issues adapting to the change. I would visit his school throughout the year to bring reinforcement and praise. I needed to appoint another professional to his schools as the AAT programs grew. I was happy with my decision, and Kathlene constantly reported good news.

When we succeed at our jobs, we must allow expansion to occur. Controlling every facet of a developing business can lead to burnout. There was no time to step away, so letting others take on new tasks and responsibilities was necessary. Kathlene was a fantastic woman, and I will never forget her.

Karlo

I worked with Karlo for a year and a half. When I first met him, he was distant and somewhat shut down. He did not speak to my colleagues or me. Karlo had just changed schools and was emotionally distraught. When teens experience significant life changes, they often socially isolate themselves and become detached, frustrated, and sometimes fearful. Consequently, the limbic system triggers the individual's preferred defence mechanism and maintains it if stress remains high.

I gave Karlo space for a few weeks but never excluded him from our activities. This young man had a learning disability and was an introvert. Adolescents with learning disabilities who withdraw internally have a challenging time in school. They are often teased or bullied; sometimes, both. Hariette, the dog, changed him in ways I will never fully be able to express.

When we started the 2017-2018 school year, we picked up the group where we had left off the previous spring; however, we were one student short. The departure opened a spot in the program, and in late February 2018, the principal introduced me to Karlo. I said *Hi!* in my enthusiastic voice, but he did not answer. The young man immediately went over to his desk, put his headphones on and listened to music.

I allowed him to participate in AAT on his terms; we are not there to worsen their lives. When he finally warmed up to working with dogs, I paired Karlo with Albear because he needed immediate confidence through assured success. Albear was amazing at detecting and implementing proper strategies to draw teens out of their shells.

Connor (right) trains Albear while Karlo (left) hovers, listening to music.

Occasionally, Albear would defy commands if he perceived a better option was available. I trusted him one hundred percent, and he never let me down. I do not know how my dog did it. Still, Albear was a genius in assessing a person's character and emotional needs. Mister Boubousky, the Russian spy alias Seymour gave my dog, was terrific with Karlo. We did simple behaviour like rolling the ball, fetching, and dropping the toy in a box. Once Karlo was successful with Albear, his confidence immediately improved. Our new member slowly emerged from his shell as we moved forward in time. He started to make a few friends, but he loved the company of animals even more.

When spring 2018 finally arrived, we could take the dogs outside regularly. We welcomed the fresh air, and the group enjoyed taking the dogs and rats for walks. Students loved sitting on benches pondering life while their little AAT partner soaked in the sun's rays.

Bench reflection, as I called it, was one of my favourite activities. In a fast-paced world, taking time to experience the present moment evades us. Sitting and simply existing soothes the soul. We can breathe, check in with ourselves, and introspect about where we are and want to go. These questions are vital for adolescents. They are forging their identity, which means they try things that work and some that do not. Reflecting on the outcomes is necessary for the process.

Typically, our attachment with the teens is secure as we near the end of the school year. But many things occur between September and June. One crucial developmental aspect of AAT is the attachment style. Without knowing or telling anyone, the connection process slowly and purposefully occurs. First, we verbally reinforce the students for their accomplishments. The reinforcement steps include human treats such as candy, cookies, chips, veggies, and cake, followed by physical contact.

We added a touch on the hand and paired it with a *great job!* And eventually, we tap them on the elbow, arm, and shoulder. By the end of the year, sessions often end with hugs for the students who enjoy physical interactions. Not all teenagers like social contact; consequently, I always ask before I hug. If the student initiates the touch, then I do not question it.

Karlo had not reached the hugging stage in our attachment

process, but he was bonding with the animals and our team, and that was my reinforcement. I often say that if their happiness and joy paid the bills, I would be the wealthiest person in the world. I still consider myself the most affluent because money will never buy such powerful and impactful human experiences. I cannot express how it feels to see humans come to life before my eyes; I simply do not have the words.

I have been fortunate enough to see this process occur multiple times, and I hope to see it many more to come. Each teen fills me with love, compassion, and a more substantial commitment to AAT with each passing year. It is not always easy to hear their stories and share their hurt, but we would be less than human if we did not try. I promised myself I would never look the other way when I saw kids needing help, whether in AAT or not.

It would be highly dishonest, disrespectful, and cruel to create a false sense of attachment only to leave them without caring about their futures. Watching social media dehumanize our humanity saddens me. The pandemic severed the little connection we had left between one another, and now people view physical contact as unfavourable. We are social animals who require touch to be physically and emotionally healthy. Our skin, the largest organ, can only thrive on physical contact. I am sure some of you are reading this and cringing. You might even wonder, *Why would I want to touch another person?* The secure attachment between a mother and a child occurs during the first eighteen months (Ainsworth, 1978; Ansiworth & Bowlby, 1992). Therefore, we must reconsider the consequences of the lack of touch that so many children and teens experience.

We laugh and cry with the students in AAT because they expect us to respond to their emotions. I admit there is a time to remain strong, but that does not exclude contact. I can only hope that the secure attachment they experienced will allow them to make better choices for themselves.

I can summarize my thoughts about the process as follows. Suppose teens experienced secure attachment for only a moment. In that case, unconditional love might open the door to seeking and recreating the feeling. They are more likely to recognize the difference between positive and negative relationships. To me, that is the noblest outcome of animal-assisted therapy. That year ended without commotion; we celebrated with food, gifts, and hugs. The teens gave the animals much love and caress as they said their goodbyes.

When the 2018-2019 school year began, I was excited to find our group intact. All the boys were present with the addition of a new young lady. We get, on average, ten boys to one girl, a ratio that has proven constant over the years. It is always a pleasure to see young ladies join the AAT program. Karlo was amongst the young gentlemen. He was less introverted and shared his summer adventures with us. He told me he had played football and developed good cardio. All the teens had changed, which we expect during the adolescent phase of development.

Because we look awkward, adolescence is not easy for everyone, including our animals. People and animals awkwardly look and behave because they experiment with their minds and bodies. Being a teenager is like trying to drive an F1 Formula at full speed and trying to play dodgeball. The only problem is that the person sitting in the car does not know how to drive.

During adolescence, dogs are obnoxious and extremely rude. Your cute puppy turned into a vicious-looking killing machine. They behave nothing like the dog you knew a few months ago; consequently, many people abandon dogs during this phase of development. The average length of dog ownership in Quebec is eighteen months, and the average age of abandonment is nine months (Powell et al., 2021).

Albear, now eight going on nine, was semi-retired in 2018; thus, Hariette the Broholmer puppy joined the group. Fresh off the Hungarian plane, she immediately joined the AAT team. She grew up in the program and promptly needed to get her feet wet. Her first visit to the school was on the first day in late August. She was momentarily overwhelmed by all the students surrounding her, so she hid under a student's desk. I introduced Karlo to Hariette, and he was a little baffled about why she was hiding there. I gave him the W5 version of her story and why she was there, hiding from the world.

I related his fears and shyness to hers, and they immediately connected. In retrospect, my intense documentation of AAT allowed me to capture and share with you the exact moment

Karlo and Hariette met. The smile speaks for itself. The Broholmer puppy instantaneously made a new friend. Karlo was compassionate and kind, and she responded to him quickly. He offered her some treats, and she accepted cuddles from everyone but circumnavigated back to her new partner.

Their relationship grew stronger each week, and when I thought Hariette could not get any closer, she would. She found effective strategies through training on how to bond. On such an occasion, she wanted affection and refused to work. Karlo was frustrated and said Hariette was *broken*.

I am not obliged to divulge what I know about the animals to the teens; I prefer to let them figure it out and come to their conclusions. In this case, it came out of Karlo's mouth as perfectly as if I had written the script myself. He spontaneously said *I guess she feels just like I do and wants to be lazy today*. So, I told him to be lazy and enjoy it. Life is not exclusively about work; being in the present moment is necessary to equalize life's experiences.

In their laziness, Karlo succumbed to Hariette's desire to work. He decided to teach her how to give a paw. I guided him through training the behaviour without him discovering it was a training session. When such situations occur, other students recognize their classmates' individual needs and never fuss about inequalities in training or lack thereof. Overall, a natural balance forms between the needs and desires of each class member. To this day, Hariette knows how to give her left and right paws because Karlo felt lazy one day.

Even if students are not working on a specific behaviour, they participate in the program. Karlo was an excellent example of this phenomenon. Some days, he would do a small training session and then ask to take a rat out; I rarely said no. However, I requested that he reinforce two more behaviours to satisfy the dog's craving for inclusion. I stayed true to my word and allowed Karlo to spend time with the rats. He liked the contact and grew fonder of Akeanu (the rat) each week.

The words we use are processed by teens, even if they seem far removed from the AAT sessions. Our vocabulary impacts each individual differently; therefore, we choose our words carefully, for they could have lasting consequences on their psyche. I remember we came into the class one day, and all the students were hyper and uncooperative. It was as if they were all under a magic spell. The effervescent energy was palpable, and it became apparent within a few minutes that we would not achieve our daily goals. The team members and I looked at each other. I summoned them with a slight tilt of the head, and we discussed the situation in what I call *A minute meeting*. We decided to let them enjoy being teenagers.

As it often occurs under Murphy's law, the headteacher visited the classroom that day. She saw two groups of four conducting a training session lying on the floor with the dogs and two other teams simply petting and chatting. The acting principal asked me if this was a common occurrence. I reassured her it was not. She replied that the students had been acting hyperactive the entire morning. In our adult's mind, the session was not a failure because students were talking with one another, which is my primary goal. The staff and I aspire to see regular conversations between adolescents and adults and between their peers. To achieve our goal, I ask questions, but nobody can answer for another person. We encourage participants to find their voices and speak their minds. Effective communication is 75% listening.

Communication skills decreased proportionately to social media use. I am baffled and saddened by this reality; therefore, I emphasize how to chat and try to understand other people's points of view. We can disagree, and sometimes discussions can become passionate, but respect, acceptance, and love dictate the outcome. No one can *shush* a person in our program.

The end of October 2018 came by faster than I anticipated. During a session, I asked the group to come disguised; if they did, we would have surprises for them. The reward was to see our dogs disguised and bags of goodies for best costume. I love to give the students unexpected gifts. I was filming a video when we talked about costumes. Karlo told me he would dress up as Neo (Keanu Reeves) from The Matrix. I told him he could pull it off easily since he could pass as M. Reeves' Teenage son. Karlo resembled the actor and shared his voice, walking, running, and other mannerisms. The resemblance was uncanny, more so since Karlo fancied the actor. I wished Karlo had met the actor because they both have learning disabilities. I believe Karlo would have gained a boost in confidence.

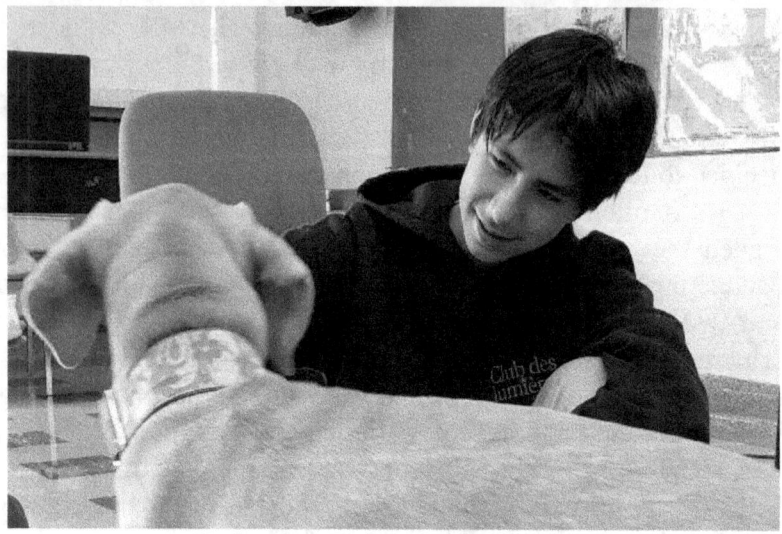

Karlo meets Hariette for the first time.

When he asked me if I knew Keanu, I said yes, a little; I lied. M. Reeves is an actor I enjoy tremendously because of his zen-full delivery of lines and his devotion to the character. Karlo has the same zen attitude, a gift at a young age. He is lucky that no one teases him about his appearance other than to point out the obvious. Unfortunately, Karlo dressed up as another character.

When I asked why, he replied *Lack of budget!* Had I known, I would have contributed to the design; nonetheless, we had fun, ate, and laughed, mainly at the dogs. The teens like it when Albear enters as Darth Vader, especially with the deep breathing adding to the role. I dressed Hariette, too, and the combination was perfect. A villain and a cowardly lion, how appropriate. We loved the mixture of characters, and Hariette was joyful and calm sitting next to her *Keanu*.

When the session concluded, I thanked the teenagers for being open-minded and congratulated them on their costumes. They represented Death well for the 2018 Halloween celebration. The students appeared stoic when they opened their bags, but I knew why. Our teens lack specific seasonal clothing;

therefore, I added gloves to their goody bags filled with toys, chocolate, and appreciation cards.

Typically, students individually come to tell me, *Thank you!* in my ear. I make nothing of it, and they appreciate the gesture. Discretion is the norm in AAT unless adolescents make it known to their peers. Some people are open about their problems, while most are uncomfortable sharing personal information. Karlo was a very discrete and reserved individual. As Halloween ended, I wished the teens a fabulous week. We could see their happiness, and we shared it. It was a successful event.

Karlo and Hariette during the 2018 Halloween celebration.

The following weeks were straining for everyone, school staff included. The grey climate shortened our outings, and I could tell the students were discouraged and anxious about the upcoming exam period at the end of the semester. I asked the school personnel if we could use the gymnasium to perfect a game I had invented the previous year. The staff was more than enthusiastic, and some teachers joined us. Dog-Ball is a mixture of sports combined into one. I combined soccer and hockey, but we played the game with a yoga ball. The canids push the yoga ball into a hocket net guided by verbal commands only—no touching allowed. Even though we were inside for the following months, the teens enjoyed the activity.

November turned into December in the blink of an eye. There were a few snow days where we went outside, but overall, we stayed inside during late autumn. The second to last week of December is the AAT holiday celebration. I bring gifts and presents to celebrate their achievements; therefore, the bags contain similar yet different products, toys, and gift cards.

I also gave them a holiday card with a picture of themselves and their dog partner, portraying their most triumphant moment. They appreciate the gesture and start showing their friends and family what they have been up to during the last few months. The picture increases their confidence and self-esteem because they can *prove* their achievements. Karlo took his picture and placed it with his things. He showed it to his mother because she told me about it during the Christmas lunch celebration.

December ends with an elaborate homemade feast, presents, music, and dancing. The dogs stay at the Dogue Shop during this event because we want to spend time one-on-one with the teens. Even though we all love dogs, we appreciate human-exclusive social gatherings. I met Karlo's mother during the holiday lunch and chatted with her. She was impressed by the changes she witnessed in Karlo's behaviour. The once introverted teen was now a socialite. She asked me how I transformed the adolescent, and I replied, *It wasn't me; it was Hariette*. I showed her videos of Karlo in action, and she smiled. I could tell she was proud of her son's accomplishments.

Unfortunately, we cannot stay the entire length of the festivities because we have other schools to attend. After lunch, we discuss the program with parents and exchange holiday wishes. We then say our goodbyes to the teens one by one. Karlo was the event's DJ, so I approached the stage and waved at him from a distance. He signalled one moment and came down to my level. We wished each other happy holidays, and Karlo asked when we would return. I told him we resumed AAT on January 9, to which Karlo added, *That's the day of my birthday!* I made a note of it, and he proceeded to hug me. On my way out of the gym, his mom winked at me. I could tell she was happy with the outcome of the emotional display. I was, too. Building secure attachments between humans and animals takes, on average, six weeks; the bonding between two people usually requires months.

In March 2018, our training sessions were in full force, and the teens were making significant progress. Unfortunately, Karlo left the group to explore other alternatives. A strange phenomenon occurred during this period. Karlo would come in before and after the AAT sessions to say *Hi!* and *Bye!* to his pet partner, Hariette. The bond between the two was analogous to the bonds between wolves and unfamiliar people. Through positive and consistent encounters, trust-based relationships are sometimes stronger than family ties.

Through observation and training, I believe teens are like wolves. Adolescent humans believe adults perceive them as wild organisms, spending most of their time plotting destruction and world dominance. The thought is often further exaggerated, and teens start thinking of themselves as conniving and tempestuous, unmanageable pack members they must avoid at all costs. The approach is not very different from that of befriending a wolf.

I kept telling Karlo that Hariette was lonely and missed working with him. He never officially told me, but Karlo returned because Hariette demonstrated unconditional love toward the young man. Hariette securely bonded with the teen to the point where she jumped and cried for him. With persistence, Hariette got his attention, and Karlo was willing to work with her; therefore, Karlo returned the following month to work full-time with us.

Teens make excellent animal trainers, and my human partner was no exception. His clicker skills were exceptional, which constitutes the foundation of classical conditioning. Karlo and the other teens in AAT were training in complex behaviours that required concentration. When participants enjoyed what they were doing, they smiled.

I would love to write that participants smiled more, but that did not occur. That said, one animal made Kris systematically smirk: Charlotte the rat. Kris loved working and spending time with rats. I often asked myself how one could dislike soft cashmere fur, delicate hand massages, and gentle licks from a debonair, charismatic mini dog. The tail is what people dislike.

Seymour and Karlo are posing for the Holiday picture.

Once they learn about rats, their prejudices fall, and people become charmed and enamoured with our rodents. When Karlo returned, I decided that each AAT session would end with rat socialization time. Karlo and another teen benefited the most from my decision. Charlotte, the one-eyed rat, and Karlo became a pair. He would go everywhere with her and was not fond of sharing her affection.

In May, we received a new rat colony. Four three-week-old baby rats joined the AAT team. The students were appointed a pup, and each teen was responsible for naming it. Karlo wanted to call the little black frisky and frolicky female Keanu after the actor, but I reminded him the name had to start with an A. Calling a rat, Keanu led my imagination down a path of lengthy explanations.

How would I explain the rodent's name on live television? But my word is my word, so Karlo named his rat Akeanu, with the nickname Aknu (A-kee-nu). Each week, group members spent time with their pups to socialize and eventually start training them. The first behaviour our rats learned was the target. The target was a retractable tent pole with a yellow tennis ball at the end. The rats knew to touch the mark with their nose or hands; consequently, we used this behaviour to create new ones.

We took longer breaks outside with the teens, dogs, and ratties as spring got warmer. The boys would take off with the dogs and run as fast as possible. Karlo was the only one capable of keeping up with the dogs. These *bathroom breaks* slowly turned into unofficial physical education sessions. Fresh air, animals, and running around, how could life get any better? The new strategy remains a viable option that the teens inadvertently added to the AAT program. I owe the boys a lightbulb moment for the idea because, without their enthusiasm, it would not have dawned on me to take them outside for a frolicking period. We cannot run outside in certain schools because the environment is inappropriate. Still, we enjoy nature whenever we can, even if it means standing around with the dogs in the parking lot.

My fondest memory is of the formidable three: Seymour, Calvin, and Karlo. We went outside on a beautiful spring day to take in some sun. The three boys sat on a park bench with their respective rats. They started a philosophical discussion about life and their future. I eventually partook in the conversation, sharing my thoughts with them. Calvin was the moderator, which allowed the teens to stay on track. The discussion eventually shifted to another topic, but I was amazed to see and hear how they shared their points of view without raising their voices. When we give young men and women the tools to dialogue, it is fascinating to witness their level of respect and compassion toward one another increase.

When we visited the Montreal Mounted Police (MMP), Karlo was not part of the group because he was in music class for a school project. I am convinced he would have enjoyed the outing and the contact from the horses. Events often unfolded in ways we were unaware of. Still, I trusted life and decided this was the best option for Karlo. When he returned the following week, the teens were still discussing the horse AAT session. Those who were present talked about their experience with those who were absent. I encouraged the communication exchange because it took precedence over actual training.

Students talked to each other without swearing, screaming or judging. The memory of seeing our teens training dogs while recalling the memorable day was, and still is, pure joy. They say it takes a village to raise a family; having homeschooled my son, I can humbly and honestly agree and am ever grateful to work with a community that believes in the benefits of AAT. We could not sustain the program without the generous help of volunteers, especially our drivers. The reason is that putting together a group of usually predators/prey animals requires constant observation. Since clients, past students, and friends' animals are in my care for the day, my responsibility is to ensure their safety. Therefore, driving and managing animal behaviour is impossible.

Karlo runs with Hariette during a spring snowfall.

Late May and early June are the busiest months of the year in AAT because we are concluding ten months of work and preparing the teens for our departure. AAT successfully creates secure attachments; consequently, we must ensure we leave the teens with a positive experience. The last thing we want is for the teens to experience abandonment; therefore, depending on the school and the student, we adjourn differently for each group and individual. Specific students receive a lifelong membership to the Dogue Academy; they can take the animal behaviour apprenticeship (ABA) as long as I am alive, or they can come to hang out and work with the animals. Either way, they are welcome at any time.

Some students took advantage of this opportunity during the school year, while others came during the summer break. Teens who cannot work because of their young age come *to do something* as they say. For some, it is an excellent way to remain off the streets. In contrast, it allows others to alleviate emotions associated with a mental disorder or disability. My colleagues and I love chatting with teens about how they experience life while we train animals. You can think of our AAT program as a hands-on approach to helping adolescents. If they have social anxiety, we work our way to conducting social outings. If teens are depressed, we give them a reason to work with us, so on and so forth.

If I suggested you train a rat to jump off a table into your hand, you probably would say *Are you crazy?* With just cause, but once the behaviour started to form, you would get excited and start believing in yourSelf. Imagine demonstrating your achievements to your current boss; you would be ecstatic. When students successfully present complex behaviours to their peers, self-esteem and self-worth immediately upsurge. The last day of school with Karlo's group was one of the most emotional endings I have experienced thus far in my career. The staff, students, and the AAT team were leaving school forever.

The EMSB had to move our school to another building in a different neighbourhood. Consequently, the school spread out the students into various locations across the city, which meant I would no longer see or work with most students unless the new school was interested in our services. Karlo was one of the students who relocated to another establishment.

Two weeks before the end of the year, Karlo rejoined the

AAT group to spend some time with us and the animals before saying goodbye. Hariette was ecstatic, and our emotions were high during the training session. The teens did not work for long; my objective was to *set them up for success*. In other words, it sets the animals and teens up to be successful and leave the school with a positive experience of detachment.

The dogs were so excited that a training session could only benefit everyone. After the exercise, we chatted and enjoyed being with one another and the animals. Karlo took a Charlotte, and she directly went into his hoodie, then down his shirt. He smiled and laughed. I was super happy to have shared that moment with him. When leaving, I asked Karlo and Seymour to stay behind because I wanted to talk with them.

I offered Karlo and Seymour a lifetime membership at the Dogue Academy to ease the transition between weekly meetings and none. To facilitate the transition, it helps to know you can still access the resource you are losing—the sense of belonging created from that knowledge benefited emotions. The student can experience the rupture as a negative or positive outcome—the choice is ultimately their own. I try to minimize negative consequences as best I can and promote positive results. It is easier said than done. When Seymour left, Karlo gave me a long and hard hug. We both held back our tears, and a deep sense of loss mixed with gratification and satisfaction overwhelmed me. Some students affect us more than others, and this was the case.

Karlo reminded me of myself and the many challenges life inexplicably threw at me as a teenager. When I returned home that afternoon, I cried. I was sad because I knew I would probably never chat or laugh with him again; conversely, I was happy knowing Hariette and I had contributed to his happiness, if only for a moment. It is soulfully satisfying to see the young man express his emotions. That meant he felt safe and trusted me enough to allow himself to cry. I told him he would do amazing things, for he was confident and authentically himself.

It was a heart-wrenching goodbye, but I would start all over again. Teens need to know they are valued and appreciated, that their ideas matter, that they make a world of difference in our adult lives, that their creativity is an exploitable resource, and that their view of the world, not yet conditioned by deceptions, contributes to the wellbeing of humans and animals alike. I was discouraged when my adolescent specialization teacher told me it was strenuous to reestablish secure attachment styles after seven years old.

This bonding mechanism means kids forge their future behaviour patterns within relationships during childhood. He added that we needed to work with kids before they entered grade school to modify attachment. I value his experience, and to some extent, he was right. Yet, I have experienced that it is possible to change insecure attachment styles to secure ones after early childhood.

> *"I rather fancy this statistic because, if true, it suggests that the contraction of childhood began to occur even in physiological terms shortly after the invention of the telegraph; that is, there is an almost perfect coincidence of the falling age of puberty and the communications revolution."*
> —Postman, 1994, p.109

If anything, Jamal, Rayvon and Karlo were prime examples of attachment style modification. It turns out all we needed were dogs, rats, horses, wolves, and training experience. Pairing them with a securely attached adult is also crucial for optimal results. Our teams are imperfect, but we achieved our goals regardless of secure attachments because animals are natural mediators. Animals seek out people who are authentically themselves, even if that version is insecure, fearful, sad, joyful, or happy. Vincent went to Markayla even though she was disgusted by the rat. Hariette bonded with Karlo, regardless of his introversion.

Seymour

The sweetest teen I have ever met came in a six-foot-tall fourteen-year-old teenager. When we first met, he was quiet and reserved with people but immediately connected with the dogs. I remember thinking to myself, *This is going to be fun!* I was right. Seymour had a phenomenal memory of historical events. He remembered dates, names, and details with such accuracy that he could have won any history competition at a world level. His recollections fascinated me; I could have listened to him for hours. Seymour was in our group because he was suicidal and was at risk of dropping out of school. This young man had other underlying issues, some physical, but most were psychological. I always tried to see the positive in negative situations to avoid focusing on the bad.

Seymour stole my heart from the beginning. When I introduced him to Albear, he rolled on the floor with him, and they immediately connected. Seymour loved animals, but I think Albear and the ratties occupied a special place in his heart. When I retired Albear from AAT, he kept asking me when he would return. During the last years of his life, Albear only participated in social events like Halloween, Christmas, and other valuable non-training days. Do not get me wrong, Albear loved to work; he did so two days before he passed, but severe arthritis meant that if he ran or stood for too long, it would take him days to recover.

Living with Hariette was a pawful for M. Boobouski[10]; therefore, managing his health was my fundamental concern. Seymour understood these challenges, for he had a twenty-one-year-old cat. He affectionately disclosed one day that *It's* [cat] *older than I am!* Seymour verbalized his inner thoughts in the purest of ways. One would say he spoke without filters, and they would have been right, but I did not mind, for I loved his honesty. These days, people get offended by factual observations and do not appreciate that *what you see is what you get* approach. A mind can alter reality to its benefit, but facts and truth will always remain unscathed.

Seymour's first session with dogs and rats occurred in

---

[10] Seymour named Albear M. Boobooski during a discussion of the cold war. He thought Albear needed a Russian spy alias.

September 2017. He immediately loved the ratties and fancied their presence on his skin. Over the years, the young man helped socialize multiple murinae mischiefs. He took the baby rats, bonded, nurtured, and trained them to the best of his abilities.

My goal was to encourage Seymour and his classmates to try novel things, challenge themselves, and believe in the results they achieve. The students demonstrated a fondness for rats that adults found strange and sometimes disgusting. Far from being dirty, rats are excellent at evaluating peoples' emotional states.

I have known Seymour for many years, and although he has experienced many difficulties, his love of animals has never changed. I have never asked him why he loved animals so much. If I did, I am confident his answer would have been: *They love me unconditionally!* Growing up differently from others always leads to judgment. It is an unavoidable reality. Animals do not care about the colour of your hair or if you can spell arithmetic without using autocorrect. Most importantly, animals only cared about teenagers being themselves.

For most AAT students, animals enriched their lives by loving them unconditionally. That goes for the AAT staff, too. During his last year of high school, Seymour only came when the AAT team was present, and that filled my heart with joy because I knew just how difficult it was for him to show up. One day, I messaged Anne, Seymour's mother, to offer free sessions at the Dogue Shop. We discussed options to help him further, and I was happy he accepted. We conducted weekly sessions with Hariette. Albear was Hariette's emotional support dog. When she got too excited, Albear would tell her, in canine behaviour, to relax. Seymour was quick to pick up on social animal cues. He would have been a fantastic dog trainer because he quickly adjusted his behaviour to dogs. That said, maybe one day, Seymour will cash in his Dogue Academy pass and join the ABA alums. He convinced me that his training abilities would benefit many future generations of AAT students.

Seymour came to work with the dogs and rats every week for months, and during the summer break, he would make random visits. He never told me why he wanted to come on those specific days, and I never asked. I thought he had his reasons, which was good enough for me. I could often figure out what was troubling him, but I kept it to myself. Motivation is a force that pushes an organism to exhibit a behaviour, and sometimes, it is best to go with the flow and let behaviour manifest itself. Adolescence is about creating a version of yourself that you can live with. When push comes to shove emotions, teenagers will retreat. Being a good parent is knowing when to stop pushing and start supporting.

The secure connection between parents and children taught them how to explore their sense of self. Insecure attachment styles forge discrepancies between what parents ask and what they do. Adolescence is a phase of detachment from the parental figure; creating one's identity and future societal role is vital. Two outcomes generally occur when parents try to be their children's friends: dependency or detachment. I have observed the same outcome in humans and dogs. Insecure attachments create dysfunctional relationships. Dogs will solve problems independently (insecure avoidant) or become confused and reactive (insecure ambivalent). Dogs with secure connections check in with their humans for feedback on how to solve the problem, but ultimately, they can solve it on their own; trust is the crucial factor in relationships.

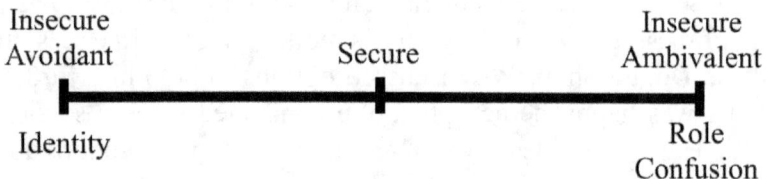

Granted, relationship types are not as straightforward as the previous image; however, it gives us a better understanding of the consequences of insecure attachment styles. When people develop secure attachments, they have a strong sense of identity and understand their roles as men, women, future parents, siblings, employees/ers, and friends. Looking at social media, we see the effects on human behaviour. People develop identity disorders favouring the ego, leading to narcissism, entitlement, borderline, or histrionic. The other end of the spectrum is as problematic. Without clear roles, people cannot integrate groups like friends, family, work, or leisure. Parenting frightens them, and so, too, does having responsibilities. They are never at fault, which can lead to isolation and despair.

People desperately attempt to harness the unconditional love emanating from animals, only to recreate their attachment styles. Unfortunately, when it comes to animal interactions, the harder you try, the less successful you become. Newton's third law applies to the human-animal bond; an equal and opposite reaction occurs. When someone forces an animal into a relationship, the animal retreats out of self-preservation. When you understand Newton's law, you can harness the human-animal bond and let animals come to you based on trust. Allowing an animal to enter your critical space is faster than the other way around.

Seymour meets Albear for the first time.

When I wanted to include Seymour in a conversation, I would ask him for an analogous historical event, and he could talk about that event for hours. Our discussions would also include relationships between past and current events or how a historical figure might act today. I loved to see his mind at work.

One of my favourite Seymour moments was a conversation we had as a group. When we came together at the beginning of the session, I asked random questions like *Has anybody seen a good movie lately?* I cannot recall who answered first, but the film was 1917. The dialogue started with the topic and plot of the movie. Within minutes, Benjamin had taken the floor and corrected the inaccurate historical events in the film.

> *"Oh, I do hope that you get going at James Lyng as well! That would be amazing. Dog training was Benjamin's favourite thing about Focus! It made him want to stay in school."*
> —Anne, Seymour's mother

Seymour's personality was always full of surprises, some fun and some less enjoyable. The AAT program always focuses on the positive side of things. If a participant is experiencing negative emotions, I will ask the person to find one thing, just one, that is positive. It doesn't matter what they choose or how important it is. They can like the colour of their shoes, a favourite song, a delicious meal, or their best friend. If they can focus on one positive experience, we can build on it. The exercise is simple, but it yields significant changes.

AAT is about paralleling animal behaviours and emotions to people so we can help change undesirable behaviours into desirable ones. Family, friends, and society condition most children and adolescents before the age of reason. The damage is even more significant with social media being omnipresent in our lives. Social media platforms can and do change the developing mind in negative ways.

Certain platforms know their content hijacks the limbic system, yet they purposefully develop algorithms to harness young people's minds. To the extent of monitoring what children see on social media, parental control is crucial for their developing minds. When we take the teens outside, I see the teens being kids. They love to run around and frolic; they even invent games with their pet partner.

Social media is like the dark side of human consciousness. I am not a pessimist; there is good content on social platforms, but unfortunately, there is very little of it since algorithms push what people watch. I work hard to tailor my feeds to positive content; however, it is a constant struggle. Parents must teach kids how to use their security settings private features and tweak their algorithms. I remember a student telling me *I never get a break from the bullying, even when I'm at home.* We talk about social media in AAT because I find it pertinent that students have a safe place to chat about the damage and fake content that influences their lives.

Major platforms cause increased anxiety, poor self-image, and suicidal tendencies (Korte, 2022). Yet, companies refuse to change their policies in exchange for money. I bring my own animal training experience to demonstrate how fake social media truly is. I pull out animal videos and show them to teens. We then critically break down the content and discuss behaviour and what the animals scientifically say or do. I believe it is our role, as adults, to talk about these matters. I had this approach with my son, and today, he critically thinks about what he sees before deciding if this represents who he is in any way.

> *"One of the outcomes of this study was that extreme use of social media* [7.5 h/d] *and virtual reality environments can lead to an increase in risk of anxiety, fewer real social interactions, lack of social skills and human empathy, and difficulties in handling solitude."*
> —Marin Korte, 2022.

An example of content we discussed was a video made by McGill computer engineering students in Montreal titled A Golden Eagle Snatches Kid (MrNuclearCat, 2012). The video went viral, and news channels worldwide reported the event. Critical thinking tells us that this is physically impossible for a few reasons. An eagle cannot lift a weight equal to or heavier than itself. Furthermore, golden eagles are rarely seen in the province of Quebec, let alone in one of the busiest parks in Montreal. Finally, birds of prey do not fly or catch their meal next to people, putting themselves at risk. A final piece of information might be unavailable to outsiders: Mont-royal Park has a constant source of dogs entering and exiting the park at any given time of the day. An eagle would not risk its life in such a place.

Students concluded that the video was fake because the child was too large for an eagle to pick up a child, even if it immediately dropped it. They also pointed out that the adult would have seen such an enormous bird *swoop in*. I like to use multiple animal species to teach our AAT participants how to think critically and use the Google Chromesearch engine to find information. There is a right and wrong way to conduct research on the Internet, a skill schools seem to forget to teach.

The brain stops growing at age twenty-five (Rochester University, 2022). Consequently, the longer people wait to seek help for their condition, the harder it will be to modify neuro-connections. I chose to work with teenagers because it is our last chance to easily undo negative conditioning before the brain settles into its adult form. When negative thoughts become habitual, they can turn into disorders. Changing these thought patterns will take years to revert to positive inner dialogues. Consequently, preventing behaviour problems from occurring is much easier than intervening once disorders or negative thought patterns are well established.

Golden eagle snatching a child in the park.

When the brain starts to weed out neuro-connections to keep the pathways we use the most active, it becomes clear that we lose some of the knowledge we had as children. This process is normal and necessary. The brain has plasticity, but there is so much an organ can do. Seymour and his classmates never used their phones. A phoneless class is a norm and safety measure we all agree on. I take pictures and videos for documentation purposes. I then send photos to the teens via the school's e-mail address or upload some images to social media and tag them. Sometimes, I NFC transfer my document at the end of the school year. When we train animals, distractions can be hazardous because we might miss a signal from the animal. If we ignore or do not see a hard-eye, we expose ourselves to bites.

> *"The rational part of a teen's brain isn't fully developed and won't be until age 25 or so."*
> —*RUMC, 2022*

Imagine trying to take a selfie with a horse, and it steps on your toes or with a wolf, and you back up on its toes. I will let you imagine the consequences of those actions, but rest assured, our teens are not allowed to make this faux pas. It would be a tragedy to stop conducting AAT sessions with teens because of a 100% avoidable accident. When I was young, a horse kicked me in the knee because I looked at another horse being goofy. It was a painful lesson in being in the moment. Animals live in the eternal present; allowing the human mind to wander leads to accidents or tragedies. AAT participants are under our care; thus, my team and I are incredibly prudent when we let our teens interact with one another while they work with their pet partners.

> *"This neuronal "prunings," which culminates in the transition from adolescence to adulthood, occurs first in the posterior area of the brain and finally in the frontal cortex, which is what controls reasoning, decision-making and emotional control."*
> —*Tuarez, 2023.*

Seymour always mesmerized the volunteer staff, and my emotions did not exclude me from those moments; I am human, after all. Unfortunately, Seymour was absent for an extended period because of a medical condition. I was so excited the day he returned that I wanted to hug him, so I asked for his permission. I knew Seymour did not like to be touched, but he said yes, and off I went. He extended his arms out, and I walked into them. I was so happy for him to be back in school with us.

Seymour changed significantly during his passage in the AAT program. Unfortunately, I recently moved my business, which is too far for Seymour to travel to the Dogue Shop. Sometimes, life complicates things, but I am confident he has the tools to continue growing. We keep in touch because I promised him a puppy when Hariette has a litter, and I will not back down on that promise. The puppy will be fully trained and ready for duty. I usually do not offer free training or free dogs. Still, Seymour has worked so hard on himself that the reward needs to be significant. If you watch my YouTube channel, I always say *Don't be cheap, and pay up!* Well, this goes for humans, too, but that is a topic for another book.

Seymour snuggles puppy George on the floor.

Connor

The case of Connor was a short but intense journey. He joined the group in January 2018 and only stayed for one year. Some of his classmates disliked, even despised, the teen. The main reason was that he screamed profanity at everyone who did not do as he wished. Connor was rambunctious and hyperactive; some students called him a spoiled brat. I did not consider him as such. Connor was misunderstood; he wanted attention, not things or technology. My experience with Connor was different.

The first day he joined the group, I explained the safety rules and norms, which he agreed to, and never once broke any of them. I saw him as a young man desperate for parental attention, to be more specific, and he screamed for it. Connor wanted someone to acknowledge him for who he was, and screeching was a sure way of getting people's attention.

Connor never once screamed or uttered profanity. Once, he was telling a story that happened to his friend and said f***; he immediately placed his hand on his mouth in horror. I told him it was OK to say the *f*-word because his friend had said it in the story. He never swore in my presence. The change was so dramatic that staff and students knew when we had arrived at school because Connor was silent. It was so noticeable that the head teacher once took me aside and thanked me for our work. I was happy and shocked. Connor was such a different person in AAT; it was hard to imagine they were telling the truth.

One day, during snack time, a student walked by the class. The door was open because the dogs were outside on bathroom break. The student passing by backtracked and said *Oh, you're here; that's why he's shut up!* I told the student that was mean and uncalled for. He added that I did not know how he behaved. I told the student that Connor was a good kid and not currently disrespectful, so his comment was uncalled for. The student told me Connor was a lousy person. I declined his explanation. I put my arms around Connor's shoulders and said I liked him and *would adopt him if he needed a family.* Connor looked at me in shock and disbelief at what I had said. I meant every word. Connor's personality shined through during his passage with us, and I can honestly say he was terrific. I wish we had had more time with him; I know he would have liked the many activities we conducted. My heart broke when I learned Connor's parents had sent him to live with his grandmother in Ontario. We grow close to the teens, making our attachments real.

When people fixate on a problem, they prevent growth. The label identified Connor as bad, and no amount of change in his behaviour would modify that; that is the sad truth. I see the teens in our program as needing love, guidance, appreciation, and belonging. After six months in AAT, Connor finally realized he belonged somewhere and appreciated us. The dogs and the rats allowed him to grow and demonstrate that he could be the best version of himself. I never doubt that process, for if I do, I limit his potential for development.

Connor was an intelligent teen, and he was a fantastic dog trainer. In retrospect, I wish I had given him a free pass to the Dogue Academy. But I forgot, and the following year, he was gone. Should he ever read these lines, I would tell him he is welcome to the Dogue Shop and Dogue Academy anytime; if he wanted to become a dog trainer, I would happily offer him that opportunity for free.

Connor's first outing with the dogs was another memorable moment in his case. I have an unwritten rule in AAT; if a student walks the dog and it poops, the student has to pick it up. Learning responsibilities is part of maturing. Connor disliked picking up poop because, in his own words, *It grosses me out!* He did not appreciate it when I said those were the rules, and the other student confirmed the fact. Surprisingly, he never screamed profanity or expressed anger; instead, he agreed and took the dog out. Connor's desire to walk the dog and be like the others was more motivating than gagging.

So, Connor set out with the leash in his hand, securely tied, and placed a poop bag in his pocket. When his puppy defecated, it was big and messy. Connor looked at me and signalled with my head that it was okay. He said to himself; *It's just poop, no big deal!* As he bent over, bag on hand, Connor picked up the poop and gagged the entire time. He accepted the rule and challenged himself. When we leave room to grow, teens spread their wings and fly. Time after time, I witnessed participants push themselves to be better versions of who they are. I can never state that enough. All teens want is someone to guide them and give feedback, acknowledging their success or encouraging them to try again.

Connor meets his new puppy partner after the safety class.

Connor continued to walk his puppy partner that day and all subsequent ones. He continued to pick up after the dog, and strangely, his gag response decreased over the semester. By June, Connor could pick up poop without gagging. He even started describing the various consistencies, smells, and colours. Connor even predicted, based on the number of treats he had given to the dog during his first training session, what kind of poop the dog would excrete. Teens will often start discussing the various topics they once experienced as unfavourable. It is a coping mechanism that trains the mind to accept that these events are normal, thus turning the experience into a favourable outcome.

Connor had a breakthrough the day I told him I would adopt him.

Trust proves that if you allow teens to act according to their beliefs, they flourish. Yes, they will make mistakes, But if you support them, they will learn from their errors. Have you ever seen a perfect adult? I have not; we all make mistakes. We are humans, and with humanity comes a great responsibility. I partly stole that quote from Spiderman to illustrate my point. AAT changes the world, one animal at a time. The only ingredients we need to achieve our goal are unconditional love and a sense of humour. Without laughter, life is terribly sad.

In the following image, many things are occurring that you are unaware of, so let me point them out. Connor and Jacob never got along, but they were standing close to one another. Seymour hated groups and social contact, but we squeezed him in for his Lion King pose. Jacob smirked after telling a joke, and Calvin relaxed enough to remove the headphones from his ears. The magical thing about this picture is that all the teens are smiling. After one year of animal-assisted therapy, we changed *troubled teens* into happy young men, at least momentarily.

I took ten to fifteen pictures of this group, not because they were terrible photos. I took many photographs because I wanted the teens to feel happy for longer than a second. For half a minute, these young adults were free to be themselves, not judged by anyone, and relaxed enough to enjoy the present moment. I like to be silly because it demonstrates that adults, too, can enjoy themselves. Life is too short to live by unwritten rules and codes of conduct that curtail curiosity and creativity. My motivations often go unnoticed, but in my heart, I know we did the right thing by them; we showed up and cared.

Standing: Connor, Faith, Seymour, Jacob, Ann-Marie. Sitting: Calvin.

Connor's moment of glory came when we visited the Montreal Mounted Police. I wanted them to experience a new species and parallel their training with rats, dogs, and horses. Some students had never seen a horse up close and personal, so the experience was new for Connor and Calvin. Seymour had some experience with horses but not with the police. Teens within youth protection services, group homes, or foster care often have negative experiences with the police; consequently, being with the mounties and watching them train horses changed their perceptions.

The moment we arrived, Connor remained distant from the group.

Connor's reaction to the horses was so enlightening and joyful that we all cried, police included. I believed him when he whispered that he did not want to leave. I did not want him to go. To see humans change who they are within a fraction of a moment is like seeing the Big Bang. Suppose that experience had the power to change their lives, even at an infinite level. In that case, I believe conducting AAT is not only valuable, it is indispensable.

Our humanity is directly linked to the animals of this world. If you do not believe me, open your social media platform and look closely; you will observe people desperately seeking unconditional love from the human-animal connection. If we cannot be one with other humans, being one with animals is the next best thing for our humanity and the expression of our unity.

Connor did not need prescription glasses. His eyewear was his defence mechanism; he hid behind his transitional lenses to escape the pain of abandonment. Connor spent much time with his glasses on, even inside. I realized that his glasses and his backpack represented security. He never removed his backpack, even after I offered to put it on my back for the time being. So, when Connor removed his glasses, I was so happy for him. He subconsciously wanted to see, to experience without filter, the moment of pure connection between him and a horse. I knew he was grateful for the experience because his physical tensions disappeared.

Connor says his last goodbye to the horse without his glasses.

Connor's experience was his, and I hope he enjoyed it with all his being. I am happy to offer such opportunities, and before you say they are lucky, stop. AAT has nothing to do with luck. My team and I work hard to provide the fantastic opportunities we think will help us reach our goals and objectives.

I knock on doors and ask. I went to the mounted police headquarters and asked if they would allow us to bring our group. I explained what we did and who the teens were. They initially agreed, with a bit of reluctance, but in the end, they invited us back any day. The policewomen present were in tears and awe at how well-behaved and respectful these young men were.

There are so many small moments in AAT that you will never experience them again if you miss them. But, if you are attentive, the program becomes an awe-inspiring practice. When you add up the small changes over a year, you can see how hard these young adults have worked to get where they are. I miss the students who have left AAT, but I am happy to have met every single one of them. Another Connor moment was when we wanted to tell a story, but everybody was chattering. He desperately looked at me like a deer caught in the headlights.

The young man did not know what to do, so I gave him an example. Instead of shouting at the group to stop, I lifted my arm and gently said, *Silence, please*. It took a few seconds, but the teens policed themselves and quieted down. I looked at Connor and said; *The floor's all yours*. Without hesitation, he began telling his story.

I want to emphasize that I am not criticizing parents; we do our best with what we have at any given moment. Parenting is the most demanding job in the world, and AAT strives to fill in the gaps. We are not perfect, but our animals take over when or where we lack attention. We trained our AAT animals to step in; zootherapy animals are not; thus, they do not know how to take over the relationship.

Jacob

That said, not all cases are success stories. Teens change schools, parents relocate, or youth services move them, which puts an abrupt end to their passage in AAT. Another reason for poor outcomes is the length of the programs themselves. Some schools select the ten-week program, while others employ us year-round. One case that did not successfully end was that of a teen named Jacob. The school staff placed him in AAT for reasons I did not control. Jacob was a complicated case, with details I did not possess. When the school proposes a student for AAT, I ask the staff and other professionals to give me the necessary tools to do our job safely. What I knew about Jacob was that he had difficulty integrating into regular academic programs. He was one of the oldest members I had in AAT.

Jacob had anger management issues, which I later came to experience directly. He had a derogation to remain in school to receive his high school diploma. The mandatory education period in Quebec is sixteen years old; Jacob was nearly three years past that deadline. His age meant that Jacob was much older than our average teenager in AAT. He was almost eighteen when the outreach program coordinator placed him in my group. Although Jacob was in my class for two years, he never truly integrated or participated.

I know he listened to everything we were saying because he would laugh at my mom jokes. The young man would also follow us into the gymnasium and sometimes outside. However, he would spend 95% of his time on his cell phone or laptop. As long as he did not cause trouble, which he never actually did, I was OK with him being part of the *gang*. The older students are, the longer they have established their defence mechanisms and attachment styles. I never abandoned him; unfortunately, this adolescent was one of those people for whom AAT had come too late and could not help.

In retrospect, Jacob would have benefited from private sessions. It would have been easier for him to have forged an attachment away from judging minds and peer pressure. He identified as a specific persona, and we could not pull him away from the *character* he had built. The last two weeks of his passage in high school were the best we both had experienced. If only we had had more time.

Throughout his time in AAT, Jacob went through many difficulties, but the one incident that stands out was a fight that broke out. I want to write about it because it escalated into an avoidable event. In reality, I had the situation under control. I started the day as usual with training sessions, and we enjoyed a few discussions. The group went outside with the dogs for a bathroom break. I stayed inside with Jacob and Albear because our next activity was rat painting; I wanted to organize the room and prepare the equipment. Albear was older, and he no longer enjoyed walking without a purpose.

During the break, it was common for non-AAT students to come and pet the animals. This practice ended following this event. An unfamiliar student walked into class to pet Albear. Jacob asked him to leave because he had no business in *our room*. Although Jacob's original request was straightforward, he was not disrespectful. The student disagreed with the demand by swearing and threatening to kill him. Jacob stood and asked him to leave again, this time in a threatening way. At that moment, I decided to intervene. I placed myself between the two young men. I used negative reinforcement to persuade the gentleman to leave our classroom.

> *Therefore, in spite of the therapeutic benefits of AAT, with these youths it might not have the desired effect because their representations, however maladaptive, are deep-rooted and resistant to change.*
> —Balluerka et al., 2014

By this time, Jacob, the nineteen-year-old, and the fifteen-year-old student were spewing death threats and racial slurs at one another. I knew that if Jacob hit this kid, he was not going to regular jail; he was an adult and would be trialled as such. I did not want that for him. I managed to bring the student to the door frame with Albear in tow. My loyal dog had followed me, smelling trouble in the air. After a few more exchanges, Jacob was standing at the doorway, too, but he had his fist in the air a few inches from my face, threatening to kill the intruder.

I took a deep breath and softly said to Jacob *If you want to punch him, you'll have to go through him*, pointing down to Albear. Because it was break time, Albear did not have his vest on; he was a free dog. This fact reminded Jacob that this highly trained dog was not in service, so he could react if I ordered him to. Although completely false, the threat was enough for Jacob to think twice and return to his seat. Unfortunately, a teacher came to the class and grabbed the exiting student by the neck to force him into the hallway. This action immediately triggered Jacob. He got angry and stood up within a fraction of a second. Jacob, yelling to himself, walked out the door into the hallway, kicking the double doors and breaking its glass. The school suspended Jacob for two weeks because of this, but at least he did not punch the teen, effectively avoiding jail.

When social animals, humans included, get angry, pulling them away during conflict does not decrease the response; it increases. The situation did not require a teacher's intervention. The teen left without much protest, and Jacob returned to his seat. I never got a chance to talk to Jacob about the event, but I know why it started.

When the student came into class to pet Albear, Jacob interpreted the situation as someone taking value away, making him insecure and angry. AAT gave him something the other student did not have: an attachment. The unfamiliar student's presence threatened Jacob's connection to Alber, as fragile as it was, and he was unwilling to surrender that bond. Perceived loss always turns into anger. When I told Jacob he would have to go through me and Albear, he knew he risked losing a lot more. He risked losing his dog friend, attachment, and freedom.

He came back to class later on and was more relaxed with us. I think he recognized that someone was finally on his side. I have always told my son *I'll fight his battles, no questions asked, but never make me wrong for having done so*. I guess my mother's instincts kicked in to save the day. Most teens want respect. Jacob knew who was honest and who was not. Nothing had changed between us and the other participants. The human heart remains the same; it wants to love and be loved.

Jacob had another minor incident during his last year, but nothing serious. That time, I made sure I handled it my way. This event concerned Connor. The situation unravelled during a session in the gymnasium. The students were training the dogs for Dogball, a game we invented together. Connor worked with Albear, and Jacob was sitting on a bench, busy on his cell phone. Jacob took it upon himself to start degrading and teasing Connor. The latter was getting frustrated and agitated. I asked the young man, *What do we do when dogs are acting silly, annoying, goofy, or rambunctious?* He replied *We ignore them!* I added *This is what you need to be doing; ignore Jacob. Do you remember why?* His reply was gold. He said something along the lines of *We ignore the dog, so it doesn't add fuel to the fire.*

I smiled, and he knew what I meant. He did another trial with Albear, and this time he was successful. I told him to end his session on a good note and to take a break. I added that I needed to go to the bathroom and that he should completely ignore Jacob until I returned.

My need to go to the bathroom was a ruse. Instead, I went to see the director of the outreach programs. I asked him if he could come nonchalantly get Jacob in 5 minutes. I returned to the gymnasium and sat with Connor. The director asked Jacob, without making any fuss, to go and help them in the kitchen. Connor did not need to know I intervened on his behalf because I wanted him to learn that ignoring other people's unpleasant behaviour does make it cease. My second lesson for Connor was that if he found out I intervened, he could rely on adults to act on his behalf; there was no reason to scream profanity, and grownups could be trustworthy.

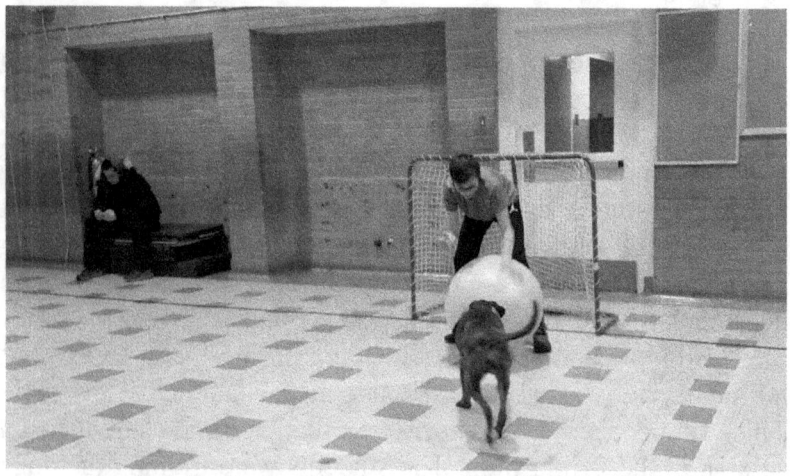

Jacob (left). Connor (right) works with Albear on Dogball.

Jacob, to this day, has no idea I intervened either. My reason was to prevent Jacob from feeling unwanted and abandoned for his bad behaviour, which would have fueled the fire. He felt the gymnasium feeling wanted and appreciated for something. Kids and teenagers do not always need to know why things happen; people require respect, confidence, happiness, and appreciation for who they are. If we continuously mettled and told kids we purposefully did so, it would intensify the negative feelings they often already have towards themselves.

I do not know what Jacob's were about, nor is it essential that I do. All that matters is that we did our best with what we had to work with. However, I can report to you that I surprised him on his last day. He was sitting on a chair in the corner of the classroom with his cell, and I decided to train Albear to tap on his phone in exchange for petting. I can shape behaviour from a distance, so I sent Albear in his direction. In no time, Albear figured out what I was up to and started to touch the phone, but Jacob ignored him, which Albear dispised.

On the last send-off, Albear tapped the phone. Realizing Jacob refused to interact with Albear, the veteran AAT dog decided to improvise. Albear went over to Jacob and perfectly tapped on the cell phone. When Albear didn't get the desired response, he stepped back and uttered a deep growl at Jacob, who immediately looked at Albear. The young man looked at me, confused. I explained to Jacob that Albear wanted to be acknowledged, so he did. For the first time in two years, the recluse student patted Albear's neck. My little dogo returned as happy as could be and got a gigantic reward.

Letting dogs improvise is essential in AAT because the animal might solve a problem in a way we did not think of. Throughout the years, each dog in the program has, at some point, improvised and got highly rewarded for it. Never let your dog always do what you want them to do; let them come up with new ideas and solutions; you will be surprised at how often they think of novel behaviours.

During his last year, I teased Jacob that I would get a picture of him smiling. He would give me his *piss-off* face, and I would respond with a wink and a smile. He did not know how patient I was. You can see in the Photo Annex that I got my photo and a smile to the extent that Jacob smirked. I see victories in every moment, even if they are infinitely small. I can build from that, but we cannot create from anything. At least, that is how I see life. It was strange to see an empty seat the following school year. I missed Jacob's mischief in our group.

A video screenshot of the moment Albear growled at Jacob.

Wolf Animal-Assisted Therapy

Barely out of adolescence, Michael and Jessie were two young participants in the wolf animal-assisted therapy (WAAT) pilot project—a program designed to establish an attachment faster than domestic animals. With dogs, rats, and horses, teenagers started coming out of their shells between six and ten weeks. With wolves, that connection required half the time. The reason is simple: they could kill us if they wanted to. That knowledge keeps the mind in the eternal present. No ego-wandering, also known as self-sabotage, occurs in the mind. In a wolf enclosure, the self-fulfilling prophecy ceases to exist.

My initial goal with the pilot project was to conduct a run-through of the program to identify what parts were functional and what aspects needed improvement or modification. Without practical application, hypotheses remain just that. I had contact with Park Safari in Hemmingford, where I had previously socialized wolves for ambassador programs. I contacted the manager and discussed what I envisioned the wolf animal-assisted therapy program to become. The management agreed, and I reached out to my media friends.

TV5 filmed the first interaction for Les Guérisseurs (The Healers), a French television documentary. You can find the link at the end in the Contact Information section. We had a large group of young adults to choose from, so we needed to make some selections. We selected three participants; unfortunately, one was removed because of a substance abuse relapse and stopped attending the Youth Employment Hub (YEH).

Ultimately, we only selected two people; therefore, my colleague and I picked specific criteria to refine our selection. Presence was the number one condition; the person had to show up. It was hard to take them seriously if they were not present for their appointments or meetings. The second criterion was remaining sober.

When people stopped attending scheduled events, it was often because of relapses. The YEH had rules concerning substance abuse, and so did I. I could not allow people under the influence into a wolf enclosure for safety concerns. Finally, respect for peers, staff, and oneself was mandatory. The participants needed to trust us and their peers as we trusted them.

Michael

Micheal was a young man who overindulged in life's guilty pleasures. Drug and alcohol consumption had taken over his life, and he was heading toward the proverbial brick wall at an alarming rate. A psychologist referred the young man to the local YEH in downtown Montreal. The YEH is a resource-based center focused on developing life skills. The organization provides young adults with various employment possibilities, from writing a Curriculum Vitae (CV) to filling in a tenancy agreement and cooking. Micheal demonstrated his dedication to the Hub by working on the various developmental programs suggested to him.

Michael remained sober throughout the program, which was a safety requirement. I remember Michael asking me during a session if his tattoo would be problematic for the wolves. I answered that he would be okay because our wolves had not learned to read yet. The word on his arm was that of an ex-girlfriend, so he laughed. Micheal was the perfect candidate for the WAAT program, so we placed him on the list. Plus, I loved his sense of humour. When wolves want to *hang around*, having jokes to tell comes in handy.

Ten years ago, I uploaded the WAAT episode from TV5 to YouTube. Michael commented that he would never forget the experience. True to his word, on the tenth anniversary day, Micheal commented again, stating *Ten years later, I am doing very well :D – Michael*.

Jessie

By the time I met this young lady. Jessie had been through a lot. She had been homeless, fighting addiction and depression. Her psychologist referred her to the YEH. We integrated the young woman into the group because of her commitment and desire to change her life. Jessie attended every class, meeting, or appointment that would move her path forward. I admired her motivation and her curiosity. Her desire to change her life around was palpable and authentic. She knew her limitations and was outspoken about them.

My colleague kept me posted on her case progress. There are often setbacks in recovering from addiction, but Jessie wanted me to choose her for the WAAT program. Even though she struggled, she managed to stay sober. Before she relapsed, we decided to include her in the WAAT program. We reasoned that telling her I accepted her candidacy into WAAT would motivate her to stay sober longer. It worked.

Making WAAT History

We picked Jessie and Michael for their dedication to YEH and themselves and their desire to meet wolves in front of the world. When Michael learned about meeting the wolves, he became overwhelmed with excitement. Wolves were his favourite animal, and he would not let this opportunity slip through his hands. He talked about it constantly, making him smile every time. Jessie's response was similar, but her love included all the animals.

Although I required 48 hours of soberness, we extended the prerequisite to four weeks. The group finished their regular programs, and we switched them over to WAAT. We first met to talk about their expectations and the event schedule. Safety was one aspect of meeting wolves, but there were other criteria. Participants could not braid their hair, wear leather, or have shiny objects like watches or jewellery, shorts, open-toed shoes, and flowy clothing. Wolves are experts at spotting things they want, and they are unequivocal thieves.

Canis lupus has mastered the art of grab-and-go. First, they greet people and pretend to sniff them, but they are searching for prizes. Once they find something they want, they test the person. Wolves can poke, push, paw, nibble, pull, or rip to see how a person reacts. If people respond suddenly, they have confirmed to the wolf that the object is indeed valuable. Once you release the thing, a wolf's next move is to grab it and run. Wolves regularly steal mittens, gloves, beanies (tuques), tissues, snacks, glasses, and whatever hangs from one's hands.

Wotan once tried to steal my treat bag. I gently placed my hand on the pouch and said *Mine!* He looked up at me, and I softly said *You will have to fight me to the death.* Knowing perfectly well that I would never win that struggle, I had previously attached my pouch with a quick release. If he had truly wanted it, he would have taken it. Wolves are like British gentlemen; their intentions are clear, but they respect your wishes. Dogs, on the other hand, are unmannered hooligans.

Michael and Jessie received dog behaviour and training classes to prepare them for the big event. When I designed this program, I never thought we would be doing our first session for a television documentary. Consequently, I modified the program to adapt to our reality. On the morning of the event, I had to give a crash course to the television staff on safety, movements, and how to safeguard their equipment. The wolves had previously been on television; however, they were outside their habitat, which is very different from entering their home.

Jessie and Michael enter with me behind them.

My primary concern was the windshield microphone cover; it looked like a little furry creature with which the wolves would have wanted to appropriate themselves. So we made sure we prepared for the possibility. Thankfully, we noticed the wolves' eyes focus on the microphone and instructed the person to raise the perch upwards. No microphones were harmed during this filming. The television crew entered the enclosure with wireless equipment, which meant they would have to swipe batteries.

Another problem we encountered was the heat. We filmed the episode on July 21, the hottest day on record, at the time. It was a wapping 36°C in the shade with a humidity index of 77%. The temperature felt by our bodies was 54°C. I would have rescheduled if it were not for the television crew, but we moved forward. We did not have water bottles because wolves would have stolen them; we had shade and much patience, so we proceeded.

Jessie, in a deep reflection in the wolves' enclosure.

After the animal behaviour crash course, the television team and the group moved toward the enclosure. We conducted a few interviews along the way, which distracted Jessie and Michael from getting overly excited and overwhelmed at the same time. Once we arrived at the wolves' pen, everybody reacted like those before them who agreed to enter such a cage. People about to walk into a wolf enclosure gasp, squeeze their gluteus maximus muscles, nervously giggle, and often say *Why did I agree to do this? What in god's name possessed me to do this?* No worries, it is a natural reaction.

Excitement builds, nervousness intensifies, and questioning one's life decisions, up until this moment, are reviewed in .30 seconds. This realization has three reactions: freeze, fight, or flight. Everybody freezes, then decides to fight (move forward) or flight (leave). The camera crew was the first to enter because they wanted to film Jessie and Michael coming in. We moved the equipment and passed it on to the regular staff. The television crew was next. Some of the men were excited to meet the wolves, but one of them was reluctant. He was insecure and jokingly said he did not want to die. I smiled and reassured him.

We are discussing relationships and anticipation.

We always allow the wolves to investigate whatever comes into their enclosure. It is their habitat, after all. The crew was nervous, for nobody had ever conducted wolf animal-assisted therapy before. I expected their reaction because the team could not look out for themselves. We were their eyes, ears, and bodyguards; they needed to trust us, so they did. We had planned for any eventuality, most of which the participants and television crew were unaware of. Calming the mind is quite the endeavour when filming and watching out for wolves trying to steal your equipment.

Both Micheal and Jessie froze between the gates. Jessie decided to confront her fears and enter. Before walking into the enclosure, she told me that meeting wolves would probably never reoccur; thus, she would rather die happy than miss the opportunity. I laughed and assured Jessie that no one had ever died. Michael was excited and entered first with Jessie in toe. We made our way to a rock and sat on it. We remained there for the next two hours. It was excruciatingly hot and humid. We had to film at high noon to avoid as many shadows as possible, which meant it was the hottest part of the day. Thank goodness the humidity had dropped from 95% the previous day, which made it a little more tolerable.

Michael gets liked by Akiak.

The wolves were hot and did not want to interact much, but the group understood our constraints. As I always say, *We're on animal time!* Wolves are no different; we can not force them to interact. Regardless, I made parallels with their lives. We talked about the many challenges they had faced and what lay ahead. We discussed relationships, work, school, addiction, recovery, and self-care; every topic was on the agenda. Then, out of the blue, Jessie and Michael had a profound realization about their respective life.

Michael realized relationships take time to establish. We cannot appreciate the minor, more joyful moments that build memories when we force or precipitate things. Michael moved too fast, fearing he would miss out on life; consequently, he missed many simple moments. The young man also realized he needed to take his time to find the right job. Michael was able to acknowledge, through his interaction with the wolves, that anticipation is an integral part of life. If we cannot long for something, events are merely consumed, not enjoyed. Within one two-hour session, two wolves changed a young man's life forever. Years later, he still was grateful for the WAAT program and what he had learned and experienced.

Jessie gets licked by Akiak.

Jessie's realizations were similar but focused more on her family and running away from home. During the session, she described how *wild* she had been all these years. I took the opportunity to ask her if she considered wolves as wild. She admitted she believed all the wolf propaganda recited in books, stories, television, movies, social media, and people in general. However, Jessie added she was astonished at how well-behaved wolves indeed were. She spontaneously exclaimed *They're nothing like what people say!* I added *Just like you're not what other people say.* Her look was worth all the gold in the world. Sometimes, you need a wolf to teach you who you really are.

Jessie was introverted during the session, while Michael became the extroverted. Wolves have strange effects on people, mainly because they keep people in the present moment. Self-actualization occurs in the eternal now, and I believe Jessie became self-aware that day. The young lady later told me she realized she could accomplish whatever her mind conjured. Living on the street was easy, she thought aloud. I commended her for her bravery and self-preservation. I would summarize substance abuse as silencing one's mind to avoid the heart's pain. Wolves reach the heart by quieting the mind, which is why WAAT is such a powerful approach to healing.

After a few more human-wolf exchanges, it was time to exit and let the wolves rest. We left the enclosure in the opposite order we had entered. The television crew headed out first and the staff last. Michael came out of the pen before Jessie and felt lightheaded, not from the heat, but from all the emotions he experienced in two hours. He needed a moment to introspect, so I turned to Jessie. Her comment was *I feel like going back to school just to be able to do what you do.* My answer was, *Why not?*

> "Sometimes you gotta say 'What the Fuck' and make your move. Joel, every now and then, saying 'What the Fuck' brings freedom. Freedom brings opportunity. Opportunity makes your future."
>
> —Miles, Risky Business, 1983

I love working with animals, but wolves hold a special place in my heart. From watching them in the wild to being in their presence, sharing that moment alone makes a person question their existence. Michael and Jessie broke the ice on a project I knew would be successful because I have been through it as a child, a teen, and now an adult. Working with wolves is my calling, and I want to share that with teens and young adults needing acceptance and guidance. When people understand that wolves serve a purpose by keeping ecosystems functional and robust, perceptions change.

You see, adolescents relate to wolves because of the way society perceives them. Wolves are dire, disorderly, vicious, murderous animals whose only thoughts are persecution and destruction of others. I might be exaggerating their description; however, many countries have killed, to extinction, their wolf populations, primarily out of fear and misunderstanding. Teens think adults view them as wild wolves; Michael was the first to point it out. When we entered the enclosure, he hid his arm, a reflex he had developed to avoid judgment. I told him not to worry; wolves were unaffected by trivial things like body ink.

Everyone who has come and gone from the wolf or dog animal-assisted therapy was changed just as much as they have changed us. Teens remind us of the challenges we went through at their age, and those memories motivate us to offer services unavailable to us. Animals are our allies, not our enemies. We share the same planet and benefit from one another, but to live in symbiosis, we must first understand what animals tell us.

Michael quickly learned to observe the wolves and asked why they lay next to us even though they could be elsewhere. I responded that *they were as curious about you as you were about them!* They enjoy our company, which is the first step to friendship. The seven steps to friendship are: know me, trust me, love me, embrace me, help me, use me, and thank me (Walsch, 1999).

> "Dogs are not our whole life, but they make our lives whole."
>
> —*Roger Caras*

Chapter 5

The future of AAI

Animals are excellent teachers; thus, the future of AAIs seems secure. However, I believe it is the responsibility of practitioners to ensure the safety, education, and documentation of their participants. Every person who currently conducts or plans on running AAIs must ensure the well-being of their clients and animals—professionals frown upon thrill-seeking and improvised human and animal encounters. In collaboration with provinces, the Canadian government has started to limit direct contact with exotic animals because of uneducated and irresponsible people.

If one person in an AAI program got injured, even slightly, the practice could, and most likely would, disintegrate. The government would discredit AAIs, and insurance companies would refuse to cover us. Dangerous exchanges are one of the reasons I cringe when I hear of ill-prepared volunteers who visit hospitals or palliative establishments without knowledge of animal behaviour or training. Such people place our profession at risk. We must call them out and encourage them to seek educational programs. Read these words as a call to action.

The human-animal bond is nothing more than accepting that we are one. The purity of that connection uplifts people; thus, people can rise above their mental health disorders and start to heal. Knowledge is power, and through proper channels, we can all agree to make AAIs the best practices available for our clients.

You can argue we are all different, which would be an undeniable fact, but based on what? Our external differences are only skin deep. Every human on earth struggles with the same problem: filling the void, the emptiness, or the loneliness. With the underlying knowledge and experience AAIs bring, that emptiness feels whole, complete, fulfilled, and accomplished. The sensation that you are one with the universe, the state of being in which time stops, is who we are. The unconditional love between animals and people fills the void, teaching us how to love unconditionally. The magic of AAI teaches people to love each other categorically, making us holy.

Einstein once argued that travelling at the speed of light stopped time, but what if thought was faster? What if love and time were a single force? What if love, time, and thought were one combined universal energy? Would you not want to stand still in peaceful contemplation for all eternity? The energy that flows between species is nothing more than universal energy manifested in a different shape. In the song Race (1994), Prince sang, *"I mark human, cut me, cut you, both the blood is red."* Love cannot be found in anyone else because another human cannot fill you with love. Only you have the power to love yourSelf, and when you do, sharing it with others will come as naturally as breathing.

Student sitting with Akiak in peaceful contemplation.

I recommend sitting on a park bench with someone and not saying or doing anything. Simply be. If time stops, you are genuinely in love, not the ego's distorted concept of love, but in loving energy where time stops. When I write, train, paint, garden, fix things, build things, meditate, or read, time ceases to move forward. What makes you say *where did the time go?* AAT makes time stop for the teens in our program. Participants who have partaken in AAT mentioned one thing: Time flies, which means it stopped. I remember a nasty winter snowstorm a few years back. The schools did not close, so we were heading to class as usual. When we arrived, the only people present were the principal, the janitor, two teachers, and most students. When I entered the classroom, we were alone. Connor heard my voice and came into class. His exact words were *You came?* At that moment, he learned we cared enough to show up. The teens in AAT deserve all we can offer and then some.

Katye (AAT staff) gets checked out by Akiak.

Let me end with a little story about my childhood. Once, I was lying on our male German Mastiff called Alexander. My head was on his body, where it rested most of the time. He was breathing after a play session. I remember consciously breathing slowly to see if Alexander would imitate me. Not only did he slow his respiration, but he also lifted his head and looked at me. I told him I wanted to knap. He lay his head down and slowed his breathing even more; I fell asleep. I now know this is a natural response in canids, but I was five years old when I did this. My point is that if a young child can make conscious decisions that modify dog behaviour, surely, we can make those same conscious decisions as adults and change human behaviour for the better.

I have always been intrigued and captivated by human and animal interactions. Hard work blessed me with the many opportunities I experienced in the last thirty years, none of which I regret. Those interactions cumulated in AAT, and without animals in my life, I, too, would be as lost as the teens we help each year. My goal is to continue and serve many more of them. In the meantime, I hope you can find peace in your human-animal interactions as I do with mine; after all, the word dog in the mirror is god.

Student looking over Ruby's back.

Maybe some women aren't meant to be tamed. Maybe they just need to run free until they find someone just as wild to run with them.
　　　　　　　　　　　　—Carrie Bradshaw

Making Changes

I started writing this book in March 2020, at the beginning

of the pandemic. I wrote over 90% of the book in three months. However, it took me a few extra years to complete because I wanted to finish a few cases to include in the book. By now, the teens are all adults, and I can write their stories without worrying about breaching anonymity. Based on their release forms, I was allowed to publish and share their photos on social media. I excluded participants under government care, such as Youth Protection Services or the Judicial System, from this book.

Throughout my years in various high schools, I realized it does not take much to change a teen's life. If you remember your adolescence, what are some of the words or actions that would, or have, made a difference? Your answers are the same for your teens. Put down your phones, tablets, and computers to be with your kids. Being involved is as simple as asking questions. Never stop asking, especially with boys. When my son was a young teen, I asked him how his day went; the dialogue unravelled as follows.

    Me: How was your day?
    Son: Good.
    M: What did you do?
    S: Math, English, History.
    M: What did you learn?
    S: Stuff.
    M: What kind of stuff?
    S: I don't know.
    M: Tell me one thing you learned in English.
    S: The teacher is incompetent.
    M: Why do you say that?
    S: She doesn't know how to pronounce Tuesday.
    M: Hun?
    S: She says it's pronounced Tooz-day.
    M: Well, that's just wrong. What did you do?
    S: I argued with her, and she wrote you a note.
    M: Can I see it?
    S: [hands note]
    M: It says that you're argumentative and that I should see the principal.
    S: Please don't.

M: Then I'll write her a note stating the etymology of Tuesday and Argumentation. How does that sound?
S: Okay, I guess.
[code word for yes]
Me: Done!

I wrote the note. My son gave it to his teacher, and I never heard about it again. I also confirmed with my son that she had dropped the subject. Follow-ups are vital to maintaining a trusting relationship. Our dialogue resumed, and we discussed another topic; it is essential to note that this conversation occurred while we were doing the dishes. Women externalize their emotions, while men internalize them. Men, in general, like to talk while doing something. A hands-on event is a great time to chat. Folding laundry, eating, walking, commuting, and cooking are my favourite times to talk. Plus, these tasks teach teens how to be autonomous in the future. I often take my nearly thirty-year-old son to eat to catch up on life.

When your children, regardless of their age, need your help, show up. When you say something, do it; if not, do not mention it. Parenting is about building trust, not handing out money or expensive things such as technology or clothing. We bond with our students because of these simple rules. Not because we hand out treats or gift baskets at Halloween or Christmas; those are bonus rewards, not trust-building things. Another good rule to implement is to say what the consequence of an action will be ahead of time. If you can not think of one, ask the teen. They are highly talented at self-assessing punishments. Once in place, be ready to act and implement the consequences. If you do not, you will have lost your teen's trust.

Would your life have been different if your parents had followed those two simple rules? I know mine would. My team and I apply these instructions in AAT. Soon enough, teens start to police themselves using the same guidelines. I firmly believe teachers should not parent other people's children. That said, we are not teachers; we never impose our ideas or beliefs. Schools contact us because teens need help understanding who they are, and we provide such a service.

Students are working with Hariette and Penny in the background.

Petting dogs or other animals is not a form of therapy. I get backlash for this statement, but I stand by it. I have seen too many dogs placed in dangerous situations for the sake of calling it therapy. I have also witnessed dogs bite people in petting frenzies. Claiming the bite did not hurt does not render the event harmless. In structured AAIs, people carefully select, train, and conduct sessions. They give great importance to socialization and continuous training to maintain behaviours. Suppose a practitioner notices a regression in behaviour. In that case, they remove the animal from their sessions until the behaviour is functional again. The adage that *a team is only as strong as its weakest member* applies in this case.

> "You know, it's moments like these when I realize what a superhero I am."
> —Tony Stark (Iron Man 3, 2013).

I hope every animal involved in AAIs, specifically AATs and their handlers, lives by this quote. Dogs give us a sense of humanity and humility that we forget as we hyperfocus on a virtual world. Put away your cell phones or tablets, sit with your child, regardless of age, and tell them how proud you are of them. Ask questions, do chores together, ride a bicycle or walk the dog and tell them how much you love them. From my vantage point, they need you more than ever.

The Art of Living

Animal-assisted activities are increasing in popularity because they achieve the end goals we set forth. The critical takeaway is that practitioners must educate themselves in human sciences to conduct feasible and efficient sessions. Without tracking progress, there is no therapy, for the word implies that a treatment intends to relieve or heal a disorder.

Petting an animal or watching fish is relaxing; however, we do not consider zootherapy therapeutic because there is no purpose to restore or alleviate emotional suffering. AAIs reply directly on their intention to conduct their sessions. My AAT primary goal is to develop and maintain communication skills. If we let participants pet animals, they would never talk to us. If I ask them to describe the dog's feelings, then I am purposefully manipulating the outcome of their behaviour. Fundamentally, I am telling our students that I will reward them if they participate in the discussion.

Bringing a dog to school for students to interact with is, in my opinion, a disservice to the dog. My reasoning is that these animals have little to no training on how to interact with emotional humans. The dog often becomes highly stressed and insecure, leading to aggressive responses or, worse, to learned helplessness. Before you embark on the journey to AAI, I urge you to consider your objective. Making people feel good is too general of a goal to include animals. The risk of an accident is too probable to be statistically ignored.

The animal-assisted journey is a humbling adventure that soon becomes a way of living. Our animal partners are our livelihood, and I hope it remains as such, for I would be beyond saddened to see the practice end. We work zealously to implement strategic plans; thus, maximizing education is in our best interest. I am responsible for ensuring my animals' lives are as rich and fulfilling as mine.

Without animals, there is no animal-assisted therapy.

Photo Annex

Alexander and Lua
RIP 2011- 2019

Alessandro is goofing off with Chica.

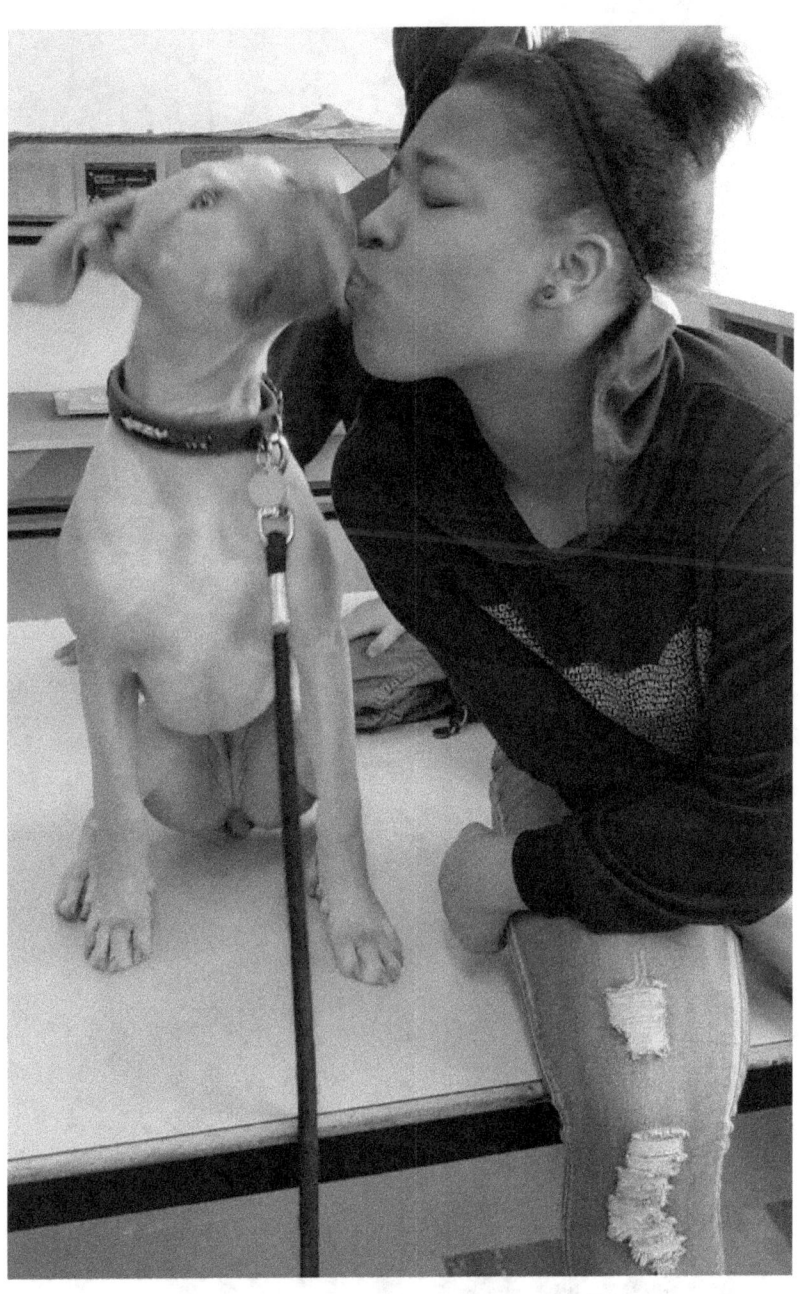

Markayla gets a kiss from Ivy.

When I asked Rayvon for a smile.

But Wild Bill showed up instead.

Calvin and Mandu.

Karlo was lost in thought with Charlotte, the one-eyed rat, in his hoodie.

Hariette meets Seymour for the first time.

Connor and Albear proudly pose after a game of Dogball.

Jacob smiles with a puppy in training for AAT.

Helene gets wolf kisses from Akiak.

Hariette is the 1st Broholmer and AAT ambassador in Canada.

Bibliography

Ager, S. (2023, 03 15). *Luwian language and script.* Retrieved 04 23, 2023, from Omniglot: https://omniglot.com/writing/luwian.htm

Ainsworth, M. D. (1978). *Patterns of attachment: A psychological study of the strange situation.* Hillsdale, N.J.: Erlbaum.

Ainsworth. M. and Bowlby, J. (1992). The origins of attachment theory: John Bowlby and Mary Ainsworth. *Developmental Psychology*, 759–775.

Anders Hviid, J. V. (2019). Mumps, Rubella Vaccination and Autism: A Nationwide Cohort Study. *Ann Intern Med., 170*, 513-520. doi:10.7326/M18-2101

Anderson, R. (2019). *When Harry Became Sally: Responding to the Transgender Moment.* New York, New York, United States: Encounter Books.

——. (2023). *Praise for When Harry Became Sally.* (B. a. UK, Producer) Retrieved 04 05, 2023, from NOOK Tablets: https://nook.barnesandnoble.com/products/9781641770491/sample?sourceEan=9781641770484

APA. (2013). *Diagnostic and Statistical Manual of Mental Disorders (5th ed.) (DSM-5).* Washington, DC: Author.

Bagnall, R. (2009). *Practical Help: Chronology, Geography, Measures, Currency, Names, Prosopography, and Technical Vocabulary, The Oxford Handbook of*

Papyrology. Oxford: Oxford University Press.

Body Dysmorphic Disorder. (2021). Retrieved 11 10, 2022, from NHS: https://www.nhs.uk/mental-health/conditions/body-dysmorphia/

Britannica, E. E. (2014, 05 12). *Suppiluliumas I*. Retrieved from Encyclopedia Britannica: https://www.britannica.com/biography/Suppiluliumas-I

Collection of Evidence-based Practices for Children and Adolescents with Mental Health Treatment Needs. (2017). Disruptive Impulse-control and Conduct Disorders. *Virginia Commission on Youth*, pp. 1-18.

Cruse, H. (2006). Neural Networks as Cybernetic Systems. *Brains, Minds & Media*.

Dhejne C, L. P. (2011). Long-Term Follow-Up of Transsexual Persons Undergoing Sex Reassignment Surgery: Cohort Study in Sweden. *6*(2), 1-8 e16885. doi:https://doi.org/10.1371/journal.pone.0016885

DSM-5. (2016, 06). *Implications for Child Serious Emotional Disturbance*, DSM-IV to DSM-5. (S. A. Services, Editor) Retrieved 11 10, 2022, from National Library of Medicine: https://www.ncbi.nlm.nih.gov/books/NBK519712/table/ch3.t19/

Dufresne-Cyr, G. (2018). *Dog in the Mirror is God: A Scientifically Spiritual Approach to Treating Human and Animal Behaviour*. (A. Editing, Ed.) Montreal,

Quebec, Canada: Dogue Shop Publishing.

Dyslexia Canada. (2023). *Dyslexia Basics*. Retrieved 01 25, 2023, from Dyslexia Canada: https://www.dyslexiacanada.org/en/dyslexia-basics#:~:text=How%20common%20is%20dyslexia%3F,reading%2C%20writing%20and%20spelling%20difficulties.

Edwards, A. E. (2022). Using robot animal companions in the academic library to mitigate student stress. *Library Hi Tech., 40*(4), 878-893. doi:10.1108/LHT-

Erikson, E. (1959). *Identity and the life cycle.* (N. Paperback, Ed.) New York, New York, United States: International Univiersities Press Inc.

——. (1963). *Childhood and society (2nd Ed.).* New York: Norton.

Feige, K. (Producer), Pearce, S. B. (Writer), & Black, S. (Director). (2013). *Iron Man 3* [Motion Picture]. United States.

Garg G, E. G. (2022, 10 16). *Gender Dysphoria*. (S. Publishing, & T. I. (FL), Producers) Retrieved from National Library of Medicine: https://www.ncbi.nlm.nih.gov/books/NBK532313/

Gender dysphoria. (2017). Retrieved 04 05, 2023, from National Health Service: https://www.nhs.uk/conditions/gender-dysphoria/#:~:text=Gender%20dysphoria%20is%20a%

20term,harmful%20impact%20on%20daily%20life.

Hafeez, D. T. (2022, 09 15). *The heyoka empath traits | heyoka traits*. Retrieved from Dr. Tahira Rubab Hafeez | Best Psychologist in Lahore: https://tahirarubabhafeez.com/blog/the-heyoka-empath-traits-heyoka-traits

Jon Avnet, S. T. (Producer), Brickman, P. (Writer), & Brickman, P. (Director). (1983). *Risky Business* [Motion Picture]. United States.

Koplewicz, H. (2023). *What are Disruptive, Impulse Control and Conduct Disorders?* Retrieved from American Psychiatric Associaton: https://www.psychiatry.org/patients-families/disruptive-impulse-control-and-conduct-disorders/what-are-disruptive-impulse-control-and-conduct

Korte, M. (2020). The impact of the digital revolution on human brain and behavior: where do we stand? *Dialogues in Clinical Neuroscience, 22*(2), 101-111. doi:10.31887/DCNS.2020.22.2/mkorte

Logan, J. (2018, 04 18). *The Equine Herald of a New Age*. Retrieved from The Current: https://www.news.ucsb.edu/2018/018903/equine-herald-new-age

Lorenz, K. (1950). The comparative method in studying innate behaviour patterns. *Symposia of the Society for*

Experimental Biology, 4, 221–268.

———. (1970). *Studies in Animal and Human Behaviour, Vol 1.* London, United Kingdom: Methuen.

———. (1970). *Studies in Animal and Human Behaviour, Vol 2.* Cambridge, Massachusett, United States: Harvard University Press.

———. (1974). *On Aggression* (1st ed.). (M. K. Wilson, Trans.) London, United Kingdom: Harvest Book.

Madison Aitken, D. P. (2016, 06). Self-Harm and Suicidality in Children Referred for Gender Dysphoria. *Journal of the American Academy of Child & Adolescent Psychiatry, 55*(6), 513-520. doi:10.1016/j.jaac.2016.04.001

MrNuclearCat (Director). (2012). *Golden eagle snatches kid* [Motion Picture]. Montreal, Canada: YouTube. Retrieved from https://www.youtube.com/watch?v=CE0Q904gtMI

Nina Jøranson, I. P. (2015). Effects on Symptoms of Agitation and Depression in Persons With Dementia Participating in Robot-Assisted Activity: A Cluster-Randomized Controlled Trial. *Journal of the American Medical Directors Association, 16*(10), 867-873. doi:10.1016/j.jamda.2015.05.002.

Phillips, K. (2022, 11 10). *Prevalence of BDD*. Retrieved from International OCD Foundation: https://bdd.iocdf.org/professionals/prevalence/

Powell L, R. C. (2021). Characterizing unsuccessful animal

adoptions: age and breed predict the likelihood of return, reasons for return and post-return outcomes. *Sci Rep., 11*(1), 8018. doi:10.1038/s4159

Prady, C. L. (Producer). (2009). *The Gothowitz Deviation* [Motion Picture]. USA: CBS.

Preston Foerder, M. R. (2021, 4 1). The Effect of Therapy Dogs on Preoperative Anxiety. *Anthrozoös, 34*(5), 659-670. doi:10.1080/08927936.2021.1914440

Reesor L, V. E. (2017, August 11). Addressing Outcomes Expectancies in Behavior Change. *Am J Lifestyle Med., 11*(6), 430-432. doi:10.1177/1559827617722504.

Richard W. Burkhardt, J. (2005). *Patterns of Behavior Konrad Lorenz, Niko Tinbergen, and the Founding of Ethology.* Chicago: Chicago Press.

Rubinstein, G. (1995). The decision to remove homosexuality from the DSM: twenty years later. *Am J Psychother., 49*(3), 416-427. doi:10.1176/appi.psychotherapy.1995.49.3.416.

Schwartz, R. O. (2015). *Love and the Brain.* Retrieved 03 15, 2023, from Harvard Medical School: https://hms.harvard.edu/news-events/publications-archive/brain/love-brain#:~:text=Being%20love%2Dstruck%20also%20releases,use%20of%20cocaine%20or%20alcohol.

The Daily — Survey on Mental Health and Stressful Events, August to December 2021. (2022). Retrieved 01 13,

2023, from Statistic Canada: https://www150.statcan.gc.ca/n1/daily-quotidien/220520/dq220520b-eng.htm

Thomas, P. (2019). *Oklahoma State University Libraries*. (O. S. Libraries, Editor) Retrieved 11 10, 2022, from 2.2 Social Development: Erikson's Eight Psychosocial Crise.: https://open.library.okstate.edu/foundationsofeducationaltechnology/chapter/7-social-development-eriksons-eight-psychosocial-crises/

Topál. J, M. A. (1998). Attachment behavior in dogs (Canis familiaris): A new application of Ainsworth's (1969) Strange Situation Test. *Journal of Comparative Psychology, 112*(3), 219. doi:10.1037%2F0735-7036.112.3.219

Tuarez, J. (2023, 02 21). *When does the brain stop developing or fully develop?* Retrieved from Neurotray: https://neurotray.com/when-does-the-brain-stop-developing-or-fully-develop/

Understanding mental disorders: Your guide to DSM-5. (2015). Arlington, Virginia, USA.

Walsch, N. D. (1999). *Friendship with God, an uncommon dialogue.* New York, New York, United States: Berkley.

Wiepjes CM, d. H. (2020). Trends in suicide death risk in transgender people: results from the Amsterdam Cohort of Gender Dysphoria study (1972-2017). *Acta Psychiatr Scand. , 141*(6), 486-491. doi:10.1111/acps.13164

Youth, V. C. (2017). Disruptive impulse-control and conduct disorders. *Collection of Evidence-based Practices for Children and Adolescents with Mental Health Treatment Needs*, pp. 1-18. Retrieved from http://vcoy.virginia.gov/documents/collection/021%20 Disruptive%20ODD2.pdf

Ziskin, L. (Producer), Schulman, T. (Writer), & Oz, F. (Director). (1991). *What About Bob?* [Motion Picture]. United States: Buena Vista Pictures Distribution.

References

Ainsworth, M. S. (1979). Infant-mother attachment. *American Psychologist, 34*(10), 932-937. doi: 10.1037/0003-066X.34.10.932

——. (1991). Attachment and other affectional bonds across the life cycle. In C.M. Parkes, J. Stevenson-Hinde, & P. Marris (Eds.). *Attachment across the life cycle.* 33–51. New York, NY: Routledge.

Ainsworth, M.D.S., Blehar, M.C., Waters, E., & Wall, S. (1978). *Patterns of attachment: Assessed in the strange situation and at home.* Hillsdale, NJ: Erlbaum.

Ainsworth, M. S. & Witting, B.A. (1969). Attachment and the exploratory behaviour of one-year-olds in a strange situation. *Determinants of Infant Behaviour, 4*(4), pp. 113-136. doi: n/a.

American Psychological Association. (2019). When working with animals can hurt your mental health. *ScienceDaily.* Retrieved March 8, 2022, from www.sciencedaily.com/releases/2019/08/190809113026.htm

Anderson, K. L., & Olson, M. R. (2006). The value of a dog in a classroom of children with severe emotional disorders. *Anthrozoos: A Multidisciplinary Journal of The Interactions of People & Animals, 19*(1), 35-39. doi: 10.2752/089279306785593919

Ariès, P. (1962). *Centuries of Childhood. A Social History of Family Life*, trans. Robert Baldick, New York: Alfred A. Knopf.

Bachi, K., & Parish-Plass, N. (2017). Animal-assisted psychotherapy: A unique relational therapy for children and adolescents. *Clinical Child Psychology and Psychiatry*, *22*(1), 3–8. doi: 10.1177/1359104516672549

Balluerka, N., Muela, A., Amiano, N., & Caldentey, M. A. (2014). Influence of animal-assisted therapy (AAT) on the attachment representations of youth in residential care. *Children and Youth Services Review*, *42*, 103–109. doi: 10.1016/j.childyouth.2014.04.007

Bandura, A. (1965). Influence of models' reinforcement contingencies on the acquisition of imitative responses. *Journal of Personality and Social Psychology*, *1*(6), 589-595. doi: 10.1037/h0022070

———. (1977). Self-efficacy: Toward a unifying theory of behavioural change. *Psychological Review*, *84*(2), 191-215. doi: 10.1037/0033-295X.84.2.191

———. (1977). *Social learning theory*. Englewood Cliffs, N.J.: Prentice-Hall.

———. (1982). Self-efficacy mechanism in human agency. *American Psychologist*, *37*(2), 122–147.

———. (1986). *Social foundations of thought and action: A social cognitive theory*. Englewood Cliffs, N.J.: Prentice-

Hall.

———. (1989). Social cognitive theory. In R. Vasta (Ed.). *Annals of child development. Vol. 6. Six theories of child development*, 1-60. Greenwich, CT: JAI Press

———. (2001). Social Cognitive Theory: An Agentic Perspective. *Annual Review of Psychology, 52*(1), pp. 1-60. doi: 10.1146/annurev.psych.52.1.1

Barker, S. B., & Dawson, K. S. (1998). The Effects of Animal-Assisted Therapy on Anxiety Ratings of Hospitalized Psychiatric Patients. *Psychiatric Services, 49*(6), 797–801. doi: 10.1176/ps.49.6.797

Beck, A. M., and Katcher, A. H. (1984). A new look at pet-facilitated therapy. *Journal of American Veterinary Medicine Association, 184*(4), 414-421.

Berridge, K. C. (2003). Pleasures of the brain. *Brain and Cognition, 2626*(3), 1-23. doi: 10.1016/S0278-2626(03)00014-9

Body Dysmorphic Disorder. (2021). Retrieved 11 10, 2022, from NHS: https://www.nhs.uk/mental-health/conditions/body-dysmorphia/

Bostan, S. (2018). Brain Signatures of Obsessive-Compulsive Disorder. Retrieved 19 August 2019, from https://www.psychologytoday.com/us/blog/greater-the-sum-its-parts/201801/brain-signatures-obsessive-compulsive-disorder

Bowlby, J. (1969), *Attachment and loss, Vol. 1: Attachment.*

New York, NY: Basic Books.

———. (1973). *Attachment and loss, Vol. 2: Separation*. New York, NY: Basic Books.

———. (1980). *Attachment and loss, Vol. 3: Loss, sadness and depression*. New York, NY: Basic Books.

———. (1988a). *A Secure Base: Clinical Applications of Attachment Theory*. London, UK: Routledge.

———. (1988b). *A secure base: Parent-child attachment and healthy human development*.

Bowlby, J. & Ainsworth, M. (1991). An ethological approach to personality development. *American Psychologist, 46*(4), 333-341.

Burgon, H. L. (2011). Queen of the word: Experiences of at-risk young people participating in equine-assisted learning/therapy. *Journal of Social Work Practice 25*(2), 165–183. doi: 10.1080/02650533.2011.561304

Busch, C., Tucha, L., Talarovicova, A., Fuermaier, A. B. M., Lewis-Evans, B., & Tucha, O. (2016). Animal-Assisted Interventions for Children with Attention Deficit/Hyperactivity Disorder. *Psychological Reports, 118*(1), 292–331. doi: 10.1177/0033294115626633

Calvo, P., Pairet, S., Vila, M., Losada, J., Bowen, J., Cirac, R., & Fatjó, J. (2017). Dog assisted therapy for teenagers with emotional and behavioural issues: A multicentre study. *European Psychiatry, 41*, S432–S433. doi:10.1016/j.eurpsy.2017.01.418

Chandler, C. (2001). Animal-assisted therapy in counselling and school settings. *Contract, Oct*, 1–2.

Cherry, K. (2019). A list of psychological disorders. Retrieved August 12, 2019, from Verywell Mind. https://www.verywellmind.com/a-list-of-psychological-disorders-2794776

CKC Welcomes a Therapy Dog Title Recognition Program. (2019). Retrieved July 24, 2019, from https://www.ckc.ca/en/News/2018/August/CKC-Welcomes-a-Therapy-Dog-Title-Recognition-Progr

Coloroso, B. (1995). *Kids are worth it!; Giving your child the gift of inner discipline*. Toronto, Canada: Somerville House.

Cruse, H. (2006). Neural Networks as Cybernetic Systems. Brains, Minds & Media.

Darwin, C. (1872). *The Expression of the Emotions in Man and Animals*. London, UK: John Murray

DSM-5. (2016, 06). Implications for Child Serious Emotional Disturbance, DSM-IV to DSM-5. (S. A. Services, Editor) Retrieved 11 10, 2022, from National Library of Medicine: https://www.ncbi.nlm.nih.gov/books/NBK519712/table/ch3.t19/

Duranton, C. & Gaunet, F. (2018). Behavioral synchronization and affiliation: Dogs exhibit human-like skills. Learning & Behavior, *46*(4), 364-373. doi: 10.3758/s13420-018-0323-4

Erikson, E. (1959). Identity and the life cycle. (N. Paperback, Ed.) New York, New York, United States: International Univiersities Press Inc. ISBN 0-393-31132-5

———. (1980). *Identity and the life cycle.* New York, NY: W W Norton & Co.

Fine, A. (2006). *Handbook on Animal-Assisted Therapy: theoretical foundations and guidelines for practice* (2ed). San Diego, CA: Academic Press.

———. (2010). *Handbook on Animal-Assisted Therapy: theoretical foundations and guidelines for practice* (3ed). San Diego, CA: Academic Press.

Preston, F. & Royer, M. (2021) The Effect of Therapy Dogs on Preoperative Anxiety, Anthrozoös, *34*(5), 659-670. doi: 10.1080/08927936.2021.1914440

Freedman, D. G., King, J. A. & Elliot, O. (1961). Critical Period in the Social Development of Dogs. *American Association for the Advancement of Science, 133*(3457), 1016-1017. doi: n/a

Friedmann, E., Katcher, A., Lynch, J. & Thomas, S. (1980). Animal companions and one year survival of patients after discharge from a coronary care unit. *Public Health Report, 95,* 307–312.

Friedmann, E., Katcher, A., Thomas, S., Lynch, J. & Messent, P. (1983). Social interaction and blood pressure: influence of animal companions. *The Journal of Nervous and Mental Disease, 171*(8), 461–465.

Gandhi, M.K. (1922). The All-India Congress Committee. *Young India, 3*(n.a.), 1022-1026. Tagore & Co. Madras

Grajfoner, D., Harte, E., Potter, L., & McGuigan, N. (2017). The Effect of Dog-Assisted Intervention on Student Well-Being, Mood, and Anxiety. *International Journal of Environmental Research and Public Health, 14*(5), 483. doi: 10.3390/ijerph14050483

Grandin, T. & Johnson, C. (2005). *Animals in Translation: Using the Mysteries of Autism to Decode Animal Behaviour*. New York, NY: Scribner.

Guo, K., Wilkinson, A., Resende, B., & Mills, D. S. (2018). Mouth-licking by dogs as a response to emotional stimuli. *Behavioural Processes, 146*(10), 42–45. doi:10.1016/j.beproc.2017.11.006

Hall, G.S. (1907). *Adolescence: Its psychology and its relations to physiology, anthropology, sociology, sex, crime, religion and education*. New York: D. Appleton and Company.

Herzog, H. (2017). *Why Kids With Pets Are Better Off*. Retrieved 21 August 2019, from https://www.psychologytoday.com/us/blog/animals-and-us/201707/why-kids-pets-are-better

Kelly, M. A., & Cozzolino, C. A. (2017). Helping at-risk youth overcome trauma and substance abuse through animal-assisted therapy. *Contemporary Justice Review, 2580*(3), 1–14. doi: 10.1080/10282580.2015.1093686

Kroger, J. (1996). *Identity in Adolescence: The Balance Between Self and Others* (2nd Edition). New York, NY: Routledge.

Kruger, K. A., Trachtenberg, S. W., & Serpell, J. A. (2004). Can Animals Help Humans Heal? Animal-Assisted Interventions in Adolescent Mental Health. *Conference paper*, 1–38

Kruger, K. A., & Serpell, J. A. (2010). Animal-Assisted Interventions in Mental Health: Definitions and Theoretical Foundations. *Handbook on Animal-Assisted Therapy*, 33–48. doi: 10.1016/B978-0-12-381453-1.10003-0

Kruk, E. (2013). *The Equal Parent Presumption: Social Justice in the Legal Determination of Parenting After Divorce*. McGill-Queens University Press.

LaJoie, K. R. (2003). An Evaluation of the Effectiveness of Using Animals in Therapy. *Unpublished doctoral dissertation*, Spalding University, Louisville, KY.

Lakhan, S.E. & Kirchgessner, A. (2012). Prescription stimulants in individuals with and without attention deficit hyperactivity disorder: misuse, cognitive impact, and adverse effects. *Brain and Behavior*, 2(5): 661–677 doi: 10.1002/brb3.78

Larkin, M. (2021). Burnout's economic toll on veterinarians calculated. (2022). Retrieved 8 March 2022, from https://www.avma.org/javma-news/2021-12-15/burnoutseconomic-toll-veterinarians-calculated.

Levinson, B. M. (1962). The dog as a "co-therapist." Paper presented at the Annual Meeting of the American Psychological Association in New York City in August 1961. *Mental Hygiene, 46,* 59–65.

———. (1965). Pet psychotherapy: use of household pets in the treatment of behavior disorders in children. Psychological Reports, *17,* 695–698.

———. (1969). *Pet-oriented child psychotherapy.* Springfield, Ill.: C. C. Thomas.

———. (1972). Pets and human development. Springfield. Ill.: C. C. Thomas.

Limond, J. A., Bradshaw, J. W. S., Cormack, M. K. F. (2017). Behavior of children with learning disabilities. *Anthrozoos: A Multidisciplinary Journal of The Interactions of People & Animals, 10*(3), 84-89 doi:10.2752/089279397787001139

Lorenz, K. (1937). On the formation of the concept of instinct. *Natural Sciences, 25*(19): 289–300. doi:10.1007/BF01492648

———. (1965). *Evolution and modification of behavior.* Chicago: University of Chicago Press.

———. (1966). *On Aggression.* New York: Harcourt, Brace & World.

———. (1974). On Aggression (1st ed.). (M. K. Wilson, Trans.) New York, United Kingdom: Harvest Book.

———. (1981). *The Year of the Greylag Goose*. London: Methuen Publishing Ltd.

———. (2002). *Man Meets Dog*. London, UK: Routledge classics.

———. (2002). *King Solomon's Ring* (2nd ed.). London: Routledge.

McClelland, D.C. (1951). *Personality*. NY: William Sloane Associates.

———. (1984). *Centennial psychology series. Motives, personality, and society: Selected papers.* New York, NY, England: Praeger Publishers.

Molenberghs, P., Cunnington, R., & Mattingley, J. B. (2009). Is the mirror neuron system involved in imitation? A short review and meta-analysis. *Neuroscience and Biobehavioral Reviews*, *33*(7), 975–980. doi: 10.1016/j.neubiorev.2009.03.010

Morris, S., Fawcett, G., Brisebois, L. and Hughes, J. (2019). *A demographic, employment and income profile of Canadians with disabilities aged 15 years and over, 2017*. Retrieved 19 August 2019, from https://www150.statcan.gc.ca/n1/pub/89-654-x/89-654-x2018002-eng.htm.

Nagasawa, M., Mogi, K., & Kikusui, T. (2009). Attachment between humans and dogs. *Japanese Psychological Research*, *51*(3), 209–221. doi: 10.1111/j.1468-5884.2009.00402.x

Nagasawa, M., Kawai, E., Mogi, K., & Kikusui, T. (2013). Dogs show left facial lateralization upon reunion with their owners. *Behavioural Processes*, *98*, 112–116. doi:10.1016/j.beproc.2013.05.012

Nestor, R. (2013). Bruce Tuckman's Team Development Model [.pdf]. Aurora. Retrieved August 22, 2019, from https://www.lfhe.ac.uk/download.cfm/docid/3C6230CF-61E8-4C5E-9A0C1C81DCDEDCA2

Ng, Z. Y., Pierce, B. J., Otto, C. M., Buechner-Maxwell, V. A., Siracusa, C., & Werre, S. R. (2014). The effect of dog-human interaction on cortisol and behavior in registered animal-assisted activity dogs. *Applied Animal Behaviour Science*, *159*, 69–81. doi: 10.1016/j.applanim.2014.07.009

Ofner, M., Coles, A., Decou, M.L., T Do, M., Bienek, A., Snider, J., & Ugnat, A.M. (2018). *Autism Spectrum Disorder among Children and Youth in Canada 2018*. Publication: 170433. Ottawa, ON: Public Health Agency of Canada.

Ortolani, A., Vernooij, H. & Coppinger, R. (2008). Ethiopian Village Dogs: Behavioural Responses to a Stranger's Approach. *Applied Animal Behaviour Science, 119*(3-4), 202-218. doi: 10.1016/j.applanim.2009.03.011

Parenti, L., Foreman, A., Meade, B. J., & Wirth, O. (2013). A revised taxonomy of assistance animals. *Journal of rehabilitation research and development*, *50*(6), 745–756. doi: 10.1682/JRRD.2012.11.0216

Pelletier, L., O'Donnell, S., McRae, L., & Grenier, J. (2017). The burden of generalized anxiety disorder in Canada. Le fardeau du trouble d'anxiété généralisée au Canada. *Health promotion and chronic disease prevention in Canada: research, policy and practice*, *37*(2), 54–62.

Pet Partner Terminology. (2019). Retrieved 11 July 2019, from https://petpartners.org/learn/terminology/

Phillips, K. (2022, 11 10). Prevalence of BDD. Retrieved from International OCD Foundation: https://bdd.iocdf.org/professionals/prevalence/

Plutchik, R. (2002). *Emotions and Life: Perspectives From Psychology Biology and Evolution*. Washington, DC: American Psychological Association.

Postman, N. (1994). *The disappearance of childhood*. New York, NY: Vintage Books.

Premack, D. (1959). Toward empirical behavior laws: I. Positive reinforcement. *Psychology Review, 66*(4), 219–233

———. (1963). Rate differential reinforcement in monkey manipulation. *Journal of the Experimental Analysis of Behavior*, *6*(1), 81–89. doi: 10.1901/jeab.1963.6-81

Pryor, K. (1984). *Don't shoot the dog!* [Ebook]. New York, NY: Simon and Schuster.

Purewal, R., Christley, R., Kordas , K., Joinson, C., Meints, K., Gee, N. and Westgarth, C. (2017). Companion Animals and Child/Adolescent Development: A Systematic Review of the Evidence. *International Journal Environmental Research and Public Health, 14*(3), 1-25. doi: 10.3390/ijerph14030234

Reesor L, V. E. (2017, August 11). Addressing Outcomes Expectancies in Behavior Change. Am J Lifestyle Med., 11(6), 430-432. doi: 10.1177/1559827617722504.

Richard W. Burkhardt, J. (2005). Patterns of Behavior Konrad Lorenz, Niko Tinbergen, and the Founding of Ethology. Chicago: Chicago Press. ISBN: 978-02260-809-0-1

Rizzolatti, G. (2005). The mirror neuron system and its function in humans. *Anatomy and Embryology, 210*(5-6), 419-421. doi: 10.1007/s00429-005-0039-z

Rizzolatti, G., & Craighero, L. (2004). The mirror-neuron system. *Annual Review of Neuroscience, 27*(1), 169–192. doi: 10.1146/annurev.neuro.27.070203.144230

Rizzolatti, G., & Fabbri-Destro, M. (2008). The mirror system and its role in social cognition. *Current Opinion in Neurobiology, 18*(2), 179–184. doi:10.1016/j.conb.2008.08.001

Rubinstein, G. (1995). The decision to remove homosexuality from the DSM: twenty years later. Am J Psychother., 49(3), 416-427. doi:10.1176/appi.psychotherapy.1995.49.3.416.

Salamone, J. D. & Correa, M. (2012). The Mysterious Motivational Functions of Mesolimbic Dopamine. *Neuron*, 76(3), 470–485. doi: 10.1016/j.neuron.2012.10.021

Sapolsky, R. (2017). *Behave: The Biology of Humans at Our Best and Worst*. New York, NY: Penguin Press.

Satir, V. (1988). *The new peoplemaking*. Mountain View, CA: Science and Behaviour Books.

Schultz, W. (2007). Behavioral dopamine signals. *Trends in Neurosciences, 30*(5), 203–210. doi:10.1016/j.tins.2007.03.007

———. (2004). Neural coding of basic reward terms of animal learning theory, game theory, microeconomics and behavioural ecology. *Current Opinion in Neurobiology, 14*, 139–147. doi: 10.1016/j.conb.2004.03.017

Scott, J.P. (1958). Critical Periods in the Development of Social Behavior in Puppies. *Psychosomatic Medicine, 20*(1), 43-54.

Scott, J.P. & Fuller, J.L. (1965). *Genetics and the Social Behavior of the Dog.* Chicago: University of Chicago Press.

Sentoo, G. S. (2003). The influence of animal-assisted play therapy on the self-esteem of adolescents with special needs. *Masters, University of Pretoria*, (5), 1–124.

Serbia, C. C. (2009). Animal-assisted therapy – A new trend in the treatment of children and adults. *Psychiatria Danubina, 21*(2), 236–241.

Skinner, E. A. (1996). A guide to constructs of control. *Journal of Personality and Social Psychology, 71*(3), 549-570. doi: 10.1037/0022-3514.71.3.549

Smith, L., Munteanu, A., Villa, D., Quinnell, R., & Collins, L. (2019). The Effectiveness of Dog Population Management: A Systematic Review. *Animals. 9*(1020). doi: 10.3390/ani9121020.

Statistics Canada. (2012). Table 13-10-0465-01 Mental Health Indicators. Retrieved 19 August 2019 from https://www150.statcan.gc.ca/t1/tbl1/en/tv.action?pid=1310046501. doi: 10.2531/1310046501-eng

———. (2019). Table 13-10-0096-03 Perceived mental health, by age group. Retrieved August 14, 2019, from https://www150.statcan.gc.ca/t1/tbl1/en/tv.action?pid=1310009603

———. (2018). Table 13-10-0096-11 Heavy drinking, by age group. Retrieved August 20, 2019, from https://www150.statcan.gc.ca/t1/tbl1/en/tv.action?pid=1310009611

Stefanini, M. C., Martino, A., Bacci, B., & Tani, F. (2016). The effect of animal-assisted therapy on emotional and behavioral symptoms in children and adolescents hospitalized for acute mental disorders. *European Journal of Integrative Medicine, 8*(2), 81–88. doi: 10.1016/j.eujim.2016.03.001

Tannock, R. (2019). *DSM-5 Changes in Diagnostic Criteria for Specific Learning Disabilities (SLD)1: What are the Implications? – International Dyslexia Association.* Dyslexiaida.org. Retrieved 19 August 2019, from https://dyslexiaida.org/dsm-5-changes-in-diagnostic-criteria-for-specific-learning-disabilities-sld1-what-are-the-implications/

Tinbergen, N. (1951). *The Study of Instinct*. Oxford, UK: Oxford University Press.

———. (1953). *Social behaviour in animals: With special reference to vertebrates*. London: Methuen.

———. (1969). *The Study of Instinct*. Oxford, UK: Clarendon Press.

———. (1974). Ethology and stress diseases. *Science, 185*(4145), 20-27. doi: 10.1126/science.185.4145.20

Team building with bite. (2019). Retrieved 27 June 2019, from https://teambuildingwithbite.com/corporate-team-building

Teglas, E., Gergely, A., Kupan, K., Miklósi, A., & Topál, J. (2012). Dogs' Gaze Following Is Tuned to Human Communicative Signals. *Current Biology, 22*(3), 209-212. doi: 10.1016/j.cub.2011.12.018

The Brain From Top to Bottom. (2022). Retrieved 9 March 2019, from https://thebrain.mcgill.ca/index.php

The Radical Academy. (2003). "*The Philosophy of John Locke.*" Retrieved 13 June 2019, from Thomas, P. (2019). Oklahoma State University Libraries. (O. S. Libraries, Editor) Retrieved 11 10, 2022, from 2.2 Social Development: Erikson's Eight Psychosocial Crise.: https://open.library.okstate.edu/foundationsofeducationaltechnology/chapter/7-social-development-eriksons-eight-psychosocial-crises/http://www.theradicalacademy.org/phillocke.html

Toich, L. (2017). *Ritalin Poses Cognitive Risks to Those Without ADHD*. Retrieved 20 August 2019, from https://www.ajpb.com/news/ritalin-poses-cognitive-risks-to-those-without-adhd

Topál, J., Miklósi, A., Csányi, V., & Dóka, A. (1998). Attachment Behavior in Dogs (Canis familiaris): A New Application of Ainsworth's (1969) Strange Situation Test. *Journal of Comparative Psychology, 112*(3), 219-229. doi: 10.1037/0735-7036.112.3.219

Tuckman, B.W. (1965). Developmental sequence in small groups. *Psychological Bulletin, 63*(6): 384–399. doi: 10.1037/h0022100

———. (1992). *Educational Psychology: From Theory to Application*. Fort Worth, TX: Harcourt Brace Jovanovich College Publishers.

Tuckman, B.W. & Jensen, M.A.C. (1977). Stages of Small-Group Development Revisited. *Group & Organization Studies, 2*(4), 419-427.

Understanding the Teen Brain - Health Encyclopedia - University of Rochester Medical Center. (2022). Retrieved 8 March 2022, from https://www.urmc.rochester.edu/encyclopedia/content.aspx?ContentTypeID=1&ContentID=3051

Van Ameringen, M., Mancini, C., Patterson, B., & Boyle, M.

(2008). Post-Traumatic Stress Disorder in Canada. *CNS Neuroscience & Therapeutics*, *14*(3), 171-181. doi:10.1111/j.1755-5949.2008.00049.x

Van Der Kolk, B. (2014). *The Body Keeps the Score*. New York, NY: Penguin Books.

When Does The Brain Stop Developing Or Fully Develop? - NeuroTray. (2020). Retrieved 8 March 2022, from https://neurotray.com/when-does-the-brain-stop-developing-or-fully-develop.

Zeanah, C. H. (1990). A Secure Base: Parent-Child Attachment and Healthy Human Development. *The Journal of Nervous and Mental Disease*, *78*(1), 62. doi: 10.1097/00005053-199001000-00017

Zilcha-mano, S., Mikulincer, M., & Shaver, P. R. (2011). Pet in the therapy room : An attachment perspective on Animal-Assisted Therapy. *Attachment & Human Development*, *13*(6), 541–561

Contacts Information

The following links are clickable on e-readers or .pdf formats.

- Autism Canada
- Dogue Academy – Website
- Dogue Academy – Instagram
- Dogue Academy – Youtube
- Dogue Shop – Website
- Dogue Shop – Dogue Academy LinkedIn
- Dreamcatcher Association – Alberta
- Dyslexia Canada
- Lakeland College – Animal-Assisted Wellness
- Made by Dyslexia
- Mobility Assistance Dog Reimbursement Program
- Montreal Autism and Psychological Evaluation Clinic
- Montreal English School Board

Your Notes

Your Notes

Your Notes

Your Notes

Your Notes

Your Notes

www.ingramcontent.com/pod-product-compliance
Lightning Source LLC
Chambersburg PA
CBHW071222080526
44587CB00013BA/1465